Memory Card Full

Liz Weber

memory card full

liz weber

Greenpoint Press

New York, NY

ISBN 978-0-9886968-7-7

Library of Congress Cataloging-in-Publication Data

Cover design by Joseph Maruca
Interior text design by Kozue Yamada

**Greenpoint Press,
a division of New York Writers Resources
greenpointpress.org
PO Box 2062 Lenox Hill Station
New York, NY 10021**

New York Writers Resources:
newyorkwritersresources.com
newyorkwritersworkshop.com
greenpointpress.org
ducts.org

Printed in the United States
on acid-free paper

I have tried to recreate events, locales and conversations from my memories of them. In order to maintain their anonymity in some instances I have changed the names of individuals and places. I may have changed some identifying characteristics and details such as physical properties, occupations and places of residence.

To Karol, whose support and commitment to healing helped me dig into the dark corners. Thank you for guiding me toward my true self. I owe you my life.

For Andrea and Mia: If it means something to you, don't stop trying...even if it gets hard.

Acknowledgements

I am one lucky lady. I am surrounded by some wildly amazing people and would like to thank them from the bottom of my heart.

Mom and Dad – For walking this journey alongside me with patience, wisdom, understanding and a thick skin. You continue to teach me how to love without strings, judgment and expectation. Thank you for always being in my corner.

Maris – For loving me through thick and thin and possessing the unique ability to crack me up no matter what. Your belief in me has been a source of strength and motivation my entire life. Thank you for always trying to understand—no matter how annoying I can be.

Jared and Pam – For always being in my corner and raising two truly incredible human beings. I love you guys!

Charles Salzberg – Who once told me, "You're a writer, so just write" (or something like that). I could go on for pages here listing all of the wonderful gifts you have bestowed upon me since I walked into that Intro to Personal Essay class a million years ago. You are a true mensch whose honest feedback, unwavering encouragement, and sheer generosity is the very reason why I've gotten to this point. What an honor it is to be in your universe. Go Greenpoint Press!

Catherine Lowe – My editor extraordinaire, who not only whipped this book into shape with her keen eye and straight-from-the-hip feedback, but has been a true friend—the kind who can share a laugh, a cry, glass of wine and an apartment all in the course of an hour. I love you, Iris!

Scott Luxor – For lending me your eyes and video expertise to make a great Kickstarter video.

Eric "FrAHncis" – You saw my power and strength long before I did. Thank you for being patient and forgiving while I grew into it.

To "Team Liz" at Prophet – To Peter and Andres whose support has been paramount in getting this from a Word document to the beautiful piece of work it is today. Joe: you have been patient and a true gem. Thank you for designing such a kick-ass cover. Kozue: You held my hand through the wonders of page numbers and chapter headings. Thank you for your great work. Donna and Dolores: For taking the time from your ridiculously busy schedules to help *me*. Your input was essential in getting this project to completion.

To my "big guns": **Julia and Daphne** – Words don't do justice to how supremely grateful I am to have you both in my life. I literally could not have done this without you. Thank you for always having my best interest in mind—even if it means kicking my ass around now and again. I love you both.

Karen – Your incredible gift of unwavering support and encouragement through this process (and our friendship) leaves me unable to find the proper words, so simply, *thank you*.

Renee, Deb and Rebe – My sisters from another mister. I love you all very much and feel truly blessed to have so many people in my life who *get it*. Thanks for getting me and being in my corner.

Saul – How do I express my gratitude for being one of the most important people in my life? The memories span far and wide, as does the love and appreciation I have in my heart for you. If only you were straight…

Todd – Your friendship means the world to me. Thanks for always reminding me of the best sides of myself.

I'm running out of room here, so I'd like to give a shout-out to the following people for their contributions to the project. DJ Eldon, Alexis Jacobs, Anya Hoffman, Mike Brenner, Linda Yellin, Joan Garrison, Scott Fuller, Kelly Caldwell, Margo K, Mark Chambers, Mary Buser, Rebecca Kendall, Sara J, Jean M, Melinda T, Alice C, Seana A, Anita Z, Matt Wells and Dan Rosenfeld.

I'd be rude if I didn't thank Arthur at Archway Café in Dumbo, who never got sick of me camping out at the best table in the house for hours on end.

Finally, I'd like to thank my new family at Greenpoint Press for welcoming me with open arms. I am lucky to be on the shelf with such amazing talent.

Prologue

•

March 2009

It was my last full day in Mexico, and I was already missing the place. As I drove through the sleepy town of Tulum, the late afternoon sun warmed my face through the open windows of my dusty rental car. I'd driven the main drag so many times those last few weeks that instinctively I knew when to slow down in preparation for the oncoming *topes*—random speed bumps every hundred feet or so—that prevented drivers from speeding through the four short blocks known as the *pueblo*.

Checking my rearview mirror, I rolled slowly over the first one, catching a glimpse of the handlebars peeking out of the trunk. I held my breath going over each of the bumps, as I did for pretty much the entire ride back from Playa del Carmen, a heavily populated town about forty-five minutes north of Tulum.

With a population of around 10,000, Tulum sat in stark contrast to Playa, where there was a Walmart, an Office Depot, and thousands of high-rise resorts lining the beaches. Tulum was filled with small cafés and eco-resorts whose electricity shut down after 11 each night to conserve energy.

"Hola!" I called to Manny through the passenger window as I made my way over the last of the *topes*. Manny ran the little store where I'd been buying eggs since my arrival and was nice enough to explain to me that asking "*Tienes huevos?*"—the literal translation of "Do you have any eggs?"—was the equivalent of asking someone if they had the balls to do something crazy.

He waved back with a wide smile and watched me pass, saying something in Spanish and pointing to the trunk of my car with envy.

The bikes.

My friend Kara had told me I could stay at her newly built condo, rent-free in exchange for readying the apartment for prospective renters. The condo was just past the edge of town, where the main road turned back into a two-lane highway and civilization thinned out into the surrounding jungle. I pulled into the driveway and maneuvered around the unpaved dips and bumps with the ease of an expert, frequently checking to make sure the bikes hadn't fallen out of the trunk.

Buying the bikes was just another adventure to add to the list of many during my stay in Mexico. The couple who lived next door had told me that Playa was the place to go for bikes, so I took a trip north early that morning.

At the shop, the owner kept saying, "No problem, lady, no problem" as I watched three of his men work the bikes into the car for over an hour. They even tied a small red rag to one of the wheels, I suppose to indicate I was carrying some sort of "wide load."

I wondered how I'd get them *out* of the car. *Maybe Memo is still here*, I thought as I opened the car door and reached back to find the flip-flops I'd brought for the journey south. Memo was the maintenance guy for the condo who'd do anything you asked as long as he understood what you were asking.

While looking for Memo, I decided it would be funny to have a picture of the bikes all tied up to the car to document my latest Mexican adventure. I ducked into the condo and grabbed my digital camera, happily distracted by this new task.

Outside again, I angled myself to the right of the rear of the car, making sure to get it all in—the red rag, front wheels, handlebars and baskets, all sticking out of the trunk like something out of *Sanford & Son*. My camera beeped when I pressed the button to take a picture, and across the screen the message read "Memory Card Full."

Shit. I knew why it was full. I still had his pictures on there. They were the last photos I had of him before he died. The ones where he had to lie down while eating when the arthritis got so bad.

The camera was a functional purchase from Target years ago, when I needed digital pictures of the furniture I'd planned to sell to fund my move back to New York from Los Angeles. I rarely saved the pictures I took, but Rufus's pictures were different.

I looked at the bikes and swallowed hard. It was like being at a great party where the speakers blow unexpectedly and just like that, the mood turns flat. My mind searched for ways around having to delete the pictures, but with no USB cord on hand, uploading them wasn't an option. The moment felt much bigger than it actually was, and I knew the choice I had to make.

Erasing some of Rufus's photos meant erasing the past. Was I ready to do that? I couldn't fathom the idea of letting go of anything that reminded me of Rufus, yet I'd made it through most of the trip not thinking about him. It was time to move forward, but to where? I knew I had to or else I'd be stuck in the past forever, coveting pictures of my dead dog.

Next week marks a year since he's been gone.

It'd been such a great trip, with so many new experiences and new friends, and it was the first time since Rufus's death that I had felt alive and really free. My stomach tightened as I flipped through the fifteen or so pictures on my memory card, toggling between past and present. I could keep his photos and erase the ones I'd taken on the trip.

But it was time to let go. I decided I would keep just three. It felt like a good compromise. Just because someone was out of your life didn't mean you had to forget him completely. Three pictures would be enough. I stood in the parking lot trying to choose the best ones.

Erasing the first one, I noticed I was holding my breath. It felt like I was betraying him, casting him aside to embark on a new life. I tried to focus on my breath, and as I did, I considered another perspective.

Maybe I should celebrate. I was finally moving on and ready to create the space for something new. I knew Rufus would dig that—in fact, I'm pretty sure that was the reason why he finally let go in the end.

PART I

1

It was August 2007, and I knew Rufus wasn't going to live much longer. He wasn't sick or showing any blatant signs of aging. I just *knew*. I didn't tell anyone because if I did, that would make it true, at least for me, and I didn't want that. Instead, I ignored it because really, what can you do with just a feeling?

Besides, I had to call Charlie back. Why did I always feel tense when he called? He was supposed to be my boyfriend, though I didn't call him that. He was just the "guy I'm seeing"—my way of committing without the commitment. We'd been together since May and had already had "the talk" once, when I asked him to back off a little.

Since then, I kept asking myself if I really liked this guy. He was good to me, completely available and not afraid to express himself—all the makings of a great boyfriend. Plus, Rufus really liked him.

When I adopted Rufus eleven years ago, I was living in Atlanta and severely homesick. My boyfriend Kenny, whom I didn't have the guts to break up with, suggested we get a dog. Like a couple on the verge of divorce who announces, "We're having a baby!" I agreed, relieved to avoid the inevitable.

Rufus didn't warm to me immediately. The first few weeks, he slept close to the front door and spent his days sniffing around the apartment, looking in open cabinets, standing on his hind legs to get a better glimpse of the bathroom sink and investigating the laundry basket.

Our shaky start continued as Kenny and I had sex one night. That we were even having sex was surprising, since things hadn't improved, despite the dog.

"What is that?" I said mid-coitus. There was a loud scratching and ripping sound coming from somewhere in the bedroom.

"Nothing, baby," he said, stroking my face and trying to coax me back to the moment.

"Is it Rufus?" I said, sitting up and pushing Kenny aside. "WHAT the…RUFUS!"

There he was, on the floor, ripping Jeffrey, my most prized teddy bear, which I'd had since I was five, to pieces. Though it might seem strange that I still had that bear at twenty-six, I insisted on bringing him everywhere. And Rufus was tearing him apart.

I flew off the bed, naked.

"STOP IT, RUFUS! STOP!" I screamed, grabbing his collar and yanking him from Jeffrey.

I hated Rufus in that moment and wanted to throw him off the terrace and into the parking lot. Instead, I pushed him out of the room, closed the door behind me and crawled around the floor, sobbing and gathering up pieces of poor, scattered Jeffrey.

Jeffrey got re-stuffed thanks to a tailor in Alpharetta, but Rufus's journey back into my good graces wasn't as easy. I was angry and he knew it, following me around the apartment, lying outside the bathroom door while I showered and licking my face any chance he got.

Despite the rift, Rufus was more attached to me than he was to Kenny, which is why he ended up coming with me to New York when I finally decided to move back home. The adventure solidified our bond and he became the only constant in my busy life.

His paperwork from the pound read: "Terrier Mix — around two years old." Rufus was less tall than he was long, with a big head, floppy ears and soulful eyes. His silky charcoal-gray fur covered most of his ill-proportioned body, while the white markings on the bottom of his front paws and a patch of white running from his chin to his chest made him look like an English butler wearing a tuxedo and spats.

His original name was Seymour, but I had a great-uncle with the same name who'd always left a trail of flatulent fragrance behind each time he visited, so I decided a name change was in order. Plus, Rufus just looked like a Rufus.

Wherever we went, people would notice him. With his front legs shorter than his back ones, Rufus loped more than he walked, which added to his awkward charm. He was a big hit with the ordinarily scary guys from the projects we lived next to on the Lower East Side.

"Look, look! He be struttin'!" they'd call out each time we passed, before giving me a respectful nod and a "What up, snowflake?"

Rufus was an easygoing dog, but he didn't like it when I had a man in the apartment. He'd never growl or bite; he'd just sit there and stare at us like a disapproving parent, never letting me out of his sight. Sometimes he'd jump up on the couch and get between us, but that was when he liked the guy. And Rufus knew. If he liked him, it usually meant the guy was a good one.

Charlie *was* a good guy, but I wasn't sure I even wanted a boyfriend. Being taken out and doted on felt good and was a great distraction, but there was really nothing more for me than the attention. Maybe I was addicted to that. A lot of times, I'd find myself forgetting about him, like the homework you wished would do itself. Definitely a bad sign.

Speaking of bad, Charlie had shown up at my job the other night— again. I'd already told him I didn't want a ride, but he ignored me and waited outside at the curb, all proud of himself. "I thought I would surprise you," he'd said.

I decided to file that encounter in the red-flag file, my secret mind file for any strange behavior, conversation or comment that made me stop and wonder if the person had major issues. I'd try to forget it once filed and not to jump to any conclusions. Getting to know someone was clunky and awkward, and we've all had those moments where we've done something that wasn't completely in our character.

If a boyfriend's red-flag file got full, I'd use it as supporting evidence in my longer than normal breakup-contemplation period. I always had the unfortunate habit of staying in a relationship long after the writing was on the wall. Tino. Jason. Jordan. The Exes of Evil, the only ones I didn't stay friends with. Their behavior blew the red-flag file away. Tino was a cheater; Jordan ran up $800 worth of unpaid parking tickets on *my* car; and Jason borrowed a large sum of money from me before going to jail for insurance fraud. I should have had another file called "Freaks and Assholes." Charlie wasn't showing any signs of ever making it into that file, but I still wasn't sure what to do about him.

"How's your day going?" I asked, hoping to get the conversation going.

"Eh, okay. Boring. Same old, same old."

It had been two minutes and already I wanted to hang up because talking to him was like being on a bridge to nowhere. When I told him I had to get ready for work, he replied, "Why are you trying to get rid of me?"

Rufus stirred from his slumber, looked at me as if to say, "Boring!" and rolled over with a sigh.

"Charlie. I'm not trying to get rid of you," I pleaded, my patience starting to fade. "I have to walk the dog and get to work, that's all."

He sighed. "Alright. Call me later." I knew I wouldn't call him later, especially after such stimulating conversation. I liked to keep my word, so I wasn't going to promise a call when I knew there wouldn't be one. The problem was, if I told him straight out, it would turn into a whole other thing.

I tried for something in between. "Okay, but it might be late. So let's talk in the morning."

"You know I don't really sleep," he said quietly.

Subtlety wasn't looking like a good option.

"Let's just talk tomorrow, okay? I know I'm going to be tired and I'd rather just come home and go to sleep."

I felt like I was negotiating with a child. While I held my breath waiting for his response, I checked the clock to see how much time I had before I had to leave. Thankfully there was no drama, and we hung up with just enough time for me to feed Rufus and go to work.

2

"I think you have a problem setting boundaries."

Stephanie and I were having lunch at our usual spot, PS 450 in Murray Hill. Seated at the bar, which was quite large with around twenty seats, she wasted no time in getting right down to it.

"What makes you say that?" I said, leaning back against the bar stool.

It was late in the day, and the place was pretty empty. The bartenders were cool, always leaving us alone while we talked.

"You've been dating Charlie for what, three months now? And it's been the same thing over and over. He pursues you and you get freaked out. You back up and he pushes harder."

I repositioned myself on the stool but couldn't get comfortable. I didn't want to talk about it. Ignoring it was so much easier! I looked at Stephanie and couldn't help but envy her strength of character. She had such presence, and it wasn't just because she was gorgeous. Her skin was so dark it glowed. She wasn't much taller than me—5'7"—but her neck was long, which made her seem taller. Her hair, a cross between short dreadlocks and an Afro, sat on her head like a crown you see in one of those cartoon caricatures of the sun. With her personality added to the mix, forget it—when Stephanie walked into a room, everyone knew it.

She was fiercely loyal and very good at getting to the heart of my matters, even when I wanted to do anything but. I didn't like to be pushed sometimes, but I always took her advice seriously. She had that determined look in her eyes, which meant avoidance was *not* an option.

"I can't distinguish between whether I just don't like him or if it's that having to set these freakin' boundaries all the time is turning me off."

"Well, what do you like about him?"

I paused, shifting my eyes upward and to the right, the way you would if you were trying to remember what you needed at the market.

"I like that he's consistent, reliable. I like that he takes care of me. I've never had that before! It's nice to not have to worry about paying or opening doors." I took a sip of wine and continued. "Last week, my air conditioner broke. It was supposed to be in the nineties and I had to work. I was worried about Rufus being in the apartment in the heat, ya know? So I called Charlie to tell him what was going on—something you *know* is out of character for me."

"What? You mean *asking* for help? Hmph."

I rolled my eyes. "Yeah, yeah, but I did. And he's like, 'Don't worry about it. I'll take care of it.' And I'm like, 'Uh, okay. How?' He's like, 'Just leave the keys with the doorman. I'll go pick up a new air conditioner and put it in for you.'"

"That's great, girl!"

"Wait…" I said, lowering my voice. "So he picks me up from work, we come home, and sure enough the A/C is in and working perfectly. Rufus is happily lying under the coffee table and Charlie turns to me and says, 'You see how I take care of you? This could be all the time if you'd just stop running away.'"

"Ohhh." Stephanie winced as if she'd been hit in the back of the head.

"I know! And I'm thinking, *Do you always have to make everything about me and you?* ARGH! He also won't let me pay for the A/C, so now I feel like I'm indebted to him because he's buying me all sorts of shit."

"Whoa. Whoa." Stephanie held her hand up. "I get the part about him coming on a little too strong, but if he wants to buy you an air conditioner, so be it. Plenty of people have bought me things. Do you think I felt like I owed them anything?"

"Yes, but that's crazy. I don't even know if I want to be with him! I can't break up with a guy who just bought me an air conditioner!"

"Yes you can," she said matter-of-factly. "That's your problem. You think people are keeping score. And frankly, if they are, let 'em. Why shouldn't he buy you an air conditioner? It is HIS choice, girl. You don't owe him anything. Now, the other stuff about the taking care of you, blah, blah, blah, that's annoying. But you can tell him, 'Uh, Charlie. I appreciate your generous gesture, but you gotta back off here, okay?'"

• • •

I couldn't sleep that night. I kept thinking about my conversation with Stephanie and wondered if I was being a fool. Maybe I was one of those girls who had problems with good guys. Why *not* Charlie? Was it because sometimes it felt like he liked me more than I liked myself?

I got out of bed and walked to where Rufus was sleeping. My apartment was a large studio with a dressing area and bathroom separate from the main room. Rufus liked to sleep in the small space where my dresser stood, just next to the closet. Beaded curtains hung in the doorway for separation, and he liked the feel of them rubbing across his back each time he passed through. Sometimes he'd stand in the doorway and peek through the wooden beads, letting them fall, like braids on each side of his face, while he watched me put my makeup on in the bathroom.

The space was small, and maneuvering onto the floor without disturbing him wasn't easy. I lay down on the floor and faced him. Rufus wiggled into a more comfortable position, stretching his front paws forward with a long sigh before he leaned in to kiss my nose.

"Yeah, buddy. I can't sleep again," I whispered, rubbing his back. The connection soothed me, and the noise in my head began to die down. "Let's just lie here for a while, okay?"

3

I'd been working at Stella Maris, a bar/restaurant in the South Street
Seaport, since June. It was okay. The owner was nice and the customers
were cool, but the manager was completely nuts. Sabrina, who'd been
in the restaurant world for many years, acted like a mean girl from high
school. Her dark hair, olive skin and thick eyebrows made her look
more Greek than the Sicilian roots she loved to remind people about,
any chance she got.

"I'm not Italian," she'd say. "*I'm Sicilian.*"

I'd have to bite my tongue each time and resist the urge to add,
"Don't forget crazy, too!"

She wasn't a bad-looking woman, and by the way she carried herself,
she was probably pretty hot in her twenties. Now she looked a lot
older than her thirty-four years. Worn-out and puffy, she constantly
complained about having only three good outfits that fit while she
dove into a plate of French fries.

Sabrina was also one of those people who demanded respect instead
of earning it. I felt many things for her, but respect wasn't one of them.
And I wasn't someone who had a problem following rules. Unlike Pan,
a guy I once dated who lived in a van. That guy got off on bucking
the system.

We were walking along the Hudson River one early spring
afternoon when Pan got in the face of a security guard who enforced
basic rules like scooping dog poop or honoring the bike lanes. Pan
decided to hop up onto the fence that ran along the waterfront to get a

better view of the Hudson. When the guard told him to get down, Pan screamed, "Is there a *law* that says I can't sit here? An *actual* law, man? And even if there is one, you can't enforce it—you're just a rent-a-cop."

"Let's just get out of here," I said, tugging at his arm. "We can go back to your place—I mean, your van."

Pan's red-flag file filled up quickly, and after that, I vowed to only date guys who lived in an apartment.

I was all about respect until you did something that made me lose it. I first lost it for Sabrina when I watched her lie to the owner about some missing bottles of wine a couple of weeks back. Right in front of me, she'd told him, "Oh yeah, Liz was moving the case, it dropped and the bottles broke. Right, Liz?"

I wanted to say, "Uh, no, freak. You *drank* half that case last week and took the rest home with you."

But I was still pretty new, and she *was* the general manager. Keith, the owner, was a gentle man who I believed had a crush on her. Instinct told me to keep quiet, so I nodded my head and said, "Sorry, Keith."

Stella Maris was smaller than the other places I'd worked, with fifty seats in the dining room. The bar was large, with twenty seats. I loved the open, airy feeling of the room. The sliding glass doors opened in the warmer months, flooding it with natural light and fresh air, adding a nice contrast to the dark chocolate woodwork and white walls, making the place look like something out of a West Elm catalog.

The bar had separate stations at each end of its 15 feet, allowing enough room for two bartenders to work, provided they were courteous and aware of each other. I worked with a girl named Danielle when I first started there. Courtesy and awareness were not her strong suits, and I spent most shifts like a commuter dodging rush-hour crowds, trying to avoid being plowed over each time she needed to get by. She trained me, so I had to play the game and let her be queen bee. Unfortunately, she became a little too queen bee for Sabrina and was let go under mysterious circumstances, which Sabrina explained with a "She's no longer with us" announcement one afternoon.

The restaurant was empty when I walked in, as it was too early for the evening rush. Keith, sitting alone at the far end of the bar, had his nose buried in paperwork. He looked up as I approached and gave me a wave and a smile.

"Your drawer's already in the register," he said, gesturing toward the bar.

I liked Keith so much better than Sabrina. His soft voice and unassuming vibe made me want to pull up a chair and chat with him for hours instead of working. And Keith liked to talk. On nights we'd close the bar, we'd talk about everything from his days growing up in Ireland to astrology. It took me a while to get used to his thick Irish brogue. When I first started, I'd shake my head and laugh when he laughed, pretending I understood exactly what he was talking about.

"Ah, Liz. Life's an interesting ride, ya know?" he mused the one night as I cleaned the beer taps. "That Sabrina. Jeez, she's such a loovely purson, but I tell you, she's got ta get her act together."

I looked up to acknowledge I was listening but stayed silent, not sure where he was going with this.

"I know ya didn't drop that case of wine."

Shit. Now I was a liar in his eyes. I put down my rag and started to say something, but he cut me off.

"It's ookay, Liz," he said holding up his hand. "I oonderstand why ya did it. But I need ya ta say no ta her when she asks for a glass of anything—wine, liquor, it doesn't matter. She's not ta drink while she's in the restaurant."

I'd been bartending long enough to know that anyone who drank as much as Sabrina wasn't going to take no for an answer, especially when it related to her getting her drink on. I couldn't argue with Keith— he was the owner and on to Sabrina's antics—but I knew policing Sabrina wasn't going to work. She'd just stolen a case of wine! Instead, I mumbled something about it being a full moon and how it would probably work itself out.

As I settled into the bar for the evening, checking juices, wines and supplies, Sabrina came bursting out of the kitchen.

"KEITH! There's no more paper for the printer in the office. How am I supposed to print out the specials with no paper? I thought I told you to get some."

Keith hung his head like a scolded child. "I'll goo to tha store nooow, Sabreena," he said quietly, gathering his stuff and disappearing into the kitchen.

Sabrina acknowledged my presence by looking past me and into the large mirror hanging behind the bar. She tousled her hair and announced, "The boys are here!" while applying her gooey pink lip gloss—something she'd do about thirty times during my shift, never self-conscious about admiring herself in the mirror for all to see.

Bart, Chris and a guy whose name I never remembered walked in and over to their usual spot in the middle of the bar, spreading out as if to claim the space as their own.

"Hi, guys!" I called, grabbing a few beverage napkins as I made my way over to them. These three weren't my favorites but they tipped well, so I had to do my best impression of "I think everything you say is so *interesting!*" They owned a law firm around the corner and came in a few times a week, which was good for my pocket. Keith didn't like them, however, and because they needed a lot of attention, I always worried that he'd hold it against me for being nice to them.

I gave Chris my left cheek. "Hi! Good to see you."

Bart and the other guy waved hello. I immediately grabbed the Tanqueray and held it up to Bart, who gave me the thumbs-up. Bart always drank the same thing—Tanqueray and Sprite—and after about five of them, he'd switch to Heineken. Once, I poured his drink without checking, thinking it to be a nice gesture. He wasn't pleased.

"What's this, now? I don't have a choice in what I drink anymore?"

His sense of humor was dry, and I could never tell when and if he was joking.

"Noooo, I just thought it'd be nice to have it ready for you."

"So, what, now you're saying I'm predictable?"

I don't know. You come in here four nights a week and drink the same thing, what do you think? I shook my head and gave him an award-winning smile. After that incident, I always asked, no matter what.

Chris was different. He liked that I remembered. When it came to food, he'd ask for the menu, look it over and say, "Liz, honey, what should I have for dinner? You choose. I can't decide." I always found this odd because how should I know what you want to eat? That would be one of the few times I'd be grateful to have Sabrina around;

I could pull her into the mix. She loved saving the day, and I liked waiting on people who were a little less high-maintenance.

Keith kept his hatred for the guys under wraps and would usually just brood at his table in the back. I knew he was jealous that Sabrina flirted with them. He'd even gone so far as to blame them for her drinking.

I had a mental block against the other guy's name, and he came in too many times for me to ask without embarrassment. The worst part was that he knew my name and used it generously every time he'd ask for a drink.

"Lizzy! Baby! How are ya, honey?"

"Good, hon! Nice to see you. What are you drinking?"

"One of your phenomenal Raspberry Smashes, of course," he said, turning to the guys. "This girl makes that drink like nobody else—she is the BEST."

I smiled and made his drink, quickly glancing at Sabrina, who to my relief, showed no signs of discontent over Nameless Guy's praise for my drink-making skills.

A Raspberry Smash was one of the specialty cocktails that Sabrina created. Most restaurants had an array of signature drinks that required more work than they were worth; thankfully here, there were only four. Sabrina acted as though her drink creations were masterpieces and only *she* made them best.

Trust me, the drinks were not all that groundbreaking. I once worked in a place where I'd have to blanch and peel tomatoes for a tomato martini that consisted of homemade onion-infused vodka, muddled tomatoes, olive juice and a salt-rimmed glass. That's innovative! A Raspberry Smash was basically a mojito with raspberry purée.

Once the guys were settled, I went back to checking my inventory for the evening and making drinks for the people who had trickled into the restaurant. Sabrina busied herself at the service bar, the area where the servers would pick up the drinks I made for their tables. It was also the staff's private oasis where we joked, made nasty comments about customers or sometimes got chewed out by Sabrina. Tonight it was the scene of a competition I wasn't expecting.

"Do you want to send the boys some appetizers?" I asked Sabrina while I prepared a martini for Table Five.

Sabrina didn't answer right away. She was half staring at me and half staring into space, which struck me odd, but with her you never knew, so I let the thought pass without consideration.

She plopped herself onto the last barstool under an oversized vase of some Hawaiian-looking flowers. With her hands tucked under her chin, she purred, "Liz. Make me a Raspberry Smash."

"For you?" I asked, realizing as soon as it was out of my mouth that I shouldn't have said it.

"Of course for me!" she snapped.

Sabrina watched, like a cat scoping her prey, as I muddled the mint, lime and sugar together in a pint glass, my nerves rising.

"You need to put more mint in there," she commanded.

I knew where this was going. It was a competition and she had to win. The tricky part was that I didn't know what winning looked like to her. Did I make it perfectly so she could boast about how well she had me trained? Or did I make it my way? Either way, I was screwed. I knew it and frankly didn't care. I was tired of Sabrina and her bullshit drama.

But I needed this job, so I followed her orders. I added the purée and the rum and grabbed the metal mixing tumbler. I shook it vigorously, entertaining myself with thoughts of telling Sabrina to fuck off.

"You don't need to shake it so much," she said with more than a tinge of authority.

It was all I could do to not roll my eyes. I poured the drink into a short glass and turned to grab a mint leaf for garnish. Sabrina waved her hand in dismissal. "Don't be shy with the garnish," she said, reaching over the bar to grab a large sprig of mint, then defiantly putting it into the drink.

I grit my teeth, placed two straws in the glass and handed over the drink for her review.

Cheers, bitch!

The guys summoned me to their side of the bar and I was eternally grateful for the reprieve from Sabrina and her scrutiny.

Bart and Chris were in their mid-forties. Chris was the best-looking of the bunch, with deep blue eyes that went nicely with his dark hair, perfectly combed, and his permanent tan. Even in jeans he looked dressed up.

Tonight's topic was culture, and Chris monopolized the conversation with examples of how cultural he was. "I go to Lincoln Center a lot," he announced.

Nodding, I poured him another draft beer. "Mmm-hmm."

"Yeah. I go to the opera and the ballet. All the cultural stuff. You should come with me sometime."

"Hi, sexy guys!" Sabrina cooed, parking herself between Bart and Chris and holding the drink I'd just made. "I'm so glad you came to see me on a Saturday!"

Sabrina's interruption was timed perfectly as she saved me from the discomfort of explaining my cardinal rule of never socializing with customers outside the bar.

"I had to have one of Liz's cocktails!" Nameless Guy said, raising his glass. I winced, hoping she didn't hear him.

"It's actually *my* recipe," she preened.

Unwilling to go down *that* road again, I interjected, "Hey, are you guys hungry?"

I saw Keith out of the corner of my eye, standing at the service bar. Walking over to him, I called over my shoulder to the guys, "Think about what you want to eat, and I'll be right back."

Keith used his chin to point toward Sabrina and the guys. "She drinking with them?"

I nodded. "She wanted to see how well I made the Raspberry Smash."

Like a child living in a house with a volatile mother and a beaten-down father, I stood there drowning in uncomfortable silence. We both knew it was going to be a long night.

A few hours later, Bart and Chris were still there, and Sabrina was in full force. She'd taken two sips of the Raspberry Smash before casting it aside. "I can't drink that. Liz! Pour something white."

Keith retired to his seat at the back table, and I tried my best to run interference for the remainder of the night. It was slow for a Saturday, which meant I wasn't going to make much money. Sabrina got really drunk, flirting and dancing with Chris and Bart, running behind the bar, flipping her hair and applying lip gloss every twenty minutes.

I stood around trying to hide my disdain for the whole scene and wondered if perhaps Stella Maris wasn't the right place for me after all.

4

I was happy to have the next day off. By the time Keith had finished talking my ear off yet again about Sabrina's drinking last night, it was nearly 2 a.m.

Why did I always end up working for such crazy women? There were too many of them lined up in my mind, and it made me wonder if *I* had the problem. Secilia at Salute, who buddied up to me when she first started, wormed her way in between me and Joshua, one of the waiters I was sleeping with. Once she'd managed that, she started bad-mouthing me to the general manager, knowing he and I were good friends. In the end I gave two weeks' notice, but she let me go anyway—with pleasure, I'm sure—on my second-to-last shift.

Then there was Lydia at Smokehouse. She was a doozy. I was the first woman she'd hired in a long while, and she reminded me of it each and every time she called the restaurant and I answered. Working with her felt like being in seventh grade again: constantly afraid my girlfriends would decide to turn on me at any given moment. One minute she was my best pal, and then, just as I would begin to relax, she'd move in for the kill and say something like, "What the hell is going on with your hair tonight? You look very Staten Island."

And Sabrina made three. *Maybe it really was me*, I thought while walking back from the deli to my apartment. Growing up in New York, the only place we ever got coffee was the deli. My friends made fun of me and my love for "dirty deli coffee" as they sipped their $7 Starbucks lattes. I liked my coffee, and I especially liked the ritual of going to get it in the mornings. It gave me some time with myself and the chance to gather my thoughts.

Unfortunately, my thoughts today were all about the fact that I had an unusually high tolerance for crazy people. My mother was a little crazy when I was growing up, and I wondered if I had some sort of deep-seated battered self-esteem issue I was working out with all these nutty female bosses.

I tried to shake those thoughts that day during the elevator ride up to my apartment. It was my day off, for god's sake! I was going to just chill and enjoy it.

Turning the key and opening the door, I witnessed a war zone. In the fifteen minutes I'd been gone, the large full-length mirror hanging horizontally in the hallway, just inside the front door, had fallen off the wall. Glass was everywhere. My first thought was if the mirror had fallen on Rufus. Panic set in as visions of him lying in the living room bleeding to death flooded my mind.

"Rufus?" I called, trying to sound calm and upbeat as I crunched over the shards of glass, tracking them into the living room with me.

Rufus was under the coffee table. He walked toward me slowly, his tail wagging, with a large piece of mirror stuck to his paw.

"Oh, sweetie," I said, bending down and running my hands all over his body to see if he'd been cut. He was fine except for the adhesive from the mirror that was stuck to his paws and ears. What a mess!

I dropped my purse and got on the floor next to him to pull the gluey strands from his ears without hurting him. It was like pulling day-old gum from someone's hair: sticky and dense.

Once I'd finished with Rufus, I tackled the bigger issue at hand. Large pieces, small pieces and teeny-tiny pieces that looked more like glitter than glass carpeted the floor. As I stood up and tried to figure out where to start, I suddenly realized something even more upsetting.

The mirror was a major "cure" that my friend Deb, a feng shui expert in Los Angeles, instructed me to add to the wall. I couldn't remember the meaning of its placement, but I knew it was a big one. Any time Deb feng shui'd my apartment, I could feel an immediate shift in the energy. With the mirror shattered all over my floor, I started to panic and I wondered aloud, "WHAT DOES THIS *MEAN*??"

I looked at the clock: 11:30, too early to call her in California. But this was an emergency. She'd understand. Deb and I had been friends since meeting at film school at NYU almost twenty years ago. Neither of us did anything with our film degrees, but she had a budding feng shui business in Los Angeles, where she'd been living since 1995.

I dialed her number, trying to pull myself together.

"Heeeey," she answered, the sleep still in her voice.

"Are you busy?"

"What's wrong?"

"It's so fucked up," I said, the tears starting to flow. "My mirror just fell off and is in a million pieces on the floor."

Silence. "Oh. Okay, okay. That's your career corner—it's all fine."

My emotions swelled to the point where I didn't really know *what* I was crying about. Was it my confusion over Charlie, the worry that Rufus could have been seriously hurt or the fact that I had three million pieces of glass all over my apartment?

"I am standing here with a broken mirror in my career corner. How the hell is that fine?"

"Honey. The mirror breaking just means you're breaking through to the next level."

"*Next level?*" I almost spat. "What next level? I'm a bartender wishing to be a writer, working at a job with a crazy woman and going out with a guy who is smothering me."

Deb paused for a beat before answering. "Like I said, things are breaking up. Trust me. This is all good stuff. Sometimes things have to fall apart in order for us to put them back together again."

When the last of the mirror was all cleaned up, I took Rufus out for a much-needed breath of fresh air. It was a beautiful summer day, and I was determined to make something positive out of my time off. It was still early enough, so a nice long walk and a little time sitting outside would put things back on track. We exited the back door of my building that led to the grounds of the complex. Seven buildings made up the complex and there was lots of grass and trees around, making it feel more like a park than an apartment building in the middle of Downtown Brooklyn.

We spent a couple of hours outside relaxing while the madness of the morning faded away. I didn't give much more thought to what things "breaking up" in my life meant. If I went there, it would only bring me panic over stuff I couldn't control. Instead, I found a bench and sat quietly. Rufus was just happy to be outside, sniffing the grass and letting the breeze blow across his face.

Every now and then a fellow dog owner would appear, and we'd exchange a few words about the weather, the dogs, nothing important. From a distance I saw Rocco, a small bulldog, approaching off-leash. This meant his owner, who was a complainer, wasn't too far behind. I took it as a sign to head back inside. I had no capacity to sit and listen to someone prattle on and on about his fucked up life and assume I cared. *Definitely not today*, I thought, getting up from the bench, waving hello to the guy as I ducked into my building.

When Charlie called later, I was happily settled on the couch with a book.

"Can I come over?" he asked.

I was silently raging. I'd just gotten through telling him that I really needed some time to myself. I didn't bother to mention the mirror. I couldn't deal with the guilt trip he'd throw me about not calling him to ask for his help. I'd simply told him I wanted to be alone—what part of that did he not understand?

Boundaries, boundaries, I reminded myself.

"I promise I won't stay long. I just want to see you," he whined. He was in the car on the way back from spending the weekend with his buddies, white-water rafting or something.

"Charlie," I pleaded. "Not tonight, okay?" I was nearing the danger zone. The harder he pushed, the harder it would be to say no. As usual, I tried a different approach. "Let's do something tomorrow night. I'm not working and I'm sure I'll be much better company."

No deal. After a long pause he said, "I really need to talk to you."

I knew I should be stronger about sticking to my guns, but I was just too damn tired to deal with this crap. "Fine," I snapped. "But I'm serious—you *cannot* stay long."

Hanging up, it became clear that it was time to break up with Charlie. There was nothing good about the relationship anymore. Nothing! I was in over my head and felt so guilty my stomach hurt. I hated hurting people. I'd much rather be hurt. At least then I could be in control of it. If I hurt someone else, I was completely powerless over the situation.

When he arrived, no sooner was the door open than Charlie was folding himself into me like a baby to its mother's breast. I put my arms around him and he leaned on me with all of his weight. Charlie was not a tall man, but he was in very good shape. He was the first Chinese-American guy I ever dated, and though I normally went for taller men, I liked his broad shoulders and strong arms. It just didn't seem right, me holding this guy up, my balance unsteady. I felt like I was dealing with a child, not a man. *Again.*

He didn't say anything as he stood there in my arms. He was shaking slightly. Confused, I wondered if he was cold. Then it hit me. He was crying. *Charlie was crying!*

My first instinct was to push him into the hallway, slam the door and lock it tight. I didn't want to deal with this right now. I wanted to get back to the couch and my book.

Instead, I clicked into crisis mode. I was good at crisis: Any type of extreme situation called for immediate action in spite of my own needs. I reminded myself to be compassionate and just be there for him. It was the right thing to do.

I closed the door and led him into my apartment and onto the couch. Rufus retreated to the corner of the living room, where he could get the best view of the situation.

I asked Charlie what was wrong, but he was too upset to talk. I tried to remain calm while the noise in my head amped up to ninety. I felt like a fraud, pretending to care that he was upset. I also felt like a jerk. What the hell was wrong with me that I could sit there with a man I'd been dating for three months and feel so repulsed by his obvious distress?

My gestures were stiff as I offered him a tissue even though I knew he wanted me to hold him and tell him all would be okay.

"Things are really bad, Liz," he said. Finally it all tumbled out. Between sniffs and nose-blows, he told me everything. His construction business was failing, he had no idea what he wanted to do with his life and he was having major financial problems. He'd had a crappy weekend because he felt inadequate next to his friends, with their successful lives. And then the bomb-dropper: The insurance for his construction business had expired and he couldn't afford to renew it. So he and his partner had decided to forge a new insurance certificate.

I didn't think my mind could race any faster. *Forging insurance documents?* Was this guy nuts?

"Isn't that illegal?" I gulped, trying to stay composed.

He nodded.

It took everything I had to stay calm. This was not just about Charlie. This was also about Jason, who borrowed a ton of money from me and then went to jail—for insurance fraud. If I learned anything from that fiasco, it was that I wouldn't date anyone engaged in illegal activities ever again.

I held up my hand. "I really can't hear this right now, Charlie. It's wrong. You know better than this."

He dropped his head and mumbled, "I know. I'm just so confused."

"*Confused about what? It is illegal!* There is nothing to be confused about."

He squirmed in his seat and said, "It's more than just the insurance—it's my whole life. You are the only thing that is good in my life right now."

I wanted to throw up. Rufus chose that moment to walk over and park himself at my feet.

As we talked further, it became clear that Charlie didn't really want to do anything about his situation. He wanted sympathy. I just wanted to break up with him, but I knew it was wrong to kick a person when he was down. But I so wanted to kick him. A few minutes, as he'd promised on the phone, had now turned into two hours.

My phone was ringing. Normally I'd just let it ring. But that night it was like freedom calling.

I shot up off the couch and reached for the phone. It was Sabrina. Terrific. Another psycho. I declined her call and used the break in conversation with Charlie as a way to wrap things up.

He didn't want to go, but thankfully he did. I closed the door to my apartment and headed for the kitchen. I needed a drink.

Several glasses of wine later, I checked my voicemail and heard Sabrina's nasally voice, which made the hair on the back of my neck stand up.

"Liz. It's Sabrina from Stella Maris. I need you to come in and work tomorrow night. We have a private party booked and it's *very* important to have everyone there. *VERY.* Everyone is working. Please come at 5."

"FUCK!" I yelled, the buzz from the wine suddenly gone. "What the hell?" My outburst startled Rufus, and he looked up at me with concern as I paced around mumbling to myself. "This is such bullshit. It's my day off. She doesn't even ask—she tells. I hate this job. I hate Charlie. ARGH!!"

My tirade had Rufus up and under my feet. As mellow as he was, he responded immediately to any kind of excitement, especially on my part. I felt bad and bent down to him, cupping his face in my hands.

"It's okay, buddy," I soothed. "Your mama's just pissed at all the freaks in this world." As I stroked his chin, he relaxed and let his head get heavy in my hands. "I know. I know. How 'bout a treat?" This pleased him and he followed me into the kitchen, practically under my feet as I retrieved a couple of baby carrots from the fridge. You'd think the dog hadn't eaten for days the way he devoured the treats.

When he finished, he looked up at me, hoping for more. I laughed aloud, Sabrina and Charlie temporarily forgotten. "That's all for now, mister."

5

I did it. I broke up with Charlie. I'd spent most of the night before having repetitive conversations with myself over whether I should wait until he was feeling better, but I couldn't. If I didn't get it over with that morning, I'd likely chicken out and end up trapped in a miserable relationship for the next six months.

I told him I thought he should take some time to work out his problems, which really meant that *I* didn't want to deal with his problems. That's the thing about love: When you're in it, his problems are your problems. When you aren't, his problems are just a freakin' burden, and it was clear to me that I was not in love with Charlie.

It was a much shorter conversation than I'd expected, which was a relief. He didn't take it badly or well. He just sat there while I talked rapidly. When I got nervous, I hardly came up for air. When I finally did, he mumbled something about understanding, and that was that.

After I hung up, I waited for some sort of wave of emotion. There were no tears, just disappointment. I *wanted* Charlie to be the guy for me and I was so tired of being single, but at what cost? I'd much rather be lonely alone than lonely with someone else.

I wished I didn't have to work. I knew Sabrina. A private party would have her in full dramatic form. She took herself way too seriously to begin with, and I couldn't imagine the show she'd put on tonight. At least it was extra money, something that had become scarce as of late.

I was glad to be distracted by Rufus, who'd just finished breakfast and was performing his daily ritual of wiping his mouth on the carpet. Finding a spot on the area rug in the living room, he angled his body downward and he pushed himself around, groaning with pleasure. Once he was finished, he'd stand up, all four legs spread apart, with a dumbfounded look on his face, and top it off with a couple sneezes.

I settled into *my* daily ritual of checking my horoscope and email. I visited three astrology websites every day. And while I didn't live my life by what was said in each horoscope, it helped me gauge of what to expect "energetically" for the day. I'd been into astrology for many years and loved having my chart read once a year by a wonderful woman who lived in Little Italy. It wasn't so much about the predictive stuff like, "*Today is a great day for romance, Gemini! Get out there and look your best.*" I much preferred to read a horoscope that made me think, rather than go out looking for something to happen. I'd studied astrology formally when I lived in L.A. a few years back and had had aspirations of starting my own practice.

Noah Garrett was my all-time favorite. His horoscopes felt more like a therapy session with an amazing shrink than reading about the Jupiter-Pluto conjunction. He not only made me think, he also made me feel, and if I had time to read just one horoscope daily, it would be his. I'd recently responded to the call for proofreaders Noah had posted on his website. There was no pay involved, but I didn't care. I was just thrilled be a little closer to someone I'd hoped would eventually take me under his wing and show me everything he knew.

With my horoscope read and emails checked, I spent the next few hours running errands in the neighborhood. Throwing the dry cleaning over my shoulder and shifting the grocery bags to one hand, I picked up the pace and rushed home with only twenty minutes to walk and feed Rufus before heading to work. Inside, Rufus seemed strange. He didn't greet me with his usual enthusiasm; it was more like trepidation, as if my apartment had become a minefield and he was trying not to get killed. I checked the garbage under my desk because sometimes he'd take a tissue out and shred it in my absence. He knew it was wrong, and when I scolded him he'd skulk around with his tail down. He was acting like that now, but all was fine with the garbage.

I put my purse on the desk and searched the rest of the apartment.

There it was. Rufus had peed on the carpet. He did that only when he was sick, so instead of being angry, I was worried. Unsure of what I was looking for, I got down on the floor and checked him over. His gums were pink, he didn't appear to be in any pain and his nose was cold and wet. What the hell was wrong? I spent some time with him on the floor before tackling the carpet. If he doesn't eat, I told myself, then something is really wrong. I grabbed a carrot to see if he'd eat it and was stumped when he inhaled it in two seconds.

While I cleaned the pee from the carpet, a dull sense of dread filled my heart. Rufus was around 13 years old. Odd behavior wasn't just odd behavior, not at that age. I thought of Prince, Lisa's dog, who had died a couple of weeks ago.

Lisa was a close friend of mine whom I met in 1998 while living in Battery Park City. Her dog, Prince, was a golden retriever, and they lived on the same floor as Rufus and me. Prince and Rufus used to play together, and Lisa and I ran back to get them on September 11th. Prince was fine up until one day, when he appeared lethargic and had trouble breathing. Three days later, he was gone—lung cancer. His passing was a shock and a sharp reminder of what was to come for me somewhere down the road.

"It's okay, buddy," I told Rufus, tears rolling down my cheeks, scrubbing harder.

After the carpet was clean, I took him outside for a walk, watching him carefully for signs of anything out of the ordinary. He appeared to be totally fine, tail wagging, sniffing the grass.

Once we were back inside, I knew I was going to be late for work, so while Rufus was eating, I called to let Sabrina know. No answer. I decided I would try again on my way to the train, though all I wanted to do was stay with Rufus and make sure he was okay. I thought of Charlie and had a moment's regret. If I hadn't broken up with him, I could've called him to check on Rufus later.

"Pull yourself together, girl," I sighed, grabbing my stuff and heading for the door.

I tried Stella Maris one more time before getting on the subway. Luckily, Stella Maris was only one stop from my apartment, so if the trains weren't delayed, I could be there by 5:30. Still no answer.

I was so worried about Rufus that it didn't occur to me to be concerned about walking in the door a full 30 minutes late.

When I got there, the restaurant was empty, the lights were dimmed and everyone was gathered by the service bar, where Sabrina was holding court.

"This is a very important party, guys. I don't want to see empty glasses or used napkins anywhere. I'm watching all of you and I won't tolerate any bullshit." She paused and addressed me. "Nice of you to join us, Liz."

I didn't expect anything less than her tactless attempt to embarrass me, but I still felt awkward as all eyes were on me. "Sorry," I mumbled.

She wasn't impressed. "Do you want to tell me why you think you can waltz in here thirty minutes late on a very important night? VERY important."

I wanted to tell her that my dog was sick, that I called twice but nobody answered. I really wanted to tell her to kiss my ass. But I didn't. Maybe it was because I felt so put on the spot and exposed in front of both the staff and a new set of people I'd never seen before. But I had bigger fish to fry with Rufus and all.

I knew what Sabrina was doing and wasn't willing to give her the satisfaction of embarrassing me for the benefit of proving to the new people how in charge she really was. Not tonight. I looked her squarely in the eye and said, "Yes. I know I'm late. I'm sorry about that. I had an issue at home. Do you want to speak about this privately?"

Deep down, I knew I'd sealed my fate, but at that point, the conversation seemed futile. If this party was so damn important, why didn't we get to it already?

The meeting finally broke, and Sabrina introduced me to the new faces I noticed when I first arrived. "This is Rachel and Irina. They will be training with you tonight."

I scoffed at the idea of training two new people at this very *important* party. A perfect indication of her incompetence. Who the hell trained new people on a night like tonight? I hated training people, and in this place there were so many new faces because Sabrina blew through staff like crazy.

Begrudgingly I introduced myself. As I did, I realized it wasn't their fault and vowed not to punish them for my own control issues with Sabrina.

Irina, the younger and perkier of the two, immediately pulled me to the side and said, "I'm so glad to meet you. I see you guys work with fresh juices. I've never worked with fresh juices. Maybe you could show me?"

"Sure, Irina." Oh boy, she was an eager one. "Let's get the bar set up first, okay?"

Rachel ended up being really cool and had clearly bartended before. I didn't have to tell her much as she only asked for clarifications like, "Do you want the glasses here or on the other end of the bar?"

As we set up, self-doubt started to creep in. Maybe I shouldn't have been so disrespectful to Sabrina. I thought about pulling her aside to apologize but wondered if she sensed my discomfort because she was really pouring it on with the new girls. It was like being back in middle school, when one girl tried to ice out the other by being super-nice to everyone but her.

"Hey, Liz!" Keith. Finally, an ally! He was standing in the middle of the bar with some Stella Maris business cards in his hand. "Joost in case ya want tew give soom out."

"Thanks, Keith!" I was thanking him more for his presence than the cards.

The night went off without a hitch. About eighty people showed up—a party I could have easily worked by myself. I put Irina in the service bar and gave her the opportunity to learn since she was so hell-bent on doing so. The majority of the guests had gathered at my end of the bar, and Rachel was in the middle, jumping in to help. I had a chance to talk to her a little between serving drinks. I liked how easily we fell into a groove of working and chatting throughout the evening.

Rachel, Irina and I were talking more than serving once the party slowed down, trading information about previous bartending gigs, career aspirations and where we lived. We stood together in the middle of the bar, still facing forward so as not to ignore the guests.

Sabrina approached the bar. "Liz, I can't have you guys all clustered together chatting. You need to split up." We obeyed, and I was so tempted to make a snide comment about Sabrina to Rachel. But I didn't want to taint it for her.

It was close to midnight and the party was pretty much over when Sabrina started drinking. She'd clearly taken a liking to Irina, which didn't surprise me as Irina was young, like twenty-three, and hung on Sabrina's every word.

"Do you think Sabrina would mind if I take off?" Rachel asked as she polished the last of the wineglasses.

"I don't see why not." Though with Sabrina, you never knew. "Do you feel comfortable asking her? If not, I'm happy to. It's pretty dead in here." I completely got that Rachel might need someone to ask on her behalf. Getting a job as a bartender was a ridiculous process. Not only did you have to provide a headshot when applying for a job, once hired, you still weren't guaranteed the job. Some places called it "training" and others called it "trailing." Either way, you'd have to come in and work for a few hours behind the bar so management and the other bartenders could see if you were a good fit.

You also had to work for free. No pay. No tips. I'd done it, and every other bartender I knew had, too. It sucked. But I was getting paid to work the party and had made about $100 in tips. I handed Rachel a twenty and planned to do the same for Irina. I was no saint, but others had done the same for me.

Rachel approached Sabrina, which prompted a short meeting. I wondered if my job was in jeopardy. I'd never felt secure there, and Sabrina clearly had a problem with me. Here were two new bartenders who, if Sabrina wanted, could totally replace me. For all her craziness, Sabrina was smart and knew how to maintain her power. Again, I considered apologizing and fully explaining myself now that the night was almost over. The thought of getting another job was unappealing, and it might be worth it to play the game a little longer. I didn't want to work there anymore, but I couldn't just walk out without having another job lined up.

By the time the new girls left, Sabrina was pretty drunk, so I decided against talking to her. She was mostly a happy drunk, but a couple of times I'd seen her go off on one of the servers, and I wasn't taking any chances or sticking around to listen to Keith complain about her. I wanted to get back home to Rufus.

6

"I really think you should take him to the vet, Liz."

I had called my mother while walking from the subway to work the next evening and told her about Rufus's accident.

"But he seemed perfectly fine today," I said, maneuvering through the tourists on their way to South Street Seaport. "If it happens again, I'll call."

I knew what the vet would say. She'd tell me to bring him in, and I didn't have the money to do that. He was due for his annual checkup, which I'd already put off for a month. If I took him to the vet, he'd have to get his shots, and before I knew it, I'd be looking at a $350 bill. I walked the line between guilt and denial, hoping my mother wouldn't bring it up.

"Well, isn't he supposed to get his annual checkup anyway?"

It was amazing how my mother remembered everyone else's doctor appointments, meetings and birthdays. When it came to her own health, however, it was like pulling teeth to get her to go to the doctor.

"Yes, but it's not the best time right now for finances," I admitted. I was getting closer to work and needed to wrap it up.

"Just make the appointment," my mother urged. "We'll take care of the vet."

That was a sore spot. I was the youngest and an artist. My brother and sister did very well financially and I was always trying to keep up with them, contributing to birthdays and anniversaries just to save face. I didn't want anyone to think I was a loser, and taking money from parents at thirty-seven years old screamed "LOSER" in my book. Occasionally I'd let them buy things for me, like when I moved to Brooklyn and my mother took me to Bed, Bath and Beyond for apartment stuff. It was always a relief when she did things like that. I wished I were the kind of person who took money when it was offered to me, but my pride wouldn't allow it.

"Nah, Mom. It's cool," I sighed. "Next month'll be better, I'm sure." She didn't push, and for that I was silently grateful.

Sabrina was up front when I walked into work. I waved and mouthed hello to her. She looked directly at me but didn't say a word.

"Uh, Mom. I gotta go." I hung up and noticed Irina behind the bar. Great. Another night of training. I headed back to the bathroom to freshen up. Sabrina marched past me and said, "Liz! In the café *now!*"

There were no customers in the restaurant yet, only servers. One caught my eye, raising his eyebrow in wonder.

My stomach felt nervous as I walked toward the French doors separating the restaurant from the café. Out of the corner of my eye I saw Keith making his way to the café as well. That couldn't be good. But at least he'd keep Sabrina in check if she got out of hand.

I put my bag on the floor and sat at one of the high tables. Sabrina remained standing, poised for battle, while Keith sat opposite me, his body facing forward but his head turned away from my eyeline.

Sabrina started. "Liz, do you want to tell us why you decided that last night, of all nights, when we had a *very* important party, you decided it was okay to walk in *thirty minutes late?*"

Damn. I should have spoken to her last night while she was drunk.

She didn't let up, her voice rising with each sentence. "You ruined the party last night. *Ruined it.* It is not all about *you*, Liz. You are not the only person that works here. You gave me attitude when you were the one who was late. I'm sick of your bullshit. I'M the manager, ya hear me? You can't pull that shit with me!"

I began to speak, but my voice was in the back of my throat, small and weak. I collected myself and said, "I had an emergency at home and tried to call two times to let you guys know I'd be late, but no one answered the phone. I agree that maybe I didn't handle it well when I walked in. But I was just really upset and taken aback when you asked me in front of everyone. I didn't want to go into it and sound like I was making excuses."

As I said this, I hoped that at least it would make sense to Keith, but he just sat there, head down, not looking at me, like he was being scolded too.

Sabrina wasn't buying it. She was out for blood. I could smell it.

"You have no respect, Liz. NONE!" she hissed. "Your attitude last night brought *everyone* down. You set a shitty example for the new people, and frankly, I'm not sure I buy your story about trying to call. When do we ever not answer the phone?" She rolled her eyes and tossed her hair.

I decided it was probably not the best time to bring up the fact that on several occasions, customers had complained about there being no answer when they called the restaurant. I also realized that I was getting upset, and I really, really didn't want to cry. I just stood there, frozen, taking her punches like a helpless kid on a playground.

"I'm sick of your shit, LIZ! SICK of it. Who the fuck do you think you are? You and your fuckin' attitude. Ever since you started you've had this fuckin' chip on your shoulder, and ya know what? I'm done with it. DONE!"

I'm no goody two-shoes, but I was taken aback by her use of profanity. I'd heard her curse at other people, but never at me. Plus, she was full-on yelling, which was so unnecessary and…brutal. I tried to open my mouth to defend myself, but I couldn't. My head was spinning so fast. I couldn't organize my thoughts.

The right thing to do was apologize, but given her level of anger, I wasn't sure it would satisfy her. And, just off to the side, in my mind, was a tiny little voice saying, "Get out of there!" It reminded me of the scene in *Rocky III* where Rocky is getting his ass kicked by Mr. T and Mickey, his trainer, is yelling at him, in slow motion, to do anything to get out from under Mr. T's punches.

As Sabrina threw around more "fucks" and insults, I was finally ready to speak. With my voice shaking, I hopped off the chair and said, "Ya know what? I don't have to take this. I'm sorry about last night, Sabrina. I was late and I apologize. But there's no reason for you to talk to me this way. None."

She shot back, "Good! Get the FUCK out of here. GET OUT!"

Picking my bag and my dignity up off the floor, I mumbled in Keith's direction, "I wish you the best of luck." I turned and walked through the dining room, where the servers shot me looks of concern and empathy.

It felt like forever before I got outside, and once I did, I stumbled around in shock. I'd never been fired like that before. I'd never been fired *ever*.

I started walking through the crowds of tourists in no particular direction. What was I going to do for a job? How would I pay my bills? How could Keith just sit there? All the times I sat and listened to him bitch about Sabrina—and for what? In the end, his loyalty was with her.

I decided to go back to Brooklyn. I thought about calling Stephanie or my sister but was too freaked out to speak. I just wanted to be in my apartment with Rufus and the bottle of Jameson I kept for extreme situations.

Walking back to my apartment from the subway, I wondered if people on the street could tell I was just fired. I felt completely defeated, like I had a scarlet letter "F" painted on my chest.

Back home, Rufus, oblivious to it all, greeted me, his tail wagging with delight. I dropped my bag, got down on the floor and buried my head in his neck. I couldn't even cry. I wanted to, but I couldn't. Rufus sat right down and leaned into me. We stayed on the floor like that for a while. Every so often, he'd lift his head up to sniff my face and kiss my nose.

"It's time for a drink," I finally said, standing up. Rufus followed behind as I went into the kitchen and grabbed the Jameson from the cabinet above the refrigerator. I remember the first time I bought a bottle of liquor for my apartment. It felt so…*adult*. I took a glass from above the sink, filled it with ice and collapsed onto the big chair in the living room.

Clinking the bottle against the glass, I poured myself a nice tall drink with Rufus settled at my feet. I took a long, slow sip of whiskey. As it warmed my mouth and slowly traveled down my throat, I tried to process what had just happened. My thoughts were bouncing around too much for reflection. What was I going to do for work?

As I poured myself another drink, it came to me: Chris from 2i's! I'd run into him a couple of months ago, when I stopped into Angelo & Maxie's, a steakhouse in Union Square, for a drink on a Monday afternoon before a movie. We'd worked together at a nightclub in the Meatpacking District several years ago, and I was glad to know he'd since become a manager at Angelo & Maxie's.

He'd told me about the sports bar/lounge they were opening next door. The place was nowhere near ready at the time, but he had said a couple of months—which would be close to now! I considered calling him but was discouraged by the voice in my head reminding me, *You just got fired. Who'd want to hire you?* Sabrina's words had struck a chord. I wondered if I really was a bitch or difficult to work with.

Time for a refill.

The whiskey was starting to kick in and I decided to send Chris a text message to see if Angelo & Maxie's was hiring. The attempt at contact with the outside world, coupled with the warm, fuzzy feeling I'd gotten from the whiskey, prompted me to face reality.

I was now ready to speak to people.

I decided to call Stephanie first. My sister would just be worried and I didn't have the strength to make anyone feel better about my situation.

Stephanie picked up and I told her what had happened. "Are you fucking kidding me? That woman is *crazy!*" I loved Stephanie. She always said the right thing. "Girl, you are sooo much better off. Seriously."

"Steph, it was awful. I just stood there like an idiot. I didn't even know what to say." The alcohol had loosened me up. It felt good to be completely honest.

"What *could* you say? I mean really. That woman was assaulting you." She paused and chuckled. "You should sue for harassment."

"No. Fuck that. I don't want to deal with her ever again." Time for another drink—half a glass this time.

"Wait. And Keith did nothing the whole time?"

"Yes! Can you believe that shit? *Nothing!* That's what bothers me the most. I thought this guy and I had a good relationship. Do you know how many times I freakin' sat there and listened to his boo-hooing about Sabrina and everything? What the fuck?"

I was angry again. Rufus lifted his head as my voice rose. I leaned over and rubbed his neck as Stephanie declared, "Well, he just sounds like a pussy! Good riddance to all of them!"

I switched gears and told her about my friend at Angelo & Maxie's.

"Good for you! A sports bar in Union Square sounds like nothing but money to me. Don't let this get you down. It's obvious that the universe has better things in store for you. Look forward, not backward."

Though I agreed with Stephanie on some level, I still felt like this was my fault—a typical tune for me. When in doubt, make it your own fault. The Jameson had done its job and I didn't feel like thinking anymore. I hung up with Stephanie and found my way onto the floor, next to Rufus.

I lay down beside him and rubbed his back. He sighed and put his chin on my arm. Being on the floor like that reminded me of my childhood dog, Max. He was a schnoodle, a schnauzer- poodle mix. Max was my pal. Back then, my mother was always losing her temper at the drop of a hat. Once, I knocked over my water at the dinner table and my mother screamed, "Can't you be more careful? I work so hard to make dinner and this is what I get?"

Menopause chilled her out, and we're good now, but back then, I was always afraid. My dad had much more of a gentle energy, but he worked a lot. The dynamic between Keith and Sabrina was not unlike the one between my parents when I was young—with me in the middle. My dad commiserated with us kids about my mother instead of standing up for us. Max became my only ally. When my mother would go into one of her rants, I'd take him to my room and hug him and nuzzle his neck, just like I did with Rufus. The very first thing I loved about Rufus was how he loved to cuddle, sometimes for hours at a time. His presence always gave me comfort. For the rest of the night, I didn't think about the fact that I no longer had a job.

7

"I have a Millionaire Mind."

I stood in front of the full-length mirror outside my bathroom door with one hand over my heart and the other placed on my forehead, just like the book said.

"My inner world creates my outer world," I continued.

It had been two weeks since I'd been fired. I was relieved I was no longer working for Sabrina, but I had no money. I had a job, technically, but it didn't start for another couple of weeks.

Chris texted me back the day after my showdown with Sabrina and told me to come in for an interview at the steakhouse, which was next door to the new bar. He gave me a warm greeting when I arrived.

"I can't believe we're going to be working together again," he said, throwing his arms around me. Hugging Chris had always felt nice. He was in great shape: broad shoulders, strong arms. He wasn't that tall, under 6 feet, but his presence definitely made him seem taller.

He assured me that the interview was just a formality and "they all know you're like a little sister to me." I was older than Chris by several years, but I didn't care. I'd say I was his eighth-grade gym teacher if it meant getting a job.

And I did—at Maxie's Grill, an offshoot of the steakhouse. The grill was less formal, with big-screen televisions, a DJ, and more casual fare, like burgers and fries. It wasn't opening until November, but an orientation was scheduled for the following week.

While I was grateful to have secured a new job, money was running way low. Desperate for some sort of cash flow, I swallowed my pride and called Lydia at Smokehouse to see if I could pick up a shift or two. She happened to be in a good mood that day, treating me like I was her new best friend. "We'd looove to have you back. It hasn't been the same since you left. Take the Sunday brunch shift. I'm not here on Sundays and could use a strong bartender now that the summer's over and brunches are getting busy again." That she wouldn't be there sealed the deal for me.

With so much time on my hands, I decided to buy the book *Secrets of a Millionaire Mind,* which I learned about on a late-night infomercial about how to increase personal wealth. The author promoting the book was pretty cheesy, but the idea of attracting money appealed to me. Rufus sat and watched me through the beaded curtains as I recited my daily declaration and readied myself to get out there and attract some money.

He hadn't had any more accidents in the apartment. Still, at my mother's urging, I finally took him to the vet for a checkup. She even picked us up in Brooklyn and drove us to the vet's office in Manhattan. I was glad she came because Rufus freaked out and started to shake as soon as we walked into the waiting room. His discomfort made me nervous, which was the very reason I'd put off going for so long.

Good vets were hard to find, but I liked Dr. Gabriele. She combined Eastern and Western medicine in her treatments and had a sweet, soothing voice that made her sound like a teenager. She was in her twenties and had a nose ring.

"How's Rufus's balance?" Dr. Gabriele asked, moving each paw around while Rufus trembled on the stainless-steel examining table. I held his head steady with both hands under his jaw.

"Actually, I didn't even think about it, but he seems clumsier than usual." I moved closer to Rufus and rubbed his cheeks with my thumbs to calm him. "He's always been a clumsy dog, but lately he loses his footing and stumbles a lot."

"Well, he's got pretty bad arthritis in his back legs," said Dr. Gabriele, shining a flashlight in his eyes. I circled around the table to hold his backside steady. "He's also got some pretty severe cataracts in both eyes, so it may be that he's just not seeing as well as he used to."

"Is there anything we can do for him in terms of the arthritis?" my mother asked.

"We could take some X-rays and see how bad the arthritis is, and we can also treat the pain with some anti-inflammatory medication."

I held up my hand. "I don't want to do X-rays. Rufus is freaked out enough. It's not that bad, really. He just seems more stiff on some days." I agreed to take a bottle of anti-inflammatory pills in case his arthritis got worse.

My mother insisted on paying for Rufus's vet visit, which cost $350. I felt my usual mix of relief and shame, though the gratitude won. With my limited income, my main focus was on the end of the month and making the bills.

Rufus rested comfortably in the back of the car on the ride back to Brooklyn.

"When does the new job start?" my mother asked.

"A couple of weeks," I said, looking out the window. I knew she wanted to say something but was holding back.

That was yesterday. Today I was reciting my mantras, determined to have a Millionaire Mind. But my own mind kept wandering, so I sidetracked myself with e-mail.

Sitting in my inbox was an e-mail with the subject line "Hang Tag." Oh my god! It was from the model coordinator at La Jolie. They wanted me to do the shoot for their new bra. I squealed with delight, prompting Rufus to pick up his head and tilt it to the right.

I jumped up from my desk. "Rufus, baby! Your mama's boobs are going to be all over the country! Woo-hoo! That's right!" After a short celebratory dance, I settled down to read the e-mail.

> Hi Liz. We're finally shooting the hang tag. Can you come on the 15th? It will be a three-hour shoot with a day rate of $500. Let me know ASAP if that works for you.
> —Alyssa

If that works for me? *Of course* it worked for me—$500 felt like a million right now. Maybe there was something to this Millionaire Mind stuff.

I'd been a lingerie model since the mid-'90s. Whenever I told people that, they'd avert their eyes and say, "Really? Are you in, like, *Victoria's Secret* or something?"

I was a 32D fit and show model, which was far less glamorous than being featured in a Victoria's Secret catalog, but the money was good and the work interesting. I sort of fell into it after a girl I knew years ago announced that she had "just made $50 for a half hour's work." Intrigued, I asked how I could get on that boat. She referred me to Abbott Kleinman. He worked in a dingy building in Times Square with even dingier offices. His office was more like a room: small, paint peeling, saggy chairs and tons of magazine clippings of women in lingerie, bathing suits and wedding gowns. It reminded me of my room as a teenager when I went through my obsessed-with-wedding-gowns phase, plastering all my favorites on the wall next to my bed.

He was on the phone when I arrived, but he waved me to sit down. There were headshots of women everywhere, though I didn't recognize them. The pictures were all signed with personal messages I couldn't quite make out.

Abbott was about 5 feet tall and had three front teeth missing; the rest were capped in silver. He had a strong accent like my Jewish grandfather and all he kept saying to me was, "How lawng ya know me, huh?" A pause for effect, his eyes flickering with delight. "Couple-a-yeeeeahs."

He got me my first job with Lilyette, working as a show model for Market Week. During Market Week, buyers would come in to see the line and the models would file in—each of us a different size—while the salespeople discussed the "features and benefits." The pay was great and his cut was minimal. Abbott died shortly thereafter, and I've been modeling without an agent ever since.

As a fit model, I worked directly with the designers, acting as the body on which they'd fit each garment and providing input on anything from the actual fit to whether I liked the lace they'd chosen. The designers took their fit models' opinions seriously, and I loved being a part of the whole process.

Show modeling was different and felt less like a show and more like a choreographed dance. And I had it down: I'd start by entering the conference room fully robed. The sales rep would say, "What we have here is…" which was my cue to let the robe drop off my shoulders down to my waist as I turned and posed, staying in sync with her description of what I was wearing.

I got a kick out of telling people that I walked around in my bra and underwear for money, but I never felt like a *real* model. A *real* model was in magazines. I was not. I always need something tangible to make me feel legitimate.

But now I was finally legitimate! Having my boobs on a hang tag was the real deal. A hang tag was the picture attached to the bra showing what it looked like on an actual human. It was just boobs, no face. And for this particular bra, it would be in every single Dillard's store across the country.

I sat back down to reply to Alyssa's e-mail, taking a moment to compose myself, even though I wanted to write, "YESSSSSSSSSSSSSSS SSSSSSSSSS!!!!! I'LL DO IT!"

My cell phone was ringing from somewhere in the apartment. I was the worst with that. Half the time I forgot to take it off silent, the mode I always kept it on whenever I was working. Other times I left it in my purse or a jacket pocket. It drove my parents crazy that I didn't have a landline, but I couldn't justify the expense. Instead, I'd shuffle around my apartment searching for the phone, with Rufus following at my feet.

I plucked my purse from the shelf by the front door, gave it a squeeze and felt the vibration run through my fingers. I didn't bother looking to see who it was.

"Hello?" I said, a bit breathless from the search.

"Liz. It's Dad."

"Oh, hey, Dad!" I was grateful that today I didn't have to play happy. Had he called half an hour ago, it would've been another Academy Award-winning performance of me hiding the fact that I was super-stressed about finances.

"Do you have a minute?" he asked.

Uh-oh. My dad hardly ever asked that. He almost always started the conversation with "So, how ya doin'?" "Do you have a minute?" was code for "I've got something serious to talk to you about." My first instinct was that he was sick. Or maybe Mom was. But I'd seen her the day before, and she seemed fine.

"Liz? Are you there?" Now my dad sounded concerned.

"Yeah, yeah. I'm here," I said. "Are you okay?"

"Oh yeah, I'm fine. We're fine. I just wanted to talk to you about *you*. Mom tells me you're not so fine."

Shit.

"Your mother and I want to give you some money."

SHIT!

"We know you're going through a rough time, and we want to help. It's just to help you get through the next few weeks until your new job starts. What do you say? Will you let your ol' parents help you out a little?"

I wanted to speak, but my voice seemed to have stopped working. My mind, however, was in full swing. I hadn't taken money from my parents in over ten years. Ten years! Sure, I'd let them pay for the vet or a doctor's visit every now and then, but that was different. They wanted to give me money to *live*. I was thirty-seven years old. Who the hell took money from their parents at thirty-seven years old?

I wanted to tell him no, but something stopped me. I also wanted to throw myself onto the floor and sob, "Yes, Daddy. Will you please help me? I just can't do this all by myself anymore." The adult in my mind, however, shot back at the little girl, *Get a hold of yourself! There is NO way you're taking money from your parents.*

"Liz? Are you there?"

8

"To your new job," my sister said, raising an oversized glass of Chilean cabernet. "Cheers!"

Leaning in to clink her wineglass with my own, I smiled. "Yeah. Pretty cool. Thanks."

My sister Blair and I were at a bar in midtown, close to where she worked. I'd arrived early in order to score a seat at the long bar, which was now full of the professional set, like her. Watching the two bartenders hustle behind the spacious bar, I wondered what the crowd would be like at my new job.

Blair walked in looking glamorous as usual. She worked in fashion and knew how to put herself together. With long limbs that accentuated her slim, 5'8" frame, Blair was taller than me with high cheekbones and big brown eyes.

"So tell me about the place. Is it part of Angelo & Maxie's? Is it a restaurant too, or just a bar? Or is it more like a lounge vibe? When does it open?"

The more questions she asked, the more excited Blair got. I loved my sister. Her enthusiasm was a comfort, though sometimes a bit much. The girl could ask a lot of questions.

"I'm not really sure what the format is. I know it's going to be separate from the steakhouse, with a more laid-back vibe. Chris said they'll have DJs on the weekends and we'll be open 'til 2."

"2 a.m.? *Ohhhh,* that sucks," she said into her glass. "But DJs? That's grrr–ATE! You're going to do so well there. It's in Union Square—

very happening."

I couldn't deny the fact that I was excited, but I tended to downplay that kind of stuff. I didn't like to get my hopes up. It kept me from being disappointed.

"Do you know how many bartenders they've hired?" Blair asked, wrapping her perfectly manicured fingers around the stem of her wineglass.

"No. I don't really know much except that there's an orientation next week and we open November 15th."

Eyes wide, my sister exclaimed, "November 15th? What are you going to do until then for work?"

"Well, I've got Market coming up, and"—I paused, readying myself for her reaction—"I'm working at Smokehouse again."

"*What*?? Oh, Liz, noooooo." My sister made no attempt at couching her feelings. "Why would you work with that crazy bitch Lydia again? Especially after finally getting away from Sabrina?"

That was the thing I loved and hated about Blair. Her questions were always the ones I'd ask myself—over and over. When I had the answers, I appreciated how in sync we were. But when I was flying by the seat of my pants, keeping my fingers crossed that everything would work out, it irritated the shit out of me.

"Look, I need the money, fast," I said. "It's only Sunday brunch. Lydia's not even there on Sundays. With the weather getting colder, it's going to get busier, so the money will be good. And right now, I'll take what I can get."

God forbid I told her I'd decided to take the money my parents offered.

"Only as a loan," I'd told my father, finally caving in to his persistence. "I don't care if I pay you back $20 a month. I'm going to pay this back."

I accepted $1,000 with the intention of starting payments in January. By then I would be settled in at Maxie's and coming off the holiday season, which every bartender lives for.

Blair and I were close, but I'd stopped telling her everything in the last few years. It's not that I didn't want to. I just wanted to be more of an individual. Blair was two and a half years older than me, and for as long as I could remember, she was the one I'd run to when I was having problems in my life.

My mother's volatility didn't warrant much free expression from a sensitive soul like myself, so it was Blair who would listen and advise me in my times of need. She had a natural maternal instinct and a strong opinion, a great combination when I was looking for advice.

Only this time I wasn't looking for her opinion. She was much more inclined to suggest the safe route, and I'd been trying to find my *own* way of doing things, which didn't include playing it small and safe. The irony was that she'd been going through her own bout with individuality and was tired of taking care of people as well.

So for the last couple of years, we'd been in recalibration mode. It felt awkward a lot of the time, with each of us holding back in one way or another. Sometimes it was only after I'd confided in her that I realized I shouldn't have. Other times it was Blair telling me that she couldn't be there for *me*.

It all started a few years ago, when we'd made plans to spend a Saturday afternoon together in SoHo. When I called to find out where she was, she told me she was running late.

Something snapped in me, and my reaction was less than rational.

"Ya know what, Blair? Let's just forget it."

"What's your problem? I just said I was running late."

And right there on Prince Street, thirty-something years of being the younger sister always waiting for her older sister to be "ready" for her had reached its boiling point. In tears and sobs, I let her have it.

"I'm sick of being treated this way! You always do everything the way *you* want to do it and I'm tired of it. TIRED of it, ya hear me?" I didn't care about the people looking at me as they passed me on the street, ranting like a lunatic. "You have NO respect for other people's time. You're selfish!"

This really got her, and the gloves came off. "Well, Liz, I'm sick of a few things myself," she said. I could hear her fighting back the tears. "You think the world revolves around you. You're always *going through* something. Always having problems. I've had enough!"

It was ugly and we didn't speak for over a month after that. She was the one who suggested we take a break, which was more devastating than our actual fight. I felt so rejected and shut down by her request to "take some time apart," but at the same time I felt a surprising amount of relief.

Our hiatus made me realize how much *I* needed a break. I needed to stop being the younger sister constantly looking for her sister's approval. I needed to be me, and she needed to be herself. Since then, things were better but still in flux.

I had a brother too. Gregory was the oldest, with six years between us. We weren't close, nor were we estranged. I think the age difference and the fact that he didn't live nearby put us in the category of loving each other but not having much of a relationship. Despite that, I knew that if I needed him, Gregory would be there.

As the youngest and the only one in the family pursuing a creative lifestyle, I had a bit of an inferiority complex. I wasn't proud of it, but Blair and Gregory both did very well in their jobs, and I hated the fact that at holidays, they'd always say things like, "Whatever you can afford" or "You don't have to contribute if you don't have it... We'll put your name on the card anyway." I knew they meant well, but my own shit kept me from agreeing to contribute anything less than what they were giving.

Blair picked up the wine list, her chunky bracelets clanging against one another. "Should we order a bottle?"

I tried not to show my discomfort. Money. It was all I thought about these days, and a bottle of wine seemed so decadent.

Sensing my distress, she leaned into me and murmured, "Liz, I got it. Don't worry about it. You're not really working."

Yet another tricky moment: when someone offered me money or to pay the bill. It would be awesome if she picked up the bill, 'cuz right now, money was tighter than a hipster's skinny jeans. But I was too proud. My motto was, "If you can't afford to go out, stay home."

I started to protest, but she wasn't having it. "Really. I've got it. You can get me when you're making all that money at your new job in Union Square," she said, almost singing the last part with glee.

I finally agreed, and the relief at not having to pay was completely overshadowed by my shame. Time for more wine. "Wanna stick with the cabernet?"

It turned out to be a great evening as we drank and snacked on olives, French fries and grilled calamari. Blair told me about how much she hated her boss and consequently her job.

"Ugh," I said, picking up a fry and popping it in my mouth. "It sounds like you're working for a Sabrina."

"I know. This woman is crazy. Do you know that she takes some sort of medication and apparently, on the days she's such a monster, she hasn't taken her meds."

I opened my mouth in shock and mouthed, "Noooo."

Last year, Blair landed a job at a major fashion house. It was her dream job. But it had quickly become a nightmare as she dealt with a very difficult boss and the constant pressure of working in such a high-profile environment. She was definitely miserable and struggling to make the best of it.

"I don't want to talk about work anymore," she said, giving her head a vigorous shake. Quickly gathering herself back from the darkness of her job woes, she shifted gears. "Tell me about Rufus. Did Mom take you guys into the city to the vet? What did the vet say? Did she find anything wrong with him?"

I told her about our visit to the vet and how Dr. Gabriele didn't see anything unusual. "She *did* say that he has cataracts and they're most likely affecting his sight, which explains why he's been clumsier than usual. Oh, and he's got pretty bad arthritis in his hind legs. She wanted to do X-rays, but really, what's the point? He hates being at the vet enough. Why put him through that? It's not like I'm going to have him go through surgery."

"I totally agree," she said softly. "It's just old age."

"I know. Oooof. I don't even want to *think* about what's ahead of me." I swallowed a big gulp of wine and the reality that Rufus was pushing 14 years old.

"Well, look, if the vet says he's okay and there's nothing wrong with him internally, who knows, he could be around for many more years," she offered gently.

Now it was my turn to shake my head and change the subject. "So... What'cha got going on for the weekend?"

9

My job at Maxie's started out less than ideal. We were not that busy, which was standard for a new place, but we were also told in training that there'd be a lot of buzz promoting the place, and so far, I'd seen no indication of that. The other thing was that we were way overstaffed. Overstaffing was a common complaint amongst servers and bartenders. The more people on shift, the less money you made. At Maxie's, we had two bartenders scheduled every night, with a swing bartender Tuesday through Saturday. A swing shift was sometimes called a "hero shift," where a bartender was scheduled to come in just for the busy times. I'd worked a few swing shifts in other places, coming in at 5 p.m. and staying until 8 p.m., making an easy $125–150.

I had two swing shifts at Maxie's: Tuesday and Friday nights. I came in a few times on Friday nights and literally walked into Scott, the bar manager, asking me, "Do you feel like working tonight? If not, you can go home, 'cuz I don't think I'll really need you." The other times, I think he kept me there just because he felt bad; however, staying for three hours and walking out with $40 was so not worth it. I had yet to even come in for my Tuesday shift. Thankfully, Scott decided to have me call an hour before the shift to see if I was needed. And though it saved me a wasted trip into Manhattan, I could never make plans.

Tonight I was on a swing, and Scott, who looked more like a professor than a manager, with his black-rimmed glasses and light brown beard, was at the host stand when I walked into the restaurant. He gave me an enthusiastic "HEY!"—which was kind of like code for

"You're working tonight?" I gave him a "Hey!" back as I hung my coat in the coat check. It was there where I gathered myself for each and every shift. Tonight was especially stressful because I was working with Amber. And Amber liked to be the star.

That made me uneasy because I had no desire to get in that game. I liked to do a good job, but I wasn't willing to run anyone over in the process. We had nine bartenders, plus myself, for a not-so-busy bar. Seven of them were women with strong personalities and presence. And then there was Brian. One of the owners took a liking to him after meeting him at some restaurant in Great Neck. Brian was a nice guy, kind of simple and not too sharp, but at least he wasn't vying for a stronger position.

Right now, Rachel was the only one I trusted. Yes, Rachel—the girl I trained at Stella Maris. On orientation day, I sat among a group of my soon-to-be-coworkers waiting for things to get started, when all of a sudden, I looked up and saw Rachel enter the room.

"Oh my GOD," I squealed, causing more than a few stares as I stood up, raising my hands in surprise. "NO way," she breathed, making her way over to me, brown curls bouncing behind her and that megawatt smile. "I can't believe this!"

"Girl, I never even went *back* to Stella," she said when I asked if she ended up getting the job. "That manager was nuts."

Rachel, I knew, had my back. There was another girl, Judy, who seemed harmless enough, but she was quiet, so it was hard to tell. The remaining girls appeared a little cutthroat to me.

Amber was fresh-faced and a bit too enthusiastic for my taste. Her dirty-blonde hair was always pulled back in a ponytail and her makeup expertly applied. Originally from the South, she had that way about her where it was hard to tell whether she was being nice or insulting.

On the last day of training, I got paired off with Amber to practice making our specialty cocktails. I had missed a large part of training due to modeling, but Scott and Chris were totally fine with it. Amber, however, took every chance she could to remind me of how much I'd missed.

"You know that we have to rim the glass with melted white chocolate for the white chocolate raspberry martini, right? Ohhhh... You probably missed that because you weren't here. Okay, well, I *guess* I can show you."

News flash, Amber. I know how to rim a glass with melted chocolate.

Behind the bar, she was super-anal and very bossy. I'd been accused of being extremely anal behind the bar, and I'm not ashamed to agree, but I had no patience for someone who'd use their anal-retentiveness as a way of micromanaging me. We'd all started at the same time, so it wasn't like she was the head bartender or anything. I suppose I could have used my friendship with Chris for leverage, but I believed that respect should be earned, not forced down someone's throat.

On Friday nights, it was Amber, Lara and I as the swing shift. Lara was nice enough, but around here, who knew if it was just an act. She was petite, with big boobs, long jet-black hair and blue eyes. Though she was *very* flaky and a little out there, it was hard not to like Lara. Working with her was sometimes a challenge because she liked to talk much more than she liked to work.

The bar wasn't that busy when I'd arrived, but Scott didn't tell me to go home, so it looked like I was staying. I lifted the hinged countertop to get behind the bar. Amber stepped in front of me, blocking the way.

"What are you doing here?" she demanded.

Taken aback, I said, "Uh, working?" I'm not in the habit of pushing my way into any place (unless it's a crowded subway), but the counter was getting heavy in my hand. "Ya think you could give me some room here?" I said, not even trying to hide my annoyance.

She moved slightly to the right, which gave me a few inches to squeeze back behind the bar. It was an awkward maneuver with such limited space that the counter dropped out of my hand, slamming closed with a loud BOOM!

"You're not supposed to let it fall," she chastised. "Scott doesn't like us doing that."

It was going to be a fun night. I decided against telling her to go fuck herself and said hi to Lara.

"Heeeeeyyyyyy, mama!" She came over to give me a hug. "You have the best freakin' body. Man, I wish I had your shape, but I'm too short and I have no waist."

"I thought we didn't have a swing tonight," Amber interrupted, craning her neck as she looked for Scott.

"Scott didn't say anything and it *is* my scheduled shift." I couldn't believe I had to justify my presence to this little bitch. I got that having a third bartender on a slow night was no cause for celebration, but Amber's attitude wasn't cool.

I looked her straight in the eye and said, "I'm sorry, Amber. Is there a problem here? Because last time I checked, Scott was in charge of the schedule, not you."

With that, she retreated. Typical. All bark and no bite. As much as I hated getting scrappy with Amber, I'd had enough of insecure women bossing me around.

Lara, on the other hand, just wanted to know about my workout regimen. "So, Liz. How did you get your arms that way? They're so perfect—muscular, but not too butch." Amber left the bar, most likely to find Scott. Lara kept talking, oblivious to the new customer who was closer to her side of the bar. As she went on and on, I pushed past her to get the guy a drink.

While I made his drink, he had some words with Scott, who'd reappeared. Amber pranced around behind the bar, cleaning and straightening solely for Scott's benefit. Lara, being her naturally bubbly self, was talking to a couple at the other end of the bar while I just stood there, feeling like a total outsider.

There were no more customers to talk to, no glasses to wash, and inserting myself into the conversation between Scott and the newest customer was not really my style. I guess Amber saw this and asked a little too loudly if I could go in the back and get some plates. Half relieved and half annoyed, I left the bar and made my way back to the kitchen.

When I returned, Scott was standing in the service area talking to Lara and Amber. I knew what was coming, and wondered how much money I'd make for staying only a half hour.

"Good. Now that I have all of you ladies here, I need to let you know how important it is to serve people right away when they come in the door. The guy with Grey Goose and cranberry—he's a regular at the steakhouse next door, and he wasn't happy that it took so long to get him his drink."

Lara flashed a cutesy smile and practically gushed, "Oh! I'm sorry. I don't know what's wrong with me—I'm so out of it tonight." By the look on Scott's face, I could see that her dumb-blonde (though she was brunette) act was working.

Amber, of course, had to remind him that she wasn't even behind the bar. That left me, of course. I hate giving excuses when I'm in the wrong, but I really wanted to tell him that it was Lara's fault for talking my ear off and distracting me. Instead, I took the professional road. "You're right, Scott. Sorry about that." And with that, I slipped back behind the bar and did what I do best: struck up a conversation with the very regular who wasn't happy with the service.

In the end, he loved me and was singing my praises to Scott on his way out, which made me want to give Amber a forehead push with my hand and say, "'Cuz that's how I roll!"—though it appeared I was rolling home, because after regular guy left, Scott cut me for the night.

"Oh, Liz," Amber said, "before you go, can you break down the well on the far end of the bar for us, please?"

Sure, Master, whatever you say.

"Did you hear that Calli got fired?" Lara asked, looking around so as not to be overheard while I poured hot water into the ice bin.

"No! I didn't." This was interesting. "What happened?"

"I don't know. She and Chris got into an argument, and he fired her on the spot. I heard that she was bitching to him about not making any money."

"Well, duh," I said, tilting my head toward the rags. "Can you hand me one of those, please?"

"And then Brian gave his notice, too." She handed me a rag and leaned against the bar, her back to the customers. "He said it wasn't worth it for him to come in all the way from Long Island. I don't know, girl, maybe all we have to do is wait for a few more people to go and we'll all start making some money."

I nodded my head and pretended to focus on my cleaning. I wasn't saying anything on that subject.

"Has Chris said anything to you about whether anyone else is next?"

My mouth almost dropped open. Only Lara could get away with asking such a question, with her pretty blue eyes and her ditzy ways.

"Um, Lara, Chris and I don't talk about that stuff. I'm just as vulnerable as everyone else."

"Yeah, but still, you guys are friends."

With that, I pushed my head toward the bar behind her to let her know she had a new customer.

• • •

On the train ride back to Brooklyn, I thought about my conversation with Lara. So was that it? Did everyone there think I was privy to some sort of special treatment because Chris was my friend? I wasn't sure how that made me feel. I was shocked because I didn't operate that way, using my friendship with management to ensure job security. But then again, why shouldn't I? Maxie's was teeming with carnivorous energy, with everyone trying to jockey into a better position. Would it be so terrible, for once in my life, to play the game just a little bit?

10

"That's fucked up, Liz. If everyone's going to be so cutthroat there, you've got to do whatever you can, even if it means using Chris for job security."

The next morning was beautiful and unusually warm for December. Rufus was thrilled to be outside as usual, doing a lot more sniffing than peeing.

"It's just soooo not my way." I gave the leash a gentle tug to remind him we were outside for a reason. "I hate that shit. I just want to work in a place where people do their job without drama."

"Ha! Then you're in the wrong business." Lisa laughed.

Lisa and I had been friends for almost ten years. We'd met in the laundry room when we were both living in Battery Park City in the late '90s. At the time, she was working as a bartender in a popular nightclub. We became fast friends, taking long walks on the promenade with our dogs, talking about life and all the things we wanted out of it.

She eventually moved into event planning before leaving the industry altogether, but Lisa still got it, which was precisely why I decided to call her that morning. My sister, though sympathetic, worked in the corporate world; today, I needed someone who *knew*.

"How many bartenders are left?" Lisa asked.

"Seven. One just got fired, and I hear another one's leaving. Rufus!" Rufus had proceeded to get his leash and himself tangled around the legs of a bench next to a garbage can while looking for snacks.

"I say just hang in there. People will eventually start to drop off.

They already are. It's not busy enough for them to hire more people, so maybe they'll start to spread out the shifts more."

"Yeah," I sighed. "You're probably right. I just wish I were making money." I was trying to untangle Rufus. My phone balanced between my ear and shoulder, I squatted down and pulled the leash free. Rufus circled back around the bench toward me, tangling himself up on the other side.

"Rufus, wait." I was about to drop the phone. "Hang on, Lisa." I placed the phone on the ground and freed Rufus's leash up yet again while he sniffed at the phone. "Sorry about that," I said, as we headed back to my building.

"What's your plan for New Year's? Are you working?"

"No. I'm going to try and get something else. Maxie's is way overstaffed—no surprise there. I made a deal with Scott to work New Year's Day instead."

"I hate New Year's. I'm toying with the idea of renting out my apartment for the holidays to make some extra cash."

"You should totally do it! Stay with me."

We hung up after I managed to convince her to come to Brooklyn for the few nights she planned to rent her apartment.

Lisa's advice was good. I should muddle through the process, but for how long? I knew Maxie's had the potential to be a great spot to work. The location, the sports-bar theme—it *had* to be good. I just didn't know how much time I had to wait it out.

Money was tight, but if I could get a gig for New Year's, I'd be okay for this month.

"What kind of dog is that?" a voice from behind me said.

I turned around and saw a short, elderly black woman admiring Rufus as he sniffed around, stalling the end of our walk.

Everyone always wanted to know what kind of dog Rufus was. People would stop us on the street, curious about his odd looks. I got tired of telling people that he was some sort of terrier mix and had once complained about it to my dad.

"Just make up a name for him, then," he'd suggested. "Why not call him a Tibetan Schelango?"

And so it was—Rufus became a Tibetan Schelango. My friend

Jonathan reveled in telling people that, with a straight face, waiting for them to pretend they'd heard of the breed, nodding his head with conviction. "Oh, yes. It's a very rare breed," he'd say. "*Very* rare." I'd never had the balls to do it, but I was always tempted when people would ask me.

"How old is he?" the old woman asked.

"I've had him for about twelve years. I think he's around thirteen or fourteen."

"Ohhhhh…" She let out a low whistling sigh. "That's how old mine was when he died. Thirteen. Yep. It's like he got old overnight." She nodded in Rufus's direction. "He have trouble walking? Mine had all sorts of trouble. Couldn't get up on the couch anymore. I miss him so."

I was pretty sure the woman was going to cry, and I was definitely sure I didn't want to hear anymore. Why did people think it was okay to tell you how their dog died? That would be like meeting someone's grandmother and going on and on about how your own grandmother died a slow and painful death when she was about the same age. I was sorry but didn't want to be reminded of how close to death my dog might be. Nope. Time to get upstairs.

Inside, I sent out e-mails to everyone I knew in the bar/restaurant world, asking if they needed a bartender for New Year's Eve. Rufus had finished his breakfast and was doing his usual face-wipe on the carpet. I watched him for a while. Did he do it more slowly than usual? Was he really getting old? People used to comment on how great he looked for his age, always saying, "Really? Nine? Wow! He looks like a puppy." Now they were sharing their death stories with me.

"Are you getting old, Rufus?" I walked over to him. Kneeling down, I took his head in my hands, massaging his neck, just under the ears. He melted into my hands, groaning slightly, then put his head down and rolled onto his back. "That's right," I said, scratching his stomach. "What does she know?"

• • •

The following week, it was Marta and me behind the bar. After my conversation with Lisa, I was ready to suck it up and muddle through, hoping more bartenders would start to quit. Marta and I worked Wednesday and Thursday nights together. She was from Finland and on the enthusiastic side. She worked another job at a busy nightclub on the Lower East Side, and I knew from experience that in some clubs, the pace was incredible. It wasn't uncommon to work four hours straight without stopping. Unfortunately, Marta brought the same level of energy to Maxie's, which was comical because I could work that bar by myself with ease. I'm sure we looked like a bad version of "The Tortoise and the Hare," with Marta running around and me staying off to the side.

That night I was the closing bartender, which meant I came in an hour later than Marta. She was in full swing when I arrived, despite there being only two customers.

"Hey!!" she called to me as I headed over to the service area, where a few of the servers were hanging out. The tables were empty and there were way too many servers milling about, trying to keep themselves occupied. There were so many of them, it was hard to remember who was who.

The hinged countertop was crowded with glassware, which meant lifting it was not an option. I placed the essentials from my purse—lip gloss, wine opener and cell phone—on the bar and gave the group a general hello before squatting low and crawling underneath to get inside.

As I stood up, Marta was right there—like, *right* there. She was so close that I practically kissed her.

"What's up?" Though we'd worked together the night before, Marta greeted me with cheer reserved for people who hadn't seen each other in months.

I had nothing against Marta. She was nice enough, but beyond the "How ya doin'?" and long stories about her life, there was nothing more to it. She wasn't really interested in my life, and I wasn't the type to offer unless someone asked me.

She was vigorously cleaning one of the sinks. "You know me. I'm a neat freak. I've been cleaning since I got here."

Well, yeah, what else is there to do? We've got two people at the bar.

I put my purse in the little cubby under the bar as Marta came up behind me. "So, how ya doin'?"

"Good, good," I said. "A little tired. I had trouble sleeping last night, for some reason."

"Me too!" she exclaimed. And with that, Marta tossed her white-blonde hair, launching into how *she* was up all night thinking about her boyfriend, who was in jail. He had been one of the bouncers at her other job and, according to Marta, was serving time for something he didn't do. "He was totally framed." She'd told me the whole story the second time we worked together. I mostly nodded and threw in the occasional "Holy shit" and "Wow, really?" Tonight she was updating me on her latest visit with him.

Yep. So much for conversation tonight; my eyes glazed over as she talked and talked and talked.

"He's so great. I love him. We're going to get married once he's out."

"Liz!" Chris called from behind. Thank god. I walked over to the service bar and leaned in to give him a kiss. "Hi, honey. You smell good."

Chris puffed up a little bit. "Yeah. It's the new Dolce & Gabbana." He pointed to Marta with his chin. "How's it going with the Energizer Bunny?"

"I've been here five minutes and I'm already exhausted."

From the service bar, I got a good look at Marta. She had a typical Nordic look—straight, white-blonde hair cut bluntly to her shoulders, a button nose and high cheekbones. The guys loved her. She was decked out in bartender gear: wine key stuffed into her waistband, a few pens in her back pocket and a retractable bottle opener affixed to her belt. I'd never seen one of those before. It reminded me of Schneider, from the '70s show *One Day at a Time*, with his retractable key chain.

"You workin' tomorrow night?" Chris asked as he organized the glassware in the service bar. That was his thing. He hated when the glasses were messy.

"Who knows?" I practically spit. "I'm on a swing, and you know how *that* goes." Pause. "Between the overstaffing and Amber... I don't know, man."

"Yeah, well, I think we're going to put Amber next door in the steakhouse. She wants more shifts and Scott thinks she's the best, so she's basically getting whatever she wants."

"Good. Then hopefully I'll get a full shift on Fridays."

Chris leaned in a little closer so no one could hear: "Can you keep a secret?"

Did I mention Chris liked to gossip? Like an old lady. When we last worked together, he knew about everything! Gossip bored me, but I played along, giving him a look like, *Do you have to ask?*

"I'm thinking about giving you Wednesday nights by yourself."

My eyes lit up. "Really? Why?"

"'Cuz that one over there can't work Thursday nights anymore," his voice imitating a whiny child. "And I don't like her anyway. So I'm just going to tell her that I can't keep her on the schedule if she's working just one shift."

"Ohhhh," I said, lowering my eyes.

He backed up a bit and scrunched up his eyes. "I thought you'd be happy about this."

"I am! I am!" I said, holding up my hand. "I just don't want people to think I'm getting special favors."

"Fuck 'em if they do, Liz." He puffed. "I'm the GM here and I can do whatever I want."

I couldn't help but laugh. "Okay, big man. I gotta work now."

I forgot to ask Chris who'd be taking Marta's place on Thursdays, but I didn't have much time to think about that or his little "secret" because we actually had a small crowd going for the remainder of the night. Nothing either of us couldn't handle alone, but it was nice to be busy. Marta was all over the place behind the bar, constantly passing behind me to wait on people I was closest to, with annoying little jabs to my back from her index finger and announcing a bit too loudly, "Behind you!"

I finally had to tell her, "Marta. Let's split the bar, okay? You stick to that side and I'll stick to this side. Yes?" She smiled and gave me a perky "Okay!" but for the rest of the night until she left, it was Marta's show and I was just another spectator.

Maybe it wouldn't be such a bad thing to have Wednesday nights all to myself.

11

The weather had finally turned cold, and with Christmas just two weeks away, I was feeling less motivated to get out of bed in the morning. Today was a chilly one. I knew it just by looking out at the gray, leafless trees swaying slowly outside my window. I rolled over and hung my head off the side of the bed, checking for Rufus, who was curled up on his blanket.

"Good morning!"

Rufus, a bit startled, jerked his head up, trying to figure out where I was. He leaned back, tail wagging, and looked up at me in bed.

"Hey, buddy," I said, reaching down to scratch his head.

He was in no hurry to get up as he rolled onto his back, ready for some tummy rubbing. He didn't stay in that position for long and started to squirm around on the floor trying to get up. The jerky movements didn't help, and he was stuck on his back, legs flailing in a panic.

"Okay, okay," I said, jumping out of bed and onto the floor. "I got you." I helped him onto his side. "There you go, Roofer man."

Brushing my teeth, I thought about the woman from last week while I was walking Rufus. Since then, I'd been watching him like a hawk, analyzing every move to recognize signs of old age. He'd always been a bit clumsy, but getting stuck on his back? Was *that* an old-age thing? I knew he was getting older and wouldn't be with me forever, but I couldn't spend the time that he had left trying to figure out whether this was his final chapter.

Rufus waited patiently in the living room while I got dressed, his tail wagging because he knew we were going out soon. He usually followed me around, but today he was just hanging out on the floor. *Was he hurt? Was he slowing down?* Oh my god! I couldn't do this to myself.

"Let's go, Rufus!" I called from the front door, leash in hand. And with that, my "aging" dog jumped up like a puppy, bounding for the door.

After our walk, it was all about laundry and cleaning in preparation for Lisa's arrival that evening. When I invited her to come and stay, I was truly excited, but today, for some reason, I was less than thrilled by the idea of any company. My mind was in overdrive, and it would be a miracle if I got *anything* done today.

As I threw myself into cleaning and cleared off my desk for a thorough dusting, I caught a glimpse of the wall calendar that hung over my desk.

"Ohhhhhhh…"

I wasn't crazy. I was *PMSing*. According to my calendar, I was officially in the last week of my cycle. That was when I turned into a whole other person. A lot of people think PMS is bullshit since its symptoms are primarily emotional. All I knew was that right before my period, I felt like I was losing my mind, and I didn't like to feel out of control.

Over the years, I'd tried to embrace it and realized that nothing *new* really came up. It was more like an amplification of what I was already feeling. PMS is like walking into Best Buy with all the TVs turned up to full volume. All the other times of the month, the TVs are on, but there's no sound.

My TVs were in full swing today. Not only was I obsessing over Rufus's health, I was also thinking about money—what else was new? I had a marathon schedule lined up for New Year's Eve and Day, so unless I dropped dead from exhaustion, I would make some good money. Next month was January, *the* slowest month of the year in the restaurant industry. What the hell was I going to do about making the rent then? Something had to give. I just didn't know what.

Lisa arrived at 6 and we got comfortable for the evening, with me on my bed and her on the couch. Rufus was happy to stay on the floor, where he could keep an eye on both of us. I was nervous about

Lisa coming to stay while I was in PMS mode. I tried to steer clear of anyone and everyone I could for that last week. It was best for all, including me, because my patience was limited and my sensitivity high—never a good mix for socializing. But it was nice to have some company for a change.

Lying on her side, Lisa shifted toward the back of the couch, making room in front of her.

"Rufus!" she called, patting the couch. "Come up here with Auntie Lisa. Come on!"

Rufus picked his head up off the floor but didn't move. Instead, he looked over at me as if to say, "You tell her. I don't feel like talking right now," putting his head back down onto the carpet with a heavy sigh.

"He doesn't go on the couch anymore," I said, arranging the pillows on my bed so I could prop my head up while lying down and still see Lisa. "God, I can't even remember the last time he came up on the bed!"

"Wow. I didn't realize that." She sat up, examining Rufus from afar. Her movements made him pick his head up again. Still not moving, he stared at her, panting.

"Does he look old?" I said. I wasn't sure I wanted to know the answer, but before I realized it, the question was out of my mouth, hanging in the air like a bad smell.

Lisa got off the couch and went to Rufus. Holding his head in her hands, she looked into his eyes, while rubbing his chin. "Are you old, Rufus? Your mommy thinks you're old. Do you feel old?"

Lisa's voice could be a little high-pitched at times, and for some reason it had always bothered Rufus. He'd never been a growler, but certain noises definitely affected him, and Lisa's voice always got him going. Right on cue, he let out a cross between a growl and a moan, wagging his tail all the while.

Lisa threw her head back and laughed. "That's my boy! You tell her—I'm not old, Mama!"

Settling back onto the couch, her mood turned a bit more serious. "He definitely looks different to me, though."

"I know!" I said, shooting upright. "Look in his eyes! It's like he's a little checked out or something." In spite of the subject matter, it actually felt good to talk to someone about it and get their opinion.

"Yeah. He looks a little—" she cocked her head to one side— "distant. It's weird."

"He's also moving more slowly," I confessed with a low sigh. "I feel like he's starting to deteriorate right before my eyes, and I can't help but watch every move to see if he's getting worse."

"You can't do that to yourself, Liz," she soothed. "You just can't. He's still fine. Yes, he's getting older. We know this, but you don't really know how long you have left. Look at me. I thought Jakey would be around for a few more years, and within a weekend, he was gone."

Being reminded of how quickly Jake went didn't make me feel much better. Lisa sensed this. "I'm not saying the same thing will happen to Rufus. I'm just saying that we just don't know. So don't focus on the bad stuff. Enjoy all the time you have left with him."

Rufus slowly got up from the carpet and skulked into the dressing area to the bathroom.

"Well, I guess he's had enough of this kind of talk." I laughed. Lisa laughed too, stretching out on the couch. Shifting gears, she sighed loudly. "UGH! Another year gone!" She put her hands over her eyes dramatically. "I'm still not where I want to be."

This was a conversation she and I had a lot. We were both 37, single, and nowhere close to the place we'd envisioned for ourselves. My aspirations fit a bit more closely together than hers. Lisa vacillated between acting and wanting to open her own lounge.

"Girl, I know," I said, falling back onto my pillows with equal drama. "I can't tell you the last time I wrote anything. And singing?" I flicked my hand in dismissal. "Forget it."

"Maybe we should make some New Year's resolutions," she suggested, perking up a bit.

"No way!" I groaned. "I hate that shit."

There was no stopping Lisa. Convinced she was onto something, she sat up and said, "What do you want to see happen in 2008?"

JEEZ-us. Were we really gonna go there? New Year's resolutions were stupid. There was so much hype around them, and right now I wasn't so sure I believed things were going to get much better in my life. Thank you, PMS.

Despite my lack of enthusiasm, Lisa encouraged me to share my aspirations for the upcoming year. Money, of course, was at the top of the list.

"Yeah, yeah. We both want more money in our lives," she agreed. "But what about career stuff? What do you want to do?"

"What are you, my father?" I laughed. Lisa shot me a look. "Okay, okay." I paused. "Hmmmmm… I'd like to start writing again. I just don't know what to write about."

"What about singing?" she asked.

"Nah. I don't really feel like singing these days." I rubbed my eyes as if somehow, in doing so, I'd find clarity.

"Wow," Lisa said quietly.

"I'm just not feeling very outward," I finally admitted.

Lisa sighed and flopped back onto the couch. "It's probably just PMS, girl. You know how you get."

I was more disturbed than I'd let on. There was a time in my life when I was fiercely determined to be a famous singer. I spent thousands of dollars on singing lessons, musicians and demo tapes. I even left a cushy corporate job when I turned 30 to pursue my music full-time. I was so naïve, thinking Clive Davis would be waiting for me outside on my last day of work, ready to sign me to his record label.

I pursued music for a while, but the older I got and the more the music industry changed, the less I wanted to be in it. Being a famous singer was my identity for so long that even now I wasn't ready to say that I'd given up hope that it would happen. But I knew it wouldn't. I was too old and too scared to give it a real shot.

"Good night!" Lisa called out in the dark. "Thanks for letting me stay."

As I lay there, I suddenly felt panicked. What *was* I going to do with my life? I couldn't bartend forever. And Rufus—sweet, sweet Rufus. Would he live to see next New Year's? Something told me he would not. I felt a mental spinout coming on, but thankfully, I'd taken an Ambien. All I had to do was wait for it to kick in.

12

The New Year's Eve party at Bobby's bar, KingSize, was mostly low-key, with about 100 people—a perfect size for the space, which was probably no larger than 1,000 square feet. It was one of those places on the Lower East Side with no sign and a dim light hanging above the entrance. The event was private, with a crowd of people in their early to mid-thirties. As New Year's Eve gigs went, it was probably the easiest money I'd ever made.

Bobby was extremely generous, paying me $250 for just showing up. The partygoers added another $200 to that, so I walked out feeling good about my decision to take the gig.

I got back to Brooklyn at 6 that morning and walked Rufus before setting the alarm for 10:30 and popping an Ambien. Lisa decided to spend New Year's with her family, so I had the apartment to myself. Waking up with four and a half hours of sleep under my belt wasn't easy, but I managed to do it. By 11:30, I was behind the bar at Maxie's.

It was a ghost town until about 2 p.m. I needed to make $200 for the shift in order to make my December bills. Thankfully, I had a decent amount of people at the bar, who, despite their hangovers, drank their fair share of Bloody Marys.

Toward the end of my shift, exhaustion set in, and all I could think about was getting off my feet and home to Rufus. I felt guilty about being gone for so many hours at a time. Had I known Lisa would end up not staying the night, I might have asked my parents to take him for the holiday.

In spite of being tired, I couldn't help but feel proud of myself for working so hard to make ends meet. It had been a long time since I'd worked this hard, and it felt good. Plus, I'd made my numbers. As I turned the key to my apartment, I was grateful that New Year's Eve went off without a hitch.

Until I got inside.

At first I didn't realize what was going on. "Hey, buddy!" I called to Rufus, who was not in his usual spot on the carpet but on the bare floor. Hanging my coat in the closet, I thought it was strange that he didn't get up to greet me.

As I walked closer toward him, I realized something was wrong. My heart was in my throat. He was just lying there, staring at me helplessly, without even a wag of his tail.

"What's wrong, baby?" I squatted down and started to pet him. But his fur felt strange, almost matted. Did he have an accident? Had he been lying in it this whole time?

Trying not to panic, I attempted to ease him gently to his feet. But he couldn't stand up.

"Oh my god," I breathed, trying to contain my tears.

He looked so forlorn. I jumped up and turned on every single light in my apartment. I think he sensed my worry, because he started panting.

"Okay, okay," I soothed, getting back on the floor and inspecting every inch of his body. His back left paw had some sort of cut or infection between his paw pads. When I touched it, Rufus winced and let out a small whine. I could no longer control my tears. "I'm sorry, buddy," I sniffed, wiping my eyes with the backs of my hands.

I still couldn't figure out why his body felt damp. I got really close, sniffing his fur to see if it smelled like urine, but it didn't.

His paw, however, was more important. I got some Neosporin and a roll of gauze I happened to have in the bathroom. After wrapping his paw, I tried to get him on his feet and at least over to the carpet. The bandage seemed to do the trick because he was up on his feet and walking around gingerly.

Rufus was not one for anything on his paws. He hated when the groomer had to clip his toenails, and he'd dance in place, trying to dodge the clippers. I used to take him to a place in Tribeca where

Buddha, his groomer, would blast Tupac and Run-D.M.C. while he cut Rufus's hair.

"Rufus is a cool cat," Buddha told me, his wide grin exposing his numerous gold-capped teeth. "He likes it when I got the rap thing goin' here. He knows what's goin' on. Right, Rufus?" But even Buddha struggled with clipping his nails.

I wracked my brain trying to figure out what the hell had happened. He was fine this morning, so it must have taken place while I was at work during the day. Or maybe I missed something, being so tired. I sent Lisa a text message to see if she had noticed anything when she took him out the night before last. Then I called my parents.

"Happy New Year!" my father exclaimed cheerily. "How ya doin'?"

"Hello?" my mother's voice cut in as she joined my father on the line. "It's Mom. I'm on, too," she said with a giggle.

"Hey, guys."

"You sound exhausted," my mother said. "So was it worth it in the end?"

"Something's wrong with Rufus," I said, trying not to cry.

My parents both reacted at once. "What?"

"What do you mean something's wrong?" my father asked. "Is he okay?"

My mother, who was getting annoyed, took charge. "Ronnie! Let her talk. You're yelling into the phone."

"*You're* yelling into the phone!" my father shot back.

"That's because I can't hear over *your* yelling," my mother replied, her voice raising.

"Guys! Guys! Enough. Maybe it's best if I just talk to one of you at a time."

"No, no," my father said. "We'll stop talking. Right, Joan?"

"Yes!" my mother said, exasperated. "Just tell us what happened!"

I was lucky to have parents with whom I got along. They were always there for me whenever there was a crisis, and today definitely felt like a crisis.

I took a deep breath and launched into the story while my parents did their best not to interrupt.

Finally, my mother couldn't take it anymore. "Well, you have to take him to the vet," she insisted.

"I put some Neosporin on his paw and wrapped it in gauze."

"But if it's infected, he might need antibiotics," my father added.

I sat down on the floor next to Rufus, rubbing the top of his head while he rested. I knew I needed to take him to the vet and what it was going to cost, but I didn't care. I just hated the idea of taking him in when it upset him so much. "I'll call the vet tomorrow and see," I said, checking his paw to make sure the gauze was still in place. "Maybe she can prescribe something over the phone."

My father thought that was a good idea, but my mother was not convinced.

"I still think you should take him, Liz. I can drive to Brooklyn and pick you guys up tomorrow morning."

That was my mom—always ready to jump into action. Over the years, I'd really come to appreciate this part of her, though at times, like tonight, I needed a minute to process everything before I let her take over.

"Why don't you wait a few days, Liz, and see if the Neosporin helps?" my dad suggested calmly. "Who knows? It might get better on its own." Always the optimist.

My mother, who should've been a professional debater, was not having any of that. "How's she going to wait, Ronnie?" She was starting to get worked up. She'd only call my father by name when that happened. "How's she going to keep his paw clean with the snow and the ice outside?" She had a point. The silence on my end and my dad's end of the phone confirmed that.

"Okay," I said, finally. "I'll call the vet tomorrow and see what she says. If she thinks he should be seen, we'll take him. Sound good?"

That satisfied my mother.

"In the meantime," my father said, "maybe you could wrap his foot in plastic to keep it dry when you take him out."

We talked a bit about New Year's Eve and how they didn't get home until 7 a.m. My parents were not big partiers, but on New Year's they'd get together with a few other couples each year, staying out until at least 5 or 6 in the morning. I didn't know what they did for all that time, but they loved it, and I was always impressed by their stamina.

Once I hung up, I got a text from Lisa: *Happy New Year Mama!! Is*

Rufus okay? He did have a little fall on the stairs when I took him out that night, but he seemed just fine when I left him.

A fall? I wanted to hit something. How could she not tell me that he fell? I was so angry I threw my phone on the couch to keep from texting her back something nasty. I wanted to blame somebody. I *needed* to blame somebody. I hated the fact that poor Rufus couldn't move for who knows how many hours and that I had had no idea. My reaction was extreme, but I also knew it wasn't really about today. It was about what was to come.

13

The next day, I was up earlier than usual. Rufus wasn't in his regular spot on the floor by the bed, and when I called out my usual good morning, he emerged from the dressing area slowly.

Rolling off the bed, I squatted down, extending my arms to him.

"Hey, buddy! How's my guy doing this morning?" I massaged the area under his ears. Relaxing into my touch, his head became heavy in my hands. "That's a good boy. We're going to get you all fixed up, okay?"

When I stood up, I noticed the gauze wrapped around Rufus's paw had unraveled a bit. As he followed me to the bathroom, it trailed behind him like an embarrassing piece of toilet paper stuck to the foot. I got dressed, fixed the gauze and wrapped his paw in a sandwich bag.

Outside, it was another cold one, but at least the sky was bright and sunny. Rufus looked a little drunk as he did his best to acclimate to the makeshift cast on his paw. It was too early to get anyone live on the phone at the vet, so I left a message.

I knew Dr. Gabriele was going to tell me to bring him in. How would she be able to diagnose without looking at him? All I could think about was money and how shitty I felt worrying about it when Rufus's health was in jeopardy. The money I'd made from New Year's felt like enough yesterday, but today I regretted not making more.

I'd just have to put it in on my credit card, I decided as we returned to the apartment. I was afraid of going back into debt, but what choice did I have? *You'll make it up,* an optimistic voice assured me from within. But would I? I had two and a half shifts in a restaurant that wasn't busy and heading into the slowest season of the year.

"It's too early in the morning to panic," I muttered, busying myself with Rufus's breakfast. In spite of his foot, he was ecstatic over breakfast. Rufus was pretty much ecstatic over anything food-related. The day he stopped eating would be the day I knew he was ready to go. That struck a chord, and I was amazed to have had such a thought. It was truly the first time I'd gone there in my mind.

"Get a grip, Liz," I told myself, placing Rufus's bowl on the floor while he hopped around with excitement, the plastic bag on his paw making funny crunching noises.

While Rufus devoured his breakfast, I sat at my computer. *I need to start looking for another job*, I thought, scanning the listings on Craigslist. It was the worst time of the year to find work as a bartender. People tended to wait until after the holidays to quit, and bars and restaurants didn't start hiring until around March because it was just too slow in January and February to go with a full staff.

The money I made on New Year's barely cleared my bills for the month of January, and there was no way I'd make enough money for February. On the full shifts I had, I was only making about $125. The swing shifts—if they even happened—only brought in $90 or so. My mortgage and maintenance alone was $1,900 a month. Modeling didn't start up again until February, so how the hell was I going to make enough money for the month?

A call from Dr. Gabriele shook me from my growing financial panic. She wouldn't be in the office that day but thought Rufus should be seen anyway. I liked that she took the time to call back on her day off. I didn't like the fact that Rufus would have to see somebody else.

I called my parents. "Hi," my mother answered, already sounding concerned. "How's he doing?"

"He's okay," I said bending down to remove the sandwich bag from his paw. "The vet wants me to bring him in."

"What time?"

The phone clicked on the other end; my father had gotten on the other extension. "Hi!" he said. "How ya doin'?"

"The vet wants to see Rufus," my mother told him. I gave them the details of my conversation with Dr. Gabriele.

"So we'll pick you up around noon," my father announced.

"Ronnie!" my mother started in, annoyed. "That doesn't leave enough time." They proceeded to bicker about how long it would take to get to Chelsea from Brooklyn.

"GUYS!" I interrupted, my voice raising. "Let's say 11:30 to be on the safe side, okay?"

With the vet logistics in place, I went back to freaking out about money. I returned to Craigslist, scanning for potential gigs. Except for the ones always listed, the prospects were not promising. It was never a good sign if a place was constantly hiring. It usually meant one of two things: There was no money to be made so people didn't stay long, or there was most likely some sort of crazy manager there, à la Sabrina, who blew through staff left and right.

The bar and restaurant listings were less than stellar. My eyes wandered to the part-time section, and as I scrolled through the listings for office work, my stomach tightened. I couldn't do an office thing. I left that world in 2000 and swore I'd never return.

I hated the monotony of it all. Every day, it was the same people asking the same questions: "How was your weekend? What are you doing this weekend? Did you cut your hair? Are you going to the conference room for birthday cake at 3?" In spite of that, it was hard not to be momentarily enticed by the pay—$20 an hour would be really helpful. I just didn't think I'd be able to stand it, no matter how much I was being paid.

My parents arrived, and when Rufus saw the car door open, he knew he was going inside. Normally he liked to be in the car, but lately he seemed to recognize the difference between a ride for fun versus a ride to the vet.

"Mom, I can sit in the back with him," I said.

She waved her hand. "No, no, I'm fine. You sit in the front with Dad and show him how to go." She turned to Rufus, who had started to shake, changing her voice as if talking to a small child. "Hello, Rufus. You okay? Yes. We're going to get you fixed up."

Sliding into the passenger seat, I turned to check on him. He looked distressed, almost worried. "Is he still shaking? Crack the window back there, Mom. He likes the wind."

We made it to the vet relatively quickly. My father stayed in the car while my mother stood outside holding my purse as I eased Rufus out, lifting him and gently setting him down on the pavement.

Inside, there were two other people waiting, both with cats in transport boxes with holes in the sides. The waiting area was bright due to the windows, which made it feel more like a storefront than a vet's office. The receptionist sat behind a long kiosk-type desk and greeted me with a smile, then stood so she could see over the desk. "Hello. Who do we have here today?"

I really liked this place. It had a calm energy to it, for which I was especially grateful that day.

"This is Rufus," I said, struggling to keep him away from the door. He knew where we were and was desperately trying to get out. His retractable leash made loud clicking noises as he pulled himself toward the door. I gave the leash a little slack and let him look out the glass door, his heavy pants fogging up the window. My mother offered to take him while I checked us in, and I realized how glad I was to have her there with me.

After a few minutes, we went in to see the doctor. Dr. Nguyen was a short man probably in his early forties. He had a strange accent, which sounded Asian but not quite, and his clipped speech made him not nearly as warm as Dr. Gabriele. I hated getting used to a new person who didn't know Rufus.

"So, let's take a rook ah heez paw," the doctor said, lifting a still-shaking Rufus onto the stainless steel table.

His paw was infected and he'd need some antibiotics along with special ointment for the wound. I was relieved to hear it was a mild infection, but the worry started to build when he listed each thing Rufus would need. I could almost hear the sound of a cash register going off in my head as he rattled off the different medications I would have to buy.

When we finished, my mother suggested I take Rufus outside immediately, in case he had to pee. It didn't occur to me that she intended to take care of the bill while we were gone.

"Mom," I protested, "I was going to pay."

"It's okay. Don't worry about it," she said, folding the receipt and tucking it into her wallet. "It wasn't that much."

Once again, I was ashamed by and grateful for my mother's generosity. The hecklers in my head were quick to remind me of what a loser I'd become.

I offered a quiet "Thanks," trying to quell the voices in my head as we left the vet.

Rufus seemed to have calmed down, sniffing and stopping to pee as we walked up the street to where my father had double-parked. Watching him happily trot ahead of me, I tried to hold back the tears. Maybe it was because the rush was over, maybe because I was in the presence of my parents, but I felt like I was going to lose it and start bawling right there on the street. I needed to get it together before I joined my father in the car. I couldn't let them see me like that. They'd just insist on giving me more money, and I wasn't sure I'd be strong enough to say no.

Back in Brooklyn, I managed to maintain my composure long enough so my father could come upstairs and use the bathroom. Rufus, glad to be home, headed straight to the kitchen for a long drink of water.

My father emerged from the bathroom through the beaded curtains, with one long strand resting on his shoulder. He brushed it away, looked me in the eye and asked, "You doing okay?"

Damn. Didn't he know that asking me that was the worst thing he could do? He was my father, and when a parent asks a child how they are, it's impossible to feign happiness.

My nose started to burn, which meant the tears would follow. "I'm okay," I said, my voice small and shaky.

He stepped toward me. "Liz," he said, his voice gentle and pleading. "You can't keep living like this."

"I know, I know," I said, tears spilling down my face. "I'm just trying to live my life *my* way, ya know?"

"I understand that and I support it fully, but this isn't about living your life, this is about *survival*. And you've got to do whatever it takes to survive right now. Do *something*—anything—just to get on your feet. Who cares what it is. Just *do* something."

Blinking through my tears, I nodded my head and folded into his outstretched arms.

"You're going to be fine, Liz." He held me, rubbing my back. "You always are. Don't let this get the better of you, okay?"

After he left, I sat down to my computer. He was right. My life was at DEFCON 5 and it was time I took control.

I opened up my e-mail and started typing.

Dear Friends,

I hope this e-mail finds you well and rejuvenated after a busy holiday season. As most of you know, I've been busy working on many of my creative endeavors. While I continue to build that area up, I'm writing to all of you to see if you or anyone you know might be in need of some part-time office help. Though the holidays were very busy, January has slowed down a bit and I find myself in need of a little extra income. I can write; I can file; I can answer phones, do research, organize, etc. I can do it ALL!! ;)

Anyway, I thank you in advance for taking the time to read this and again, I wish you all a wonderful 2008.

Fueled and inspired by my father's words, I addressed the e-mail to just about everyone I knew, with "Got Work?" as the subject line. I sat at my desk, staring at the screen for a moment, and took a long, deep breath, like divers did just before leaping off the board.

Turning to Rufus, who had settled down on his blanket, I said, "Here goes, Roofer man, let's see what kind of work Mommy can get."

And with that, I hit send and got ready to go to work.

14

Walking into Maxie's, I felt like I'd lived four days in one. Between taking Rufus to the vet and the conversation with my father, I longed to be at home decompressing rather than putting on a happy face for the customers.

Marta was behind the bar when I arrived. Something wasn't right. She wasn't supposed to be there until 5:30. In the midst of all the chaos with Rufus, had I mixed up my in-time? Shit. I never messed up my schedule.

I left my coat on and headed over to the bar, where Marta was leaning forward on her elbows, talking to Danny, one of our regulars, in a hushed tone. She saw me but didn't acknowledge my presence. Yeah, something was definitely wrong.

I looked around for Chris, hoping he'd tell me what was going on, but the restaurant was empty and he was nowhere in sight.

"Hey, Marta!" I called, hoisting my purse onto the far end of the bar.

She looked up with a frozen smile on her face and said something to Danny before giving me a nod.

Pretending not to notice her obvious cold shoulder, I gave Danny a small wave.

"So, did I mess up? Was I supposed to come in later?"

Marta pushed herself up slowly from the bar and reached for Danny's now-empty pint glass of Coke. "I worked the lunch shift today," she said, her eyes on the glass as she filled it.

After handing Danny his drink, she headed my way. "Yep. They totally changed the schedule," she said matter-of-factly. "I only got Wednesday lunches now."

"What?" I couldn't believe it. A schedule change? What the hell? I already had a limited number of shifts. Had they taken one away from me?

Marta was talking rapidly, her accent getting stronger. "I don't know what the hell's going on, but Chris told me he's going with one bartender on Wednesdays, and since I can't work Thursdays anymore, it's either Wednesday lunch or nothing."

I didn't know what to say. I thought Chris was *thinking* about making the change on Wednesday nights, but I didn't think he'd go through with it and be such a dick about it. Plus, I was dying to know if *my* schedule had changed. But Marta needed to vent, and I didn't have the balls to ask about myself. Instead, I offered, "I don't understand."

"Oh, I understand. Chris hates me. I know he does. He never liked me from the beginning, and now that I can't do Thursdays anymore, it's a perfect opportunity for him to fuck me. He fucked with Lara's schedule, too."

"Wait, what?" I said, my eyes wide. "I thought Scott does the schedule. Why is Chris all involved now?"

Marta shrugged her shoulders. "Beats me, girl. All I know is that one shift a week—a lunch shift, no less—is not going to cut it. But ya know what? I'm not going anywhere, 'cuz that's what Chris wants. I know it. He gave me this shift because he knows I won't stay for a crappy lunch shift. Well, fuck that. He doesn't know who he's dealing with. I'm not going anywhere."

I saw Chris walking toward us. "Let me hang up my coat," I said, tugging at the zipper, trying to avoid being caught in the middle. "Is the schedule in the book?"

"Mmm-hmm," she answered, glaring at Chris as he walked past the bar and over to the host stand. "Your schedule didn't change," she sniffed. "You don't have anything to worry about."

I couldn't decide if I was relieved or stressed. Chris, on other hand, couldn't wait to talk to me. He peeked his head into the coat check. "Hey. She tell you about the schedule? She's pretty pissed, huh?" he said with a slightly wicked smile.

"Dude, not now," I said, brushing past him. "Let's wait till she leaves."

I stepped behind the bar. Danny was gone and it was just the two of us.

"Did you see it?" she asked with her back to the bar. She punched angrily at the touch screen on the computer, closing out Danny's check.

"No. I didn't look at it yet." I busied myself straightening the liquor bottles, taking way too much time to make sure all the Grey Goose bottles were lined up perfectly. "How did they fuck up Lara's schedule?" I asked.

Marta flounced past me, lifted the hinged counter and practically marched over to the host stand. Thank goodness Chris went back to the office to get my bank, otherwise I don't know what would've happened. She grabbed the schedule book out of the top drawer of the host stand and brought it back to the bar, throwing it onto the beer cooler.

I scanned the schedule. "So wait, Amber's only working two shifts now?" I was pleased about that. "And Lara's still got Saturday nights."

"Yeah, but she *asked* for Thursday nights and they gave her Thursday lunch instead," Marta pointed out.

Chris came over to the bar and handed me my cash drawer. "Marta. You ready to cash out?" he asked.

Marta turned away from Chris dramatically and hit the upper right side of the computer screen to release her drawer from the register. "Yup," she said, her back to him.

With the two of them in the office and still no customers, I had a chance to really look at the schedule. Amber would be working most shifts at the steakhouse next door, though I still had to work with her on Fridays. The best news of all was that Rachel would be working with me on Thursday nights.

But Marta was right. I was the only one whose schedule did not change. I liked having a set schedule, and though I wouldn't have minded giving up a swing shift for a full one, I'd gotten used to my shifts. The thing that worried me was whether or not it looked like favoritism. But I had to admit, it was nice to be on the good side of management for a change.

"So, what, you're not happy about having Wednesday nights all to yourself?" Chris asked later as we were closing up. He was sitting at the bar, having a Jack and Coke, while I counted the money. The last of the servers were downstairs changing, and the guys in the kitchen had just punched out.

The night turned out to be a decent one, and I was grateful it was just me behind the bar. Being busy for a few hours took my mind off all the schedule bullshit, and flying solo obviously made a difference. If Marta had been there, I'd be walking out with less than $100.

"No. I'm glad to have the shift to myself," I said, wrapping a rubber band around a stack of ones and shoving them back into the cash drawer. "I just worry that people are going to think I'm getting special treatment. Plus, what did Scott think of all of this?"

Chris looked at his drink, stirring it around with a black cocktail straw, then looked at me. "He's fine with it, Liz. We discussed it and agreed that we have to start cutting the schedule here and there. You guys have all been complaining about the fact that you're not making any money, and now that we don't have as many bartenders, we decided to make some changes so people can start making some money."

"We need customers to make money," I muttered under my breath as I went back to counting.

"Ya just gotta be patient, Liz. I'm telling you. We're still pretty new. Give it some time."

Time? I didn't have time! I just sent out a freakin' e-mail asking for part-time *anything*.

Chris finished his drink with a loud slurp and pushed the glass forward. "I'll be in the office. Let me know when you're ready to cash out."

I just wanted to get home to Rufus. The memory of coming home to find him stuck on the floor was still fresh in my mind. Grabbing the cash drawer, the paperwork and my purse, I headed back to the office, hoping Chris would be just as interested in getting out of there as I was.

Things were just fine at home. Rufus was resting comfortably, and though he didn't get up to greet me, his wagging tail was a strong indication of his good spirits. Once he was walked and settled in for the night, I was able to check my e-mail to see if anyone had responded to my plea. I was pleasantly surprised by the number of replies, most of which were well-wishes and promises to keep their "ears open." But I was disappointed that no one offered any work.

Except Katy Pressman. I met Katy a few years ago, when I responded to an ad on Craigslist looking for a bartender for a private party. She and I hit it off instantly, and after I worked the party, we stayed in touch.

Leaning forward, I edged my butt with a short hop to the end of the chair and opened the e-mail.

Hi—I passed your info on to my husband Pradeep Gupta, who has recently started his own law practice. He may have some work. Best of luck to you.

"Rock!" I exclaimed, leaning back and clapping my hands together.

Just below Katy's e-mail was one from her husband, Pradeep, with the subject line "Got Work!" I couldn't believe it. I could very well have a job by tomorrow! I was so excited and relieved, I didn't even care that it was in an office or that I had no idea what it was paying. Instead, I thought about how nice it would be to have a steady paycheck.

15

The next morning, despite my excitement, I didn't rush to call Pradeep. Instead, I did something I'd never done before—I made a plan. In the past, whenever someone offered me a job, I'd be so grateful for the offer that I'd forget to consider whether it was fair or good. Over the years, I realized I was being taken advantage of. This time I was going to aim as high as possible because I was sick and tired of being poor. *This* time I was going to make it work for me.

Fired up and ready, I made the call.

"Hi, Pradeep, it's Liz Weber."

"Oh, Liz! Hi!"

"Is this a good time?" I asked, standing in the middle of my apartment, hand on my hip.

"Actually, it's a perfect time," he said. "So, Katy tells me you're looking for some part-time work. Basically, my partner and I opened our own firm about six months ago, and we're in desperate need of organization," Pradeep began. "We're looking to expand and grow the firm, and it's become more and more difficult to do so without proper administrative support."

"Sounds great!" I said, trying to appear enthusiastic about monotonous work.

"We work mostly with music people. We share our offices with some other people in the entertainment industry."

Music? Now he was talking! My mind quickly conjured an image of a sleek, modern environment with records lining the walls.

"What type of compensation and hours were you looking for, Liz?"

There it was. The big question. I took a deep breath and said, "I'm looking for about twenty hours a week." Might as well get that out of the way first.

"As for compensation, I'm looking for $20 an hour," I continued, bending over slightly, clenching my fist in anticipation.

"Okay, well, $20 an hour at twenty hours a week would be $400 weekly," Pradeep said, more thinking aloud than to me.

That's right, brotha! $400 per week. I decided to keep quiet and let him make the next move.

"I'll have to run the numbers past my partner, Avi. We'll have to see if we can afford you," he laughed.

"I understand, though financially, I can't go any lower than that."

Look at me! Suddenly I had confidence, but I was also surprised at how easily that came out of my mouth. I could hear the hecklers stirring, getting ready to bombard me with criticism for being too cocky.

"No, no!" He assured me. "I completely understand. I think Avi shouldn't have a problem with the numbers. I'll talk to him this afternoon, and if he's on board, perhaps we can get you in here to see the office and talk further about our vision for the position."

I was pretty sure I'd gotten the job.

"Woo-hoo!" I sang after hanging up the phone. "Rufus! Mama's got a job!"

Rufus looked up at me, chin still on the floor.

I sat back down to my desk and called Deb, even though it was early in California.

She picked up the phone with a "YO!"

"YO! How's it goin'?"

"Good! Good!" she said. "Just getting ready to head to yoga."

"I've got some news," I said with a smile.

"Ohhhhhh... Do tell."

"I think I just got a part-time job."

"Shut up!!" she exclaimed. "Where? Doing what? How?"

I could picture her in her apartment, her red hair framing her milky-white skin, seated at her desk, green eyes wide, blinking with each question.

"Well, it's not a done deal yet, but it's in a law firm."

Silence. Then, "Wait, what?"

"I know. Trust me, it's not ideal, but I've got to do something to make some extra money, and it'll be nice to have a steady paycheck."

I sounded like I was trying to convince myself that it was going to be a good thing. But how could it? I was going to work in a freakin' law firm! What the hell was I thinking?

"You there?" Deb's voice cut into my thoughts.

"Yeah, yeah, I'm here." I couldn't hide anything from her, so instead of trying, I told her the truth. "Wow. I was just thinking about this, and yeah, okay, the money will be good, but a law firm... Oh, girl, what am I doing?"

"Whoa there, missy. Take it easy. This is not forever, right? It's a temporary means to an end. And while it's not ideal, the whole office thing, it's going to help you pay the bills. Think about all of the extra energy you'll have because you're not wasting so much of it worrying about money."

She was right, and I was glad I'd spoken up.

"Plus, they work with musicians," I said, perking up.

"Well, *that's* no accident, I'm sure!" Pause. "How's Rufus doing?"

"He's a lot better. The ointment and meds seem to be working pretty quickly."

Deb was pleased. "Oh, gooooood. I'm glad my boy is doing better. How about his mother? How's she doing?"

"I'm okay," I said, leaning back in my chair with a sigh. "It was scary. He's starting to look old to me."

"Well, he *is* old," she said matter-of-factly.

"I know. I just hate the idea of losing him."

"Of course you do, Liz. It's normal. But you will be fine. Wherever you are, you're right where you're supposed to be."

When we first met, Deb ate burgers, rode motorcycles and dated bad boys. Since then, she'd found yoga, turned vegan and had become one of the few people in my life I could count on to tell me like it was—with love and kindness.

"Alright, mama. I gotta get to yoga. It was good to catch up with you. Congratulations on the job! Let me know how the interview goes. I loves ya."

"Thanks," I said, flopping onto my comfy chair by the window. "I love you too."

After we hung up, I thought about my potential new job. While I was excited about finally making some money, the reality of working in an office again was starting to overshadow my excitement—and as an assistant, no less. I didn't want to take care of people.

"It's just temporary," I told myself. Just until the money at Maxie's got better—or when I won the lottery.

• • •

Later that night was my first shift with Rachel, and I was so excited to work with her again. She was already behind the bar when I arrived, her hair pulled back in a tight bun that made her look more like a ballerina than a bartender.

The bar was busy, with a nice crowd of thirty-something corporate guys in the corner and parties of two or three people scattered around the bar. As soon as I walked in, Rachel spotted me and stopped what she was doing, flashing me her fantastic smile.

"Hey, lady!" she called, lifting the counter for me as I stepped behind the bar. I put my stuff down immediately and held out my arms for a hug.

"Yay!!!" I cheered as we embraced. "I'm sooooo happy you're *here*."

"Me too!" she said. "I love that we're working together again! Ha! Screw Sabrina!" she added with a wink.

We eased into a nice work rhythm without discussion. Rachel took the service bar and the tables in the cocktail area, working the crowd with her charm. I focused on the people already at the bar. It was so nice to be busy.

Rachel came back behind the bar from the cocktail area, passing behind me to get some clean pint glasses. "The strippers are coming tonight," she said, pouring several pints of Guinness.

I fell in next to her to pour two pints of Bud Light. "No way, really? Don't they usually come on the weekends?"

"Yeah, but Chris said something about them coming in tonight for somebody's birthday. I don't know. I'm just glad, because those girls can tip."

"And eat!" I added, stepping behind her with the Bud Lights for two guys at the end of the bar.

"Thanks, sweetheart," the older one of the two said. "When did yous open?"

I hated to judge, but the "yous" was a dead giveaway: I bet these guys were from Jersey or Staten Island.

"We've only been open since November. Where are you guys from?" I couldn't resist.

"Staten Island!" the younger one piped up. "We work for the Port Authority."

"Well, gentlemen, welcome to Maxie's!" I said, sweeping my hand like one of the blonde ladies from *The Price Is Right*.

"Yeah, I like this spot," the older guy said, handing me a twenty. He was taller than the other one and wore a Yankees hat. The younger guy was on the heavy side. Both had a sweet and simple demeanor—my kind of customers.

Over at the register, Rachel was ringing in some drinks. "Staten Island or Jersey?" she asked, her back to the crowd and eyes affixed to the computer screen.

"Staten Island."

"Hell, I'll take it. It's just nice to have people at the bar." She sighed dramatically and turned toward the crowd, "Hi! Can I help you ladies?"

I didn't really mind the blue-collar set, especially the guys. They loved me because I could joke with them and flirt all at once. A lot of other bartenders despised that crowd, deeming them "bridge and tunnel." During the week, these guys were great, kicking back after work, having a few beers and a snack. They always spent a lot of money and tipped well. It was when they dressed up and took their ladies out on a Saturday night that I joined my fellow bartenders in looking down on them.

Dressed-up blue-collar went "bridge and tunnel" real fast. Saturday nights would bring out the worst in them. Maybe it was the heightened expectation—the "It's Saturday night, baby! We have to go out and live it up!"—but the women were the worst offenders. All they wanted were Cosmos and dirty martinis, which was good for business but not so good for the arms if you were making them all night long.

I tried to avoid working Saturdays whenever possible, even though it was a big money night. I made just as much money during the week as I would on Saturday nights, and with half the aggravation. On Saturdays, everyone was all about the cocktails, plopping down at the bar and asking, "What's your specialty?" Then they'd sit there and ask me about every single drink I made, which on a slow night wasn't so bad, but when I had seventeen intricate cocktails to make, conversation would mess up my concentration.

We'd been going strong at the bar for at least an hour when Chris finally appeared. "Hey!" he called from the service bar.

"Hey!" I said, grabbing a dry rag to wipe my hands as I walked over to him. "How's it going?"

"Good." But I could tell he was a bit wound up because his eyes kept darting around nervously.

"What's up?" I asked, trying to grab his eyes with mine.

"The strippers are coming in tonight," he said, rearranging the glasses.

"Yeah, I know. Rachel told me. That's *good*, right?"

"No, no. It's great! It just means Reed's going to be up my ass all night." Reed was the big boss and known to make people cry.

I put my hand on Chris's arm. "It'll be fine. Those girls are really sweet. Plus, it's me and Rachel, so you're cool." I flashed him a smile and went back to work.

"Thank god it's you two!" he called after me.

The strippers arrived at around 10. When we first opened, Reed decided it would be good business to have a bunch of sexy women having dinner and drinks in the front window for all to see. They were super-nice and extremely generous. I never remembered their names, but they loved me for some reason and always greeted me with excitement.

Tonight was no different. "Lizzzzzzzzzzz!" the tall Spanish one squealed. "I'm so glad you're here!" She was a beauty, with long, shiny black hair and almond-shaped eyes.

"Hey! How are ya?" I said, coming out from behind the bar to say hello. "I hear y'all are celebrating a birthday."

"Yes," she said. "It's Marissa's birthday. Marissa!! Come and meet my *favorite* bartender!" She motioned to the birthday girl, her blood-red nails contrasting nicely with her olive-toned hand.

"Hi," Marissa said, more embarrassed than excited.

"Happy birthday!" Turning back to the bar, I called out to Rachel, "Rachel, this is Marissa, the birthday girl!"

Rachel beamed widely. "Happy birthday! What're you drinking?"

Marissa, who was on the shy side, giggled. "I like that martini with the white chocolate on it."

"You got it!"

I knew what Rachel was thinking because I was thinking the same thing: They're all going to want white chocolate raspberry martinis, the most labor-intensive drink on our cocktail list. Sure enough, the rest of the party chimed in: "Me too! Oh, I loooove that drink!"

There were about ten of them, and the group of suits who were still in the corner was thrilled to see the busboys pushing together the remaining cocktail tables right beside their party. Sensing this, the strippers' handler stepped forward to make his presence known. A handler was a cross between security and a chaperone. The strippers were never without one while working and out in public. He paid the bill and sat with them, acting as a deterrent to onlookers who might be considering an approach.

I let them get settled and joined Rachel behind the bar. She was already dipping the martini glasses into the melted white chocolate. "Strippers," she murmured. "How is it that these women can eat and drink like this and then get up on stage and take their clothes off?"

"I know, right?" I said, lining up the mixing glasses for their drinks.

Once the strippers were happily sipping on their cocktails and the rest of the bar customers were under control, I checked my phone and saw that I had a missed call. I told Rachel I had to run outside and check my voicemail.

Outside, I listened to a message from Pradeep, asking if I would be available to come into the office the next day to meet with Avi and himself. "I realize you're probably working, so just call the office anytime tonight and leave me a message to confirm," he said.

It was going to be a stretch for me, working until at least 1 in the morning and then getting up to be in midtown by 11. But this was going to be my new reality; I might as well get used to it.

I left Pradeep a message to confirm, and as I jogged up the stairs to go back inside, I wondered if things were actually starting to turn around.

16

The next day it was pouring rain, which meant I'd need extra time outside with Rufus. He hated the rain and always tried to avoid going out in it. And with all his hair, he'd need to be dried off with a towel, another one of his least favorite things because it meant being handled.

I didn't know it was supposed to rain, so I had limited time to get him out and fed. I also had to put something together to wear. Since it was a law firm, the atmosphere was probably formal, which was definitely a problem because I no longer owned any suits. My initial plan was to wear my funeral dress, a simple black dress that was good for any kind of serious occasion. With the rain, though, a dress was a bad idea.

I settled on a pair of eggplant corduroy trousers, a black shirt and black boots. The outfit wouldn't win me any fashion awards, but it was conservative enough to pass for professional.

It was really raining outside, and I wondered if it was a sign from the universe that this whole law firm thing was a bad idea. As much as I needed the money, I was not excited at all by the fact that I'd be going back to office work. *Assistant* work, actually. As an assistant, I had to *care*, and I wasn't sure I had it in me.

Being an assistant only worked if you liked your boss. In the mid-'90s, I worked at a management consulting firm for the COO. Steve Rivkin was a miserable man in his forties who was pretty much the whipping boy for the CEO, Tim Sherman. Tim was a brilliant egomaniac who liked to call Steve into his office for every little thing. "Hey, Stevey!" he would yell from his office, which was about twenty feet from Steve's. "Come on in here and check this out." Steve would jump to it, muttering under his breath like a little boy being forced to eat his vegetables.

I should have felt bad for Steve, but I couldn't. I'm not sure if it was the fact that he was just such a sad, sad sight, standing 5'7" at most and probably weighing 100 pounds soaking wet. His curly dark hair was way too full for his narrow head. One of the partners called him "toilet brush" behind his back.

In the beginning I tried to get Steve to like me, greeting him every Monday morning with a cheerful "Hey, Steve! How was your weekend?" He would stop walking, stand beside my desk and exhale dramatically, his bony shoulders hunching even further forward, and reply in a sad little voice, "It was."

After about a month of that, I gave up asking him about his weekend. My compassion for him didn't fade until he started treating me like crap. I'd walk into his office to hand him a message, and he'd snap his fingers and point to the door, wordlessly telling me to leave.

When the company was bought out and positions were shuffled, I was assigned to work for the new CEO, Arthur Chutney. Arthur wasn't CEO material and was only given the job because the new board of directors knew they could get him to do whatever they wanted. Arthur was afraid of me and wanted me to think he was cool rather than respect him as a superior. He'd show up Monday mornings, stop by my desk, and give me the "guns"—the gesture people make with their thumbs up and index fingers pointing forward. "Heeeey, Liz," he'd say, trying to sound all smooth. I just couldn't warm up to him.

"Do you think I have a problem with authority?" I once asked Deb, who had the pleasure of hearing my rants about hating my boss of the moment.

"No," she'd said thoughtfully. "I just think it takes a lot for you to respect someone. It's like, if you can do their job better than they can, you have no use for them."

She was right. The problem was that most people couldn't live up to my impossibly high standards. A good assistant took care of everything, which meant practically *thinking* for her boss. A good assistant was always one step ahead of her boss so he could stay focused on more important things. Almost all the bosses I'd had were consultants, and they never really *did* anything.

Walking across 40th Street toward Madison Avenue and thinking about old jobs gone wrong was not helping me feel excited for my interview. *It's only temporary,* I reminded myself as I entered the elevator and pressed the button for the 20th floor.

The doors opened as I shook the rain from my umbrella and stepped off. A young blond guy sat at a desk to the right. There was no receptionist out front, just a copier and that guy.

"Uh, hi," I said. "I'm here to see Pradeep Gupta."

The man, who was wearing headphones, slid one side off his ear and said, "Down the hall and around the corner. Second office on the left." His tone was detached but friendly.

As I walked down the hall, I noticed several framed gold and silver records on the walls. I'd expected a sleek lawyers-who-work-with-musicians office, not a few measly records lining the dreary walls. I also thought there'd be a receptionist sitting at a large desk in the lobby area, not some dude with headphones. At the end of the hallway was a woman sitting at a desk to the left, just outside a large office. She looked up and gave me a friendly smile.

Turning the corner, I knocked on the open office door. "Pradeep?" I said, poking my head in.

Pradeep was sitting at a large desk, working on the computer. "Liz! Hi! Great to see you," he said, walking over to me with his hand extended.

"Great to see you, too," I said, pumping his hand firmly.

"Let's go into the conference room. Avi's just finishing up a call and will join us in a minute."

I followed him down the hallway, toward the elevator, past the blond guy's desk and into the conference room. It was dreary too, with faded yellow walls, bad fluorescent lighting and a gray Formica conference table taking up most of the room. There was no artwork on the walls. A small refrigerator and microwave sat in the corner.

I took a seat on the far side of the conference table while Pradeep sat across from me. We spent a little time chatting about the weather, his wife, Katy, and if I'd found the office all right.

Pradeep was a good-looking guy with dark skin and white teeth. He had an athletic build and short black hair. His demeanor was warm and relaxed, not what I'd expected from a lawyer, but what did I know? I was relieved to see that he was casually dressed in a blue dress shirt and khakis.

Avi walked in and announced himself by simply saying "Hi."

I stood up and extended my hand. "Hi, Avi. I'm Liz Weber."

He shook it. "Hi, Liz. Sit down, please." Avi sat down next to Pradeep, placing a copy of my résumé on the table in front of him. He was much taller than Pradeep and wearing a suit—a nice one. His curly brown hair was cut short, and his glasses were stylish. I decided he was the more serious one, although he seemed a little nervous too.

"So, Liz," he started. "Has Pradeep talked to you about the position at all?"

"No, I figured we'd wait for you," Pradeep answered for me.

Pradeep did most of the talking at first. "As I explained to you on the phone, Liz, Avi and I started the firm back in August. Since then we've been very busy, and we feel it's time to start thinking about expanding. Before we do that, we need someone to come in and help us get organized, whether it's filing or just doing the bookkeeping. Right now, we rent the office space from the guys in the corner. Even the furniture's rented," he said, then laughed. "Eventually we'd like to move into our own office space, and that could be something we would have you help us with."

Pradeep's enthusiasm stood out against Avi's more reserved demeanor. "You'd be the office manager, and when things get rolling, you'll probably need to hire an assistant, though I know you're only interested in working twenty hours to start. But you never know, perhaps down the road we could offer you full-time, with health insurance."

I nodded as if that would make me happy, as opposed to letting on to how nauseated I was starting to feel. Pradeep was long-winded, and the more he talked, the more conflicted I felt about taking this job.

Avi, thankfully, stepped in to add his own few cents.

"Pradeep mentioned that you're a bartender. Will late nights at the bar be a problem for you in terms of being here in the mornings?"

"No. No," I assured him, sitting up a little straighter in my chair. "When I have to model, it's always early mornings and never a problem."

"Modeling too?" Avi asked.

I really couldn't tell if he was being direct and professional or if he was just not a warm guy. I figured he'd be the difficult one.

"I mentioned that to you, Avi," Pradeep reminded him.

I jumped in. "Yes, I model four times a year for about a week at a time, with some appointments in between, so there would be times when I wouldn't be able to be here."

The more we talked, the less interested I was in the position. I didn't want to be an assistant again! I wanted to be in charge of my own life. I wanted to be a writer. I wanted to make enough money to pay my bills *and* live my life creatively.

Just do something, Liz. Anything. My father's words came back to me.

I clicked into sales mode. I could sell myself like nobody's business. Even if I wasn't interested in a job, I was great at telling people what they wanted to hear. Being a bartender taught me that.

"I like to do a lot of things," I said, leaning forward, clasping my hands as I placed my elbows on the table. "However, the thing I pride myself on is that I'm very committed, no matter how many things I've got going on. Modeling is a priority, for sure, which is why I mentioned it to Pradeep prior to our meeting. The good news is that it doesn't happen that often and I normally have advance notice, so I'm confident that I'll be able to work around it and give you guys exactly what you need to make your lives easier." I paused a moment for effect, then continued. "It sounds to me like you guys have a great thing going here. I'm excited by the prospect of helping the firm grow. While I lack specific legal experience, I'm confident in the fact that I'm a fast learner and I'll do whatever I need to do to get up to speed as quickly as possible. Plus, it sounds like you need more organization than you need legal assistance."

"We have a law student working with us at the moment," Avi said. "So, yes, you're correct. You'd be operating in more of an administrative capacity."

Bingo! He'd just gone all theoretical on me, which meant I got the job. Nobody talked about you having the job until they'd already decided on it.

And sure enough, they offered me the job as their office manager— twenty hours a week at $20 an hour.

I should've been excited. Or relieved. But all I felt riding back to Brooklyn after the interview was dread. The money was going to take an enormous amount of pressure off me, and I could finally start thinking about other things besides paying the bills. Working in a law firm? Ugh. But if I could hang in there until Maxie's picked up, I'd be fine.

17

The next few weeks passed in a blur, with the new schedule kicking my ass. I worked at the law firm five days a week from 10 to 2 and had Maxie's on Wednesday, Thursday and Friday nights. I was still working Sunday brunch at Smokehouse, so my only day off was Saturday.

"Something's gotta give, girl," Stephanie told me over the phone during a token free moment between jobs. "You can't keep running back and forth like this, with no time for yourself."

"I know," I sighed. "But I told the law firm guys I'd do twenty hours, and I really need that extra money."

"I'm not saying you've got to give up hours. Why don't you do longer hours, say, three days a week?"

Leave it to Stephanie to give me an idea that was somewhere in the middle. I never thought like that. It was always all-or-nothing balls to the wall.

"Yeah, I guess I could do that and do a full day on Mondays and two short ones on Wednesdays and Fridays."

As much as I liked the idea of not going in every single day, I was still nervous about asking Avi and Pradeep if I could change my schedule. It was that authority thing again. I was brought up in a household where you respected the rules set forth by those in authority, no matter what. Stephanie was brought up in a household where while you respected authority, you also respected yourself. I sure wished I'd grown up in her family.

My job at the law firm was not what I'd expected. It was worse.

There was very little to do. I spent most of the first week reading the FedEx manual and watching the clock.

My seating situation was less than ideal. Initially they were going to have me sit close to the area where Carla, the woman I saw the day of my interview, sat. Her boss, Paul, was our landlord. Paul was in his eighties, and according to Avi and Pradeep, he was quite the entertainment lawyer in his heyday, representing the likes of Mary J. Blige and other top artists.

Paul didn't like Avi and decided at the last minute to squash the seating plans. Instead, I took up residence in Avi's office, which was large enough to fit his oversized desk, a few filing cabinets and a couch. They decided I would sit in the corner of the office, just to the right of the doorway, facing the wall, with my back to Avi. My desk chair, when pushed away from the desk, blocked the door, making it awkward for people to come in and out with ease.

I also hated that Avi could see my computer screen. I never got to check e-mail or mess around on the computer to break up the day. It was the ultimate corporate prison sentence, especially when there wasn't that much else to do. A few times, I tried to sneak a look at the *New York Times* homepage to see what was happening in the world. The page wasn't even fully loaded when Avi's deep voice behind me said, "Do you need something to do?"

I also kept my cell phone off. Nobody told me to, but I figured while I was at work, personal calls would be a no-no. Plus, there was no privacy with me sitting literally less than five feet from Avi.

Stephanie was right. I had to get in better control of my schedule because it was killing me. If I cut back to three days a week, I'd have Tuesdays and Saturdays off. They weren't in a row, but at least it'd be two days instead of one. I didn't think I'd be at Smokehouse so long, but brunches had been lucrative, and if I was going to leave anywhere, I would rather it be the law firm.

"Well, I've got some good news," Stephanie said.

"Bring it!" I cheered. "I could use some good news."

"I got a part!"

"What?!" I practically screamed, giving Rufus a bit of a jolt from his comfortable slumber by the front door. "Tell me."

"I've got a principal part in the play *Gee's Bend.*" The play was a true story about three sisters living in rural Alabama during the civil rights movement whose unique quilts were discovered by a visiting preacher and later sold all over the country.

"Steph, that's freakin' a–MAY–zing! I am SO proud of you!"

"There's one thing that kind of sucks," she said, her voice getting a little lower. "It's in Denver."

Ohhhhh. That *did* suck. Denver? "For how long?" I asked, still trying to sound upbeat.

Stephanie would be gone for a little over two months. Two months! It was a huge opportunity for her and I did my best to be supportive— but it was hard.

"You're so busy, you won't even notice I'm gone!" she joked.

She had the busy part right. It wasn't like I even had time to hang out with my friends anymore.

In the meantime, I had to walk Rufus and get to Maxie's. "Okay, buddy! Are you ready to go out?" I said after hanging up with Stephanie.

Rufus, still lying by the door, shot his ears up. He tried to get up but couldn't. After a few more attempts, he managed to stand with his back stuck in a hunched position. Finally he straightened out and gave himself a shake, his tail wagging.

His paw had completely healed, but he hadn't been the same since the fall. The cold weather had really taken a toll on him, and his arthritis was worse than ever. The whole getting stuck on the floor was a new thing with him, and I worried that he was in pain.

"Here ya go, buddy," I said, giving his lower back a hearty rub, hoping it would loosen him up a bit.

Despite his slow start, Rufus was happy to be out in the hallway without a leash. He trotted to the elevator, panting and wagging his tail. Outside, the air was cold and the bare trees washed out against the gray sky. We took our usual route toward the area designated for dogs to relieve themselves. Rufus assumed his usual squat but then lost his balance and fell, butt first, into his poop.

"Oh, Rufus!" I exclaimed, hoisting him up from the ground. Damn. I'd have to clean a bunch of shit off his ass, but I was more concerned by the fact that he couldn't hold himself up. "It's okay," I soothed

Rufus as he hobbled back to our building, his backside brown and wet from the fall. We rode up in the elevator, thankfully without company, because the smell was not pretty. Standing in the elevator, he looked up at me with such sad eyes.

"Awww…baby. It's okay," I said, leaning down and scratching the top of his head.

Inside, we went right to the kitchen. I grabbed some paper towels and wet them with warm water as Rufus stood patiently and let me clean him up, only hopping around when I tried to clean his butt.

Once he was clean, I fed him. As he ate, I leaned against the counter and watched him. This wasn't good. What if he fell again and really hurt himself the next time? I couldn't go to work knowing I might come home and find him lying somewhere, stuck on the floor. And what if it got worse and he couldn't walk? Would he need to wear those awful wheels they gave to dogs who couldn't walk on their own?

I couldn't bear the thought of him suffering. How would I know when he'd had enough? It wasn't like he could just wake me up one morning and say, "Yeah, I think I'm done. Please put me to sleep now." No, unless he went naturally, that decision was going to be on me.

Rufus finished eating and headed into the living room. I, however, couldn't seem to get myself to move from my position against the counter. I made a list in my mind of the things that would confirm the right time to put Rufus to sleep.

The most obvious was when and if he stopped eating. Rufus loved to eat, and if he couldn't, that would definitely mean the end. I didn't make it past that. It was just too much to think about. I was not ready to let him go.

Rufus trotted into the kitchen, his whiskers fresh from being rubbed around on the carpet. He stared at me with his ears up and tail wagging. You never would've known he'd just had so much trouble outside.

Maybe it's just a bad day, I lied to myself as I pushed away from the counter, gave Rufus a scratch on the head, and got ready to go to job number two.

18

"Amber's gone."

Rachel delivered the latest staffing news the following week when I arrived for our Thursday night shift.

"Like, fired?" I asked, tucking my wine key into the waistband of my pants.

"Nope. She went next door—full-time. Guess we weren't good enough for her."

"She's had her eye on working next door all along," I said, nodding to a few new customers settling in at the bar.

Rachel grabbed some beverage napkins and placed them in front of the new customers, three women in their forties. Two wore wedding bands while the other, who looked the oldest, couldn't stop running her hands through her highlighted blonde hair.

"Hi, ladies!" Rachel greeted them cheerfully. "What can I get you?"

The one without the wedding band answered immediately. "Goose martini. Up. Dry. NO vermouth. Extra, extra, extra dirty."

"Damn, Kelli," her friend said. "You're on a mission."

Kelli blotted her coral lipstick with the napkin. "That's right. You two married chicks *never* come out. I'm getting my drink on."

The other two laughed, looking over the menu. Both had wavy brown hair cut to their shoulders. They seemed a little overdressed for a Thursday night with a few too many sequins and sparkles on their shirts, but hey, maybe they were going to a prom afterward.

"Oooooh...I want a white chocolate raspberry martini," said the one with the gigantic engagement ring. "Celeste!" she said, poking the girl with the smaller ring. "You should get one of those. We are ON OUR OWN tonight!"

Celeste looked the most apprehensive about "getting her drink on" but agreed nonetheless.

It was early in the night, and for the moment, they were our only customers. Rachel walked toward me and the service bar, muttering under her breath, "Yay. White chocolate raspberry martinis."

I took three martini glasses and the white chocolate from the top shelf. "So are they gonna hire someone else?" I asked, dipping a glass into the chocolate, holding its stem and turning it gently.

"I don't think so," Rachel said. "She barely had any shifts left because she was next door so much. I'm going to take her Saturday nights and Judy's going to take her Friday nights."

"Judy? On Fridays?" I asked, stopping mid-dip.

"Yep. I guess Judy asked Chris if she could have Fridays."

While Rachel poured the drinks, I tried to control my anger. How was it that Judy got Friday nights when I'd been working that stupid no-moneymaking swing since the beginning? That shift should be mine! If Judy wanted to work Fridays, let her take my swing shift while I stepped into my rightful position.

I hated this place. It was always something. What was I supposed to do, go and tell Chris I wanted that shift? I couldn't take it away from Judy. It was bad enough that Marta lost her Wednesday nights because of me.

I *needed* a full shift on Fridays. And it was only fair. Ugh. In this place, fair meant whoever fought the hardest for what they wanted always won. Maybe I could ask Rachel what she thought, but I didn't want her to get the wrong idea and think I was scrapping for shifts. If I talked to Chris, he'd just blab to Judy. Scott made the schedule, but we didn't have much of a relationship, so why would he give me preference?

Plus, if I got Friday nights, I'd have to change my schedule at the law firm again, and I'd already done that earlier in the week. Pradeep and Avi were surprisingly cool about the whole thing when I had asked. Avi had no problem with it, and Pradeep told me, "That might work out better for us, because if we only have you on set days, it will force us to be ready and have stuff for you to do on the days that you come in."

Pradeep was a funny one. Ever since I'd started, he kept talking about how I had to help him get organized. "I know you and I have to spend some time to sit down and go through all this stuff on my desk," he'd told me the week before. "Maybe Monday morning."

But Monday morning came and went with no attempt at organization on his part. I even tried a different approach, offering to sift through the papers and put them in piles to make it easier for him.

"No," he'd said. "It's better for me if you do it with me. It forces me to stay focused."

Great. I was an overpaid babysitter.

Avi was more easygoing than I'd expected. We ended up chatting a lot about the newest bars and restaurants in the city. Though he was married with kids, he liked to check out the "in" restaurants whenever he could. He was also a little kooky, which I liked, walking around some days, singing, "Lizzzzzzz. Liz-o-rama! Lizzzzzz." There still wasn't much to do there, so at least his silliness kept the mood light.

The night passed pretty quickly, which was a blessing, because I had Rufus on my mind. He was still having trouble getting up, and that morning I had to help him by gently lifting his body up from the floor and holding him steady until I was sure he could stand on his own.

Celeste and company were on their third round of martinis, which was pretty impressive considering our drinks weighed in at ten ounces compared to the standard four. Rachel was great, egging them on to do a shot with her.

"Don't ever get murried!" Celeste, the one most hesitant to order a martini, had completely come out of her shell. She slapped her hand down on the bar and said loudly, "Ah HHHAYTE my husband."

"Should we cut Rachel?" Chris asked from the service bar behind me. "We could probably just go with one."

"Yeah, I think she wants to stay and finish these ladies up," I said, leaning against the refrigerators so I could see the bar. "Hey. You got a second?"

There I went. I didn't plan it, but suddenly I felt compelled to find out why I didn't get Friday nights.

"What's up?" Chris said, neatening a row of glasses.

"So, I don't want to cause any problems or anything," I started. "But how come I didn't get Friday nights now that Amber's gone? I mean, technically I should, since I'm the swing, right?"

I was grateful that Chris was my friend, because despite his flair for gossip, I felt comfortable enough to be straight with him.

Chris seemed oblivious to the charge I had put on the situation. "Oh, you want Fridays? Judy asked me and I figured we needed someone, but yeah, I guess you're right, it should go to you," he said.

I put my hand up. "Okay, but wait. I don't want to step on any toes here. I don't want it to look like I'm trying to take shit away from people, ya know?"

Chris laughed. "Yes, Liz. I know." He straightened up, indicating the conversation was nearly finished. "Let me talk to Scott and see what he thinks, okay?"

As he walked away, I wasn't sure what to think. Part of me was proud of myself, but the other part was nervous about making waves. I liked Judy and I didn't want to screw her, but I needed that extra shift. But it was done and in Chris's hands now.

"'Bye, Liz!!" Kelli, the single one, called to me as she and her two friends stumbled outside.

"Bye, ladies!" I sang, smiling to myself and grateful for the entertainment they'd provided.

Rachel, who was much better at partying with our customers than I was, was slightly tipsy after Lydia and company left. She decided to hang at the bar to have another drink and keep me company as things wound down for the night.

"You think the Angelo & Maxie's people are coming over tonight?" I asked her as I started to clean the far side of the bar.

"I don't know," she said, sipping a gin and tonic. "I hope so. They always take care of us." They really did tip us well, but still I thought it was strange to charge fellow staff members for anything, and I never charged them for more than one drink.

As much as I'd love to have the extra money, I hoped they wouldn't come in. It was nearing the end of the night, and I couldn't stop thinking about Rufus. If they came in, things were bound to keep going for at least another hour.

Lately all I did was worry about whether or not I'd come home from work and find Rufus dead. I was sure if I told anyone this they'd call me crazy, but I couldn't help it. He was deteriorating. Most days I couldn't figure out which would be worse—finding him already gone or making the decision to put him to sleep.

My thoughts were interrupted as the crew from next door rolled in. "Hey, guys!" I called out, feigning enthusiasm.

"You guys shuttin' down?" Billy, my favorite, asked as he shrugged his backpack off his shoulder and onto the bar. I was glad Rachel was still here because she'd talk to them while I cleaned up.

"Liz! Liz! Do a shot with us!" she called from the other end of the bar.

"Yeah, Liz!" Billy chimed in. "Come down here and have a drink with us."

"Nah, I'm good," I said, throwing the rag in my hand over my shoulder and walking to their end of the bar. "What do you guys want to do?"

Shots. Great. It was going to be one of *those* nights. Billy and Matt I could handle. They were usually good for just a couple of drinks. But Cal was there, and when he was around, the party went on for hours.

Chris joined the crew at the bar.

"Hey, Liz," he said. "Pour us up some shots of Jack."

I lined up six shot glasses and ran the bottle back and forth over them until each glass was full. If Chris started drinking with them, I'd never get out of there. I wanted to be a part of things and hang with everyone, but I also wanted to get out of there and get home to Rufus.

An hour later, I was in a cab on my way back to Brooklyn. I finally told Chris that I had to get going, and he and the rest of the crew moved on to the bar next door. I'd wished there was someone I could call to take my mind off this crazy thinking, but it was way too late. I probably could have called Deb since it was still early in L.A., but what was I going to say? "Hi, can you stay on the phone with me while I walk into my apartment just in case I find Rufus dead"? Reaching out was hard for me unless it was a crisis. If I found him dead, *then* I'd reach out.

I opened the door to the apartment and stepped inside.

"Hey, buddy!" I called into the semi-darkness.

There was no sign of Rufus, but the smell of shit permeated everywhere.

"What the…" I said, walking into the living room. Rufus slowly emerged from the kitchen, and the closer I got to him, the stronger the smell. When I reached the kitchen, I stepped over a trail of what I was sure to be shit.

"Oh my god!" I said, immediately covering my mouth and nose with my hand. The combination of the winter heat and the closed windows made for one horribly potent stench.

It was everywhere—on the floor, on my cute little throw rugs from IKEA. Worst of all, Rufus's butt was covered in it, which meant he must've fallen in it at some point.

I decided to take care of Rufus first, but the smell was so bad, I first had to open every single window in the apartment. Cleaning up Rufus was easiest, and from the look on his face, I could tell he felt bad.

"It's okay, honey," I said, gently wiping his butt with a wet paper towel. In the twelve years I'd had him, he had never, ever pooped in the house.

Once he was clean, I tackled the kitchen. I didn't even know where to start. The rugs were not salvageable, so I rolled them up and tossed them down the garbage chute in the hallway. With the rugs gone, things felt less overwhelming, and as I wiped the remaining shit off the floor, Rufus stood in the doorway, panting and watching. He looked worried, so I tried to soothe him by talking while I cleaned. "Buddy, what's the matter, huh? Are you sick?"

My talking prompted him to come into the kitchen where I cleaned up the last of the shit. Without the rugs, however, Rufus's paws slipped right out from underneath him, causing him to fall to the floor, all four paws splayed in different directions.

"Oh, sweetie!" I said, dropping the dirty paper towels and lunging to pick him up. As I lifted him from the floor, he let out a small growl, reminding me that he didn't like to be handled.

"Yeah, yeah, Rufus," I answered, placing him down on the carpet in the living room. "There ya go, okay? All done."

He stayed put while I took the garbage out and threw it down the trash chute. When I came back inside, I wondered if he'd still need to go outside. Like a detective casing a crime scene, a flood of unanswered questions overtook my mind. When did this happen? Was he sick? Rufus *always* held it until I got home, and he wasn't waiting an exceptionally long time tonight—at least, no more than usual. But the usual had changed.

19

The next day at work, I could barely concentrate. All I could think about was Rufus and whether or not he was okay. I should've stayed home with him, but I just couldn't take the time off. When I called the vet first thing that morning, she didn't seem too alarmed.

"I'll leave a mixture for Rufus with the receptionist," she'd said. "Sprinkle it on each meal to help with his digestion. I've also included an antibiotic just in case he has some sort of infection. But if he continues to have accidents in the house, you're going to have to bring him in."

If he continued to have accidents in the house, someone would have to bring *me* in—to a mental hospital. It was going to be a marathon day because after the law firm I had to run down to the vet to pick up his meds, go to Brooklyn to walk and feed Rufus and then come back to Manhattan to bartend.

I was already exhausted from barely sleeping. Poor Rufus. He was so sluggish the night before. I wished he could still make it up onto the bed. It would've been a great comfort to both of us. Instead I lay on the floor for as long as I could, scratching his body in all the places I knew he loved.

The exhaustion coupled with extreme boredom was not helping my concentration at work. Avi was working on a brief—something of which I still wasn't quite sure. I was too tired to care. He was stressed, and when I asked him if he wanted two or three copies of something earlier this morning, he snapped, "I can't. I can't. I'm working."

Well, duh, Avi, I wanted to say. Whatever. Today he could work all he wanted. I'd just pretend to be busy until it was time to go.

"Hey, Liz." Pradeep stuck his head into Avi's office. "I'm going to lunch, and when I get back we'll sit down and go through the stuff on my desk." He paused. "Avi, do you want anything from outside?"

Avi didn't look up from his desk. "I'm working," he replied, waving his hand in dismissal.

Pradeep shot me a *What's his problem?* look and said, "I'll be back in an hour."

I was starting to get Pradeep's schtick. He was a procrastinator. All week long he'd been telling me how we had to "tackle" his desk, and so far, we hadn't. I was sure he wouldn't be back in an hour. Instead, he'd show up ten minutes before I was supposed to leave with some sort of apology, to which I would've loved to say, "Dude. I could care less if your desk is clean or filled with Rufus's shit from last night. I'd just like to have something *interesting* to do!"

Avi was typing away behind me—or, should I say, pounding. His fingers pecked at the keyboard as if he were beating on the thing. I could always tell when he was backspacing or hitting enter because he punched the keys vigorously, making it hard for me to concentrate on pretending to be busy.

My phone blinked with an incoming call. Although I kept it on silent, I'd leave it on. I may not have been able to talk to people, but at least I knew they were still there.

It was Maxie's, which was strange. Chris wasn't working until the evening, so I wondered who was calling. After a few minutes of shuffling papers, I discreetly grabbed my phone and headed to the bathroom. I couldn't help but laugh at the fact that I was sitting on the toilet, checking messages. Prisoners probably lived more freely and openly than that.

It was Chris. "Hey, Liz, I'm here at Maxie's with Scott, and we were just talking about the scheduling situation. We both agree that the Friday night shift should go to you, so if you still want it, give me a call."

Of course I wanted the Friday night shift, but after last night and Rufus, maybe I should be working less and not more. But I couldn't work less—I needed the money. I was *so* sick of hearing myself say that.

Leaning forward, I let out a long exhale—elbows on my knees and head resting in my hands. I felt trapped, like my life was not my own. I loved Rufus more than anything, but this running back to Brooklyn and constant worrying was killing me.

"I'll work it out," I said as I stood up and flushed the toilet for effect before returning to my desk.

"There you are," Avi said when I walked back into the office.

Was I really gone that long? I checked the clock on my computer screen. Seven minutes! What the fuck?

"What's up?" I said nonchalantly.

"Can you find out which of the FedEx places in the area stay open after 6? I'm going to need to drop this off and I won't make it by the time the place down the street closes."

"Sure," I said, trying to sound enthusiastic. Normally I liked that kind of project. I was a good detective. Give me a goal and I would find the best possible way to achieve it. But with Avi and Pradeep, the fun vanished quickly because they'd micromanage me to the end. They'd analyze the simplest things to death, squeezing the very life out of the challenge.

The week before, Pradeep wanted me to mail a letter for him. "Do you think we should send it registered mail?" he asked, handing me the envelope.

"What is it?"

"It's a letter to a client I've already spoken to on the phone, but I told her I'd send something in writing."

"Well, if you've already spoken to her about it, I don't see why it has to be registered."

"Yeah, but what if she's not there when it comes and somehow it gets lost? I don't want her to think I didn't follow through."

This went on for a good ten minutes, and I wanted to scream, "Send a fuckin' pigeon, man! At this rate, it will get there faster!" In the end, I sent the letter registered, with strict instruction from Pradeep to track it online and confirm delivery. The FedEx project today, I was sure, would be a repeat of the same thing.

It's not that they were bad guys. They were just very thorough and liked to think things through ten times more than I ever would.

I couldn't bring myself to hem and haw over every little detail of something ridiculous like postal delivery.

"I found five FedEx places in the area," I called to Avi from my desk without turning around.

"Why don't you put them on a spreadsheet and e-mail them to me so I have them?"

I'm glad he couldn't see my face. At least I had the luxury of rolling my eyes without getting caught.

As expected, Pradeep came back ten minutes before I was done for the day. "Oh, hey, sorry I didn't get back in time," he said as I packed up. "Maybe we could start now and get a little done."

In the past, I wouldn't have had the guts to say no, but something was changing in me. I was getting really tired of people taking advantage of my time. "Uh, okay, but I really have to leave at two today, Pradeep."

"Of course! Of course!" he said. "Why don't you finish up here and stop by my office and we'll see what we can get done."

What we can get done? Is this guy for real? I've got ten minutes!

"Do you really think that's going to be the best use of her time?" Avi piped in.

Oh boy. I'd seen this once before with the two of them. I got the sense that Avi was pissed at Pradeep for being out of the office for almost two hours. No one ever said so out loud, but I was good at reading between the lines. The last time Avi made a similar comment was when he was working really hard and Pradeep was gone for most of the morning doing who knows what.

I took this opportunity to get up and go into Pradeep's office to retrieve the FedEx spreadsheet from the printer. When I returned to Avi's office, the momentary tension had passed because Pradeep was sitting on the couch and talking with Avi about the brief he was working on.

"We'll leave the organizing until Monday, Liz. I've waited this long." he laughed.

Relieved, I bid them a good weekend, my mind already on getting to the vet and then home before my shift at Maxie's.

Back in Brooklyn, I managed to get a little catch-up time with Jonathan on the phone.

"I swear, lately all of my socializing is limited to the phone," I told him.

"Well, you're working all the time," he said. "You don't even have two days off in a row."

"I know," I sighed. "I really miss my Sundays. How's Bakersfield?" I asked, switching gears.

"It's Bakersfield," he said, and we both cracked up.

Jonathan split his time between New York and Bakersfield, California, where his boyfriend Ramon lived. He and I met in Atlanta, waiting tables at The Cheesecake Factory in 1995. We hit it off instantly and continued the friendship when we both moved back to New York. Ramon, originally from the Philippines, was a doctor. Several years ago his visa expired, and the only way to stay in the United States was to work in an area where they couldn't hire any doctors. Compared with New York, Bakersfield was the epitome of drab, with not much more than Costco and Starbucks dominating the area.

Jonathan couldn't take the boredom any longer and decided to move back to New York a few years ago in the hopes that Ramon's green card would soon be issued. September 11th threw a wrench in all things immigration, and they were still waiting.

After chatting about the monotony of Bakersfield, I told him about Rufus's accident.

"In the end, Liz, it all boils down to dignity. Living isn't just about breathing. If there is no quality to your life, what's the point?"

"I know. I don't want to keep him around just for me, ya know?"

"No, that wouldn't be good for either of you."

"It's just so hard to figure out *when*," I said, flopping onto the comfy chair.

Rufus, already on the floor, stretched his body toward me, resting his head on my foot.

"I know," Jonathan said gently. "And unfortunately, no one can decide for you."

"I just wish he could talk."

Jonathan erupted into laughter. "Ha! Oh *no* you *don't*! Twelve years with you? Believe me, he could talk some shit!"

It felt good to laugh. "Yeah, that's true. Besides you, he's probably the only one who knows almost everything about me. Maybe I should put you both to sleep."

"Had I not gotten out of Bakersfield, I would've taken you up on that offer in a heartbeat!"

Jonathan could always bring the laughter out in me. I wished he were in town. He wouldn't be back for another month, and Stephanie was in Denver, rehearsing like a madwoman. Thank goodness for Lisa, but I couldn't keep talking to her about Rufus all the time. I hated to be that friend who went on and on about the same thing. My sister had too much going on at work. And what would I say, anyway? Like Jonathan said, it all boiled down to dignity, and the only person to decide when Rufus had lost his was me.

20

I hated Mondays. They were my long day at the law firm, which meant I'd have to spend eight hours trying to look busy. Most days were spent creating files for new cases, which I didn't mind because it gave me something to focus on and I could do it at my own pace. What I did mind was Avi's constant pounding at his keyboard and Pradeep's funk, for which he was continually apologizing.

"I don't know. I just can't seem to get motivated," he told me earlier that day when I went in to his office to drop off his mail. "I know I should get to work on the Duffy case, but I just don't feel like it."

It wasn't the first time I'd heard that. Pradeep definitely had a case of the blahs, and I didn't want to be his counselor. I did that for Keith from Stella Maris, and look where that got me. I had my own problems and wasn't going to bite at another person's attempt at dumping his stuff on me.

I gave Pradeep a sympathetic nod and a smile without really looking at him. Looking at someone who was asking for attention was the kiss of death. "Are you going to sign up for that Bar Association Dinner next week?" I asked, handing him his mail.

"I don't know," he said, leaning back in his heavy leather desk chair. "I should go—it's great networking—but I really don't feel like it. I don't know, maybe I'll go. We'll see."

"You have to sign up by Wednesday," I reminded him, successfully controlling the urge to roll my eyes at his inability to make a decision.

I was glad I didn't have to work that night. And I needed a drink.

The stuff the vet prescribed for Rufus worked, and he'd had no other shit storms since the first one. He was, however, no longer able to control his bladder between walks. But Rufus was a good dog and only peed in the kitchen. My father suggested putting down wee-wee pads, and they made the cleanup much easier.

But his arthritis was progressing, making it almost impossible for him to get up on his own. He could still walk, though the linoleum floor in the lobby of my building had become too slippery for him. I carried him outside and down the steps.

He hadn't stopped eating; he just couldn't eat on his own. At first I thought it was because the kitchen floor was too slippery, so I moved his bowls onto the carpet in the living room, setting them on top of a couple of thick Verizon phone books to make it easier for him to reach his food. But that didn't work because Rufus couldn't hold himself up long enough and had to eat lying down.

Life, for us, had become about good days and bad days.

Yesterday was a good one. My parents came to visit for a few hours, and Rufus was in fine spirits. Still, even on his better days, he was a shadow of his old self.

"Ya know, nobody would blame you if you decided to let Rufus go," my mother said when she and I took him outside for a walk. The air was crisp, and Rufus walked gingerly on the frozen grass, looking for a spot to move his bowels. I didn't respond. Instead, I bent down, ready to catch Rufus if his legs gave out.

My mother didn't push the issue, and we headed back to my apartment in silence. Rufus attempted the three stairs to the building on his own but needed a little lift and a slight push from behind. Once we were on the elevator, my mother said, "You'll know when the time is right."

Would I? Because by the look of things, the time was definitely right. So why was I still not totally convinced? Why was I still holding onto the good days as if they were some sort of indication that Rufus was improving and would shortly return to his younger, healthier self? Maybe I *was* being selfish. Maybe he was done and I was keeping him alive just for my own comfort.

How do you truly know when to end the life of someone you love?

Perhaps that's why euthanasia for humans isn't legal in most places. The agony of coming to such decision is too much to handle. But I was sure I didn't want to come home and find Rufus dead, either.

I was ready for a drink. With only an hour to go, I took my phone to the bathroom and sent my sister a text: "*Drinks after work???*"

Back at my desk, I couldn't ignore the pang of guilt I felt for not wanting to go home right away tonight. I needed to spend some time doing something other than watching every single breath my dog took. I couldn't remember the last time I chose going out for a drink over rushing home to take care of Rufus.

"I'm just so tired," I told my sister later.

Thankfully, she was up for a drink or two, and we met at Houston's in Murray Hill. The circular bar was rather large with stools all around, making it easy to find a seat, even among the after-work crowd.

"I hate the law firm, and each day I go there it's like a little part of my soul dies off."

Blair took a sip of her wine and placed it on the bar, her long fingers resting on the base of the glass. "I know you do. But it's paying the bills right now, which has taken a huge weight off your shoulders."

My sister had always been much better at suffering through a bad job for the sake of maintaining her lifestyle. Her job sucked, but she got to go out on the weekends, have a car in the city and buy pretty much anything she wanted. My friend Todd put it best once when he said, "Your sister chooses her lifestyle over her happiness, while you choose your happiness over your lifestyle."

And believe me, having a steady paycheck and being able to pay my bills didn't suck, but why couldn't a person get paid *and* like what they did?

Walking back to my apartment a few hours later, I was glad I was able to hang with Blair for a while. Neither of us were in the greatest of places, she with her job and I—well, with everything. And though she wasn't always the one I'd talk to about Rufus, she understood how much the decision of his future was weighing on me.

The weight returned as I rode in the elevator. It was such an awful feeling to anticipate the worst every time I came home: opening the door to my apartment, holding my breath, unsure of what I might find.

That night, I didn't find Rufus by the door or in the living room. I sniffed the air, out of reflex, I guess, to make sure there hadn't been a repeat of a couple of weeks ago.

"Rufus!" I called. As I rounded the corner to enter the kitchen, I heard him moving around.

Rufus was lying on the floor, against the wall. "Oh, baby!" I cried, rushing to him and dropping to my knees.

It appeared that Rufus had gone into the kitchen to pee. The wee-wee pads were taped to the floor to keep him from slipping, but one of them must have gotten loose, causing Rufus to slip on the bare floor and fall into his urine.

He looked up at me, eyes wild with panic. "Okay, okay," I said, trying to maneuver him up and away from the wall. "I got you." I put one hand under his butt and the other on his shoulder, closest to the wall. As I attempted to ease him to standing position, Rufus squirmed around and slipped back onto the floor, his back hitting the wall with a thud.

I let him go and sat on my heels, giving us both a minute to settle before I went to him again. Sitting there, I looked at my sweet little Rufus, lying in his own pee, panting excessively. I felt the tears stinging my face as I tried not to let him know that I was crying. Rufus hated it when I cried.

He continued to look at me, and all I could think about was that my dog had lost his dignity, and as I sat there I realized that from here on out, the only reason to keep Rufus alive would be for me, and doing so would be selfish—a word that had never been a part of anything between the two of us.

21

Two days later, I struggled to get out of bed and gear up for another
day at the law firm. Rufus was lying on the carpet near the couch with
his head up, still panting. He'd barely slept, which meant I barely slept
as I listened to him walking around and trying to find a comfortable
spot to sleep.

I got down on the floor next to him and rubbed his head, just
behind his ears. "Hey, buddy. How are you doing? Did you have
another rough night?" He relaxed into my hands. "I know, I know," I
said, reaching out to grab his stuffed octopus. Placing it between his
front paws, I eased his head toward the toy, gently urging him with my
hands to rest his chin on its soft head. Rufus stayed put while I got up
and made coffee.

In the kitchen, I noticed that he'd already peed in two places. "It's
okay, buddy!" I called to him as I rolled up the wee-wee pads and put
them in the garbage. While the coffee machine purred and burped, my
mind flipped to last night. Placing my hands on the counter, I leaned
forward and flattened my back.

Praying wasn't my thing. But last night, before I went to bed, I asked
the universe to send me a sign to let me know what to do. And as I
woke up this morning, a voice inside me said, *It's time.*

I felt strangely sure it was what needed to be done. Or maybe I was
finally ready. How was that possible, to feel almost numb, now that I'd
made the decision? I walked back into the living room with my coffee.
Placing the mug on the desk, I got back on the floor next to Rufus,

who was still lying there, his chin resting on the octopus.

Sitting cross-legged to one side of him, I leaned forward and gently rested myself on his body, sniffing his scent and feeling the softness of his hair. I had no words—just tears. As I cried gently, Rufus picked up his head and continued to pant. Our bodies shook together as we just lay there together, him breathing heavily while my tears turned into light sobs.

"I love you so much," I murmured into his fur, encircling his body with my arms and holding him tightly. "It's going to be okay, Rufus."

I picked my head up slowly and reached for the phone, my free hand scratching Rufus's lower back. Dialing my parents' number, I sniffed like a little girl who'd just had a really big cry.

My mother answered. It was early and she knew something was wrong.

"Hi," she said, sounding sleepy but concerned.

"I think we need to go to the vet," I said, my voice breaking as the tears ran down my face.

"Okay," she said. "When?"

I pulled myself together enough to stand up, call the vet and e-mail Avi and Pradeep to tell them that I wouldn't be coming in that day. "Rufus is sick," I wrote. They were just going to have to understand.

"The vet has an opening at 11 o'clock," I told my mother when I called back. "Is that too early?"

"No, no, it's fine," my mother assured me. "Daddy's gonna come too."

"Okay," I almost whispered. "See you soon."

I hung up the phone and looked down at Rufus, his head still on the octopus and his eyes looking up at me. "What are you thinking?" I wanted to ask him. I wished he could tell me what to do. He was just old and couldn't walk or stand. Were those legitimate grounds to put him to sleep?

I called Lisa. "Oh, girl, I'm so sorry." She cried after I told her what was going on. "It's for the best. It really is. He's ready to go. It's the best thing you can do for him. Call me when you're at the vet if you need to. Otherwise, call me after, okay?"

I nodded, offering a small "Mmm-hmm" as I hung up the phone.

As I got dressed, my mind went into practical mode and I decided to give Chris a heads-up that I might not be able at work that night. I left him a voicemail, miraculously without crying, to let him know I was bringing Rufus to the vet and I'd keep him posted. Telling a few people, whether live or through voicemail, seemed to edge me a little closer to reality.

Rufus still hadn't moved from his position on the floor with the octopus. I lay down next to him, my stomach resting against the length of his body. He groaned ever so quietly with pleasure as I stroked his back and kissed his head. We stayed like that until the doorbell rang.

I knew it was my mother, but I couldn't move as everything suddenly went all slow-motion. If I got up and walked from Rufus to the door, I'd really have to go through with it.

The voices in my head screamed, *Don't do it! Don't you answer that door! We can stay just like this, forever. Please, please, don't take our little boy away.*

I sat up and looked at Rufus, who continued to stare up at me, the love in his eyes palpable. I leaned down and gave him a kiss on top of his head, between his eyes. "I love you," I whispered as I stood up, my body heavy, and made my way to the door.

I tried not to cry as I let my mother inside. "Hi," I managed. She gave me a hug and held me for a minute. Then, after setting her purse on the floor, she walked over to him. "Hey, Rufus," she cooed, bending down to pet his head. Rufus lifted his head slightly to acknowledge her, but he was too weak to keep it up for very long.

"It's raining outside," my mother said, standing up, ready to follow my lead.

It was a typical cold, wet and rainy March day, an external manifestation of how I was feeling inside.

There was no last meal or final farewell to the doorman. A part of me hoped the vet would find something to explain all the panting and Rufus would come back home, but I was pretty sure of what was to come. I tried to keep it simple and focus on getting Rufus out of the apartment and into the car.

I carried him outside, where the rain was falling lightly. My mother tried to keep up, shielding Rufus and me from the rain with her umbrella. It was bone-chillingly cold, but I felt nothing.

"I have to let him pee," I said, setting Rufus down gently onto the wet pavement. "Mom, you get in the car. I'll sit in the back with him."

Rufus stood there, unable to move. I wasn't sure if it was the rain or the fact that he was too stiff, but I waited with him for a few moments, gently tugging on the leash to see if he'd get himself moving. Maybe he knew. Maybe he was trying to tell me he wasn't ready. All I needed was one little sign from him and we'd go right back inside. But Rufus finally took a few steps forward, toward his usual spot, walking and peeing at the same time.

I put Rufus in the car, where my dad sat in the driver's seat. He turned around and said, "Hey, babe."

The combination of the AM radio station my father had on for the traffic report and Rufus's panting created enough ambient noise to make it easy to drive to the vet in silence. When we arrived, my father stayed in the car while I carried Rufus and my mother ran ahead to open the door to the vet's office.

Thankfully, there was only one other person in the waiting room and he was paying, so I didn't have to worry about making small talk. Keeping Rufus in my arms, I sat down, letting his backside rest against my body as I cradled him like a baby with my left arm.

My mother gave my name to the receptionist, who asked, "What is Rufus here for today?" My mother turned to me, unsure of what to say.

"Old age," I said flatly to the receptionist who nodded knowingly as she pulled Rufus's chart from the filing cabinet behind her.

After a few moments, I looked down. "Oh my god," I said to my mother. "Rufus just shit on me."

"Oh," my mother mumbled, reaching into her purse and grabbing a wad of tissues. She wiped my jacket clean and disposed of his poop outside.

"Maybe he's trying to tell you that he's ready," my mother said gently as she settled back into the chair beside me.

I was sure she was right, though I couldn't help but wonder if he'd pooped because he wasn't ready and that was his way of letting me know. The vet technician called us in, and my mother followed us down the long hallway to the examining room. Dr. Gabriele was waiting.

"Hi!" she said, her voice soft with concern as she motioned me to put Rufus on the table. "How's he doing?"

"Not great," I said, easing him onto the table. "He can't really sleep anymore; he walks around at night, panting. Then he'll stay in the same spot for hours, most times unable to get up."

She listened to his chest and said, "Well, it doesn't sound like he's got any fluid in his chest." She pulled the stethoscope off her ears and stepped to the back of the table, placing her hands on Rufus's backside, moving her hands around his lower back and hind legs. "I think it's probably his arthritis. It's pretty bad."

That made me feel worse. I was hoping it would be something internal, something I could justify in my mind that was horrific enough to warrant putting him to sleep.

"What do you suggest?" was all I could manage.

Dr. Gabriele sighed and said, "Well, we can take him downstairs and take some X-rays of his chest to be sure there's nothing going on in there. Other than that…" her voice trailed off.

She didn't have to say it. I knew what she was thinking. I knew what *I* was thinking. I was just trying to find the courage to say it.

"No," I finally said. "I think it's time."

The rest seemed to happen fast and in a blurry, very surreal way. Dr. Gabriele explained that she would sedate Rufus first to make him comfortable. And then, only when I was ready, I would give her the okay to inject the stuff that would euthanize him. There were papers to sign, which thankfully my mother took care of. The details seemed so ridiculous. All I wanted was to drink the last of Rufus in until it was time to say good-bye.

"Do you want them to cremate him?" my mother whispered uncomfortably.

I shook my head vigorously. I only wanted the memories of Rufus's life, not his death.

Somebody came in and put a towel on the table to make Rufus comfortable. He was still panting and resting on his side, though not comfortably.

"Okay," Dr. Gabriele said gently. "Here we go."

She injected Rufus with a sedative that made him extremely woozy. I was amazed at how quickly it happened. All the while, I stood next to him, rubbing his head, his body, never taking my hands off him. As the sedative took effect, his body relaxed and he rolled into a more comfortable position on his side, his head gently resting on the table.

My mother gave me a chair and I sat down, my face close to his. I didn't want him to be scared. "It's okay, baby," I said, my breath ruffling his whiskers. "Everything's going to be okay. You're such a good boy, Rufus. Such a sweet, sweet boy."

My mother was standing off to the side. I didn't take my eyes off of Rufus, but I was comforted by her presence.

His eyes closed slightly, making it look like he was stoned. The panting stopped as he relaxed, and his tongue poked out from his mouth as it did when he was in a deep sleep. I leaned in closer and he tried to give me a kiss, his tongue reaching out to my cheek in slow motion.

"That's a good boy," I said, aware that I couldn't stay there all day. I looked over at Dr. Gabriele.

"Take as much time as you need," she said, stepping forward a few inches.

I sat with Rufus a little while longer and talked to him. He looked peaceful. "Okay," I told her, pursing my lips, trying not to burst into tears.

She stepped closer to Rufus and said quietly, "Okay, I'm going to give him an injection and once I do, he'll gently slip away. No pain, okay?"

I nodded, never taking my eyes off of him, tears streaming down my face.

She finished giving Rufus the injection and stepped away from the table.

I watched him, not knowing what to expect, but when it was finally done, I knew he was gone. His eyes didn't close; there were no last movements. He just quietly slipped away. I let myself take a short, tight breath. I wanted to crawl up on the table with him and hold him one last time, but I couldn't move.

My mother put her hand on my shoulder. I turned to her and saw that she was crying too. Standing up slowly, I fell into her arms, letting the tears flow freely. We stood there for a while, both of us letting the pain hold us together.

I finally broke away from my mother and turned from where Rufus's body lay. I couldn't bear to look at him, lying there, gone. I suddenly just wanted to get out of there. Sensing that, my mother quickly gathered my jacket and asked the vet if there was anything else we needed to do.

"No," she said, putting her hand on my shoulder. "Would you like a piece of Rufus's fur?"

I felt numb, but not enough to think it was a bizarre question. Who the hell would want to keep the fur?

As if reading my mind, Dr. Gabriele said, "Some people like to keep a little fur as a memory."

I couldn't manage any words, so I shook my head no and started moving toward the door. Some of the staff was outside the door in the hallway and when I opened it, they offered me looks of sympathy and concern.

"We have a special exit you can leave through," Dr. Gabriele said, to my relief. I couldn't imagine walking through the waiting room. "Take care of yourself, okay?"

I wanted to thank her. I really did. It might sound strange, but I don't think it could have been a better experience. I wanted to tell her so. Everyone was so incredibly kind and caring, and at a time like that, it made all the difference. Instead, I offered a small "Thank you" as my mother and I left through the special exit.

I don't recall walking to the car. All I remember was throwing myself on the backseat, finally able to let my emotions run freely in the privacy of the car.

"He's gone," I wailed. "My sweet, sweet boy is gone." My cries were loud and raw as reality crashed in around me, the pain, the shock. I couldn't believe my beautiful Rufus was no longer with me.

PART II

22

Twenty-two days had passed since Rufus died, and I was completely lost. It was hard not to count every moment since I'd last felt his sticky tongue gently lick my fingers moments before he took his last breath. Some days I forgot he was gone, like a dream you woke up from and thought was real. Other days I would come home after work and cry myself to sleep. I'd taken to sleeping with his octopus—it smelled like Rufus, and that was a comfort to me. I still hadn't vacuumed. Doing so would have meant getting rid of the last remnants of Rufus, and once I did, what would I have left?

"Right now, the grief is keeping you connected to Rufus," my old friend Kelly told me when I finally called her to let her know he was gone.

Kelly and I met in the mid-'90s and had kept in touch ever since. We didn't see each other often, but the connection between us was still strong.

"Once the grief starts to move through you, the good memories will take over, and *that's* what will keep you connected to him."

Sitting on a bench between the buildings in my apartment complex, I couldn't imagine feeling anything but sadness. And anger. I was pissed—I wanted my friend back. I wanted more time with him, and I wanted to stop feeling so alone.

Mother Nature hadn't gotten wind of my grief because it was a beautiful, early spring day. Instead of sitting in my apartment among the reminders of Rufus, I'd decided to sit outside and write in my journal for a while. I hadn't written in a long time, but now, I felt the need to get it all out. Time passed quickly for those who weren't in pain, and most of my friends had stopped calling to check on me regularly. I was sure that in their minds, it was time for me to move on.

As a kid, it always seemed like whatever I was feeling was above and beyond my family's capacity of understanding. I could still hear my mother screaming from the kitchen as I stomped upstairs to my room in tears over whatever was upsetting me.

"Elizabeth!" she would say. "I don't have time for your dramatics. Can't you see I'm busy!?"

My father's approach was more gentle, but the message was the same: I had to learn how to control my emotions. I heard that so much growing up that over time, I began to think there was something wrong with me. After all, my brother and sister never had any outbursts. *I* must have been the problem.

That's when I started singing and writing. Singing came first. I'd play the most emotional songs I could find—usually Barbra Streisand or Whitney Houston—and hole up in my room with a hairbrush and audience of at least twenty stuffed animals, singing my heart out until it stopped hurting. When I was ten, my parents took me to see *A Chorus Line* on Broadway, and I was hooked. Even then, I identified with the pain and sense of alienation the characters felt. I begged my father to buy me the soundtrack, and I listened to it over and over.

My favorite song wasn't the expected "Dance Ten, Looks Three," where one of the characters sings about her "new" tits and ass. All my friends loved that song! It was the only time when, as young children, we could get away with saying bad words.

The one I liked best was a moody tune called "Nothing," about one of the dancers who didn't quite fit in with her acting class. Her acting teacher, Mr. Carp, keeps pushing her and finally tells her one day that she'll "never be an actress, never!" At the end of the song, she triumphs because she finds a class where she does fit in, though upon hearing about Mr. Carp's death, she pauses and sings sadly, that she felt…"nothing."

At 14, I began writing poetry. I never shared it with anyone, but I wanted to—not for accolades, but in the hopes that someone would understand what was really going on inside and ultimately accept me.

At 22, I began keeping a journal, and ever since, it was the only place where I could truly express myself—without judgment. Rufus was an extension of that freedom. He loved me for who I was, no matter what. On the bench that day, all I had was my journal—and a large butterfly that had been fluttering around me since I'd sat down. It was beautiful, with splashes of yellow accenting its vibrant orange wings. I'd seen butterflies before, but not so much in Brooklyn. As I sat and watched it, I wondered if it was Rufus. Reincarnation was something I believed in on a very selective basis. After my grandmother died, a dainty ladybug took up residence in my apartment for about a week, and I talked to her as if she were indeed my grandmother. A little crazy, I admit, but sometimes we all need to know we're still connected to those who have left us.

I went back to my journal. I knew deep down that Rufus's passing was to allow me to fly—*really* fly. But I was afraid to.

The butterfly landed on the upper right corner of my journal. It *had* to be a sign.

"I miss you so much, Rufus," I whispered to the butterfly, my eyes burning as the tears welled up. "I miss my friend."

The butterfly leapt off the page and circled around me, making me think of Tinker Bell from Peter Pan, dancing around the children with delight. I knew that graceful insect was trying to tell me something, but the pain in my heart was strong, and I couldn't bring myself to see past it. Its work apparently done, the butterfly flew away after a final dance around my head. "Good-bye," I sighed, closing my journal and heading back inside.

On the way back to my building, I saw Eddie, the resident dog walker, talking to a woman whose name escaped me, though I knew her dog's name: Puck. Shit. I didn't want to see them today. I'd been doing my best to avoid all fellow dog people because I wasn't ready to tell them about Rufus. But there was no way to avoid it. They were standing right in front of the back entrance to my building.

"Hey, lady!" Eddie greeted me as I approached. "How's it goin'?"

I did my best to fake a sunny smile and answer cheerfully, "Heeeey, guys!"

Puck's mom gave me a wave and said, "Where's your guy on this beautiful day?"

There it was. I felt my stomach tighten and the tip of my nose start to tingle. *Please don't cry, please don't cry*, a voice in my head chanted as I tried to think of what to say.

Eddie cocked his head and chimed in, "Yeah, where the big guy at?"

"He's...he's..." I couldn't do it. As soon as I opened my mouth, I knew there'd be waterworks. "He's gone," I sobbed.

The mood changed in an instant and Eddie moved closer, putting his hand on my shoulder. "Ohh noooo! I'm so sorry."

"I was wondering if that were the case," Puck's mom said, reaching out and squeezing my arm. "I haven't seen you guys in a while."

I managed to compose myself just enough to give them a quick version of what happened, even though all I wanted to do was get inside and have a good cry, alone.

"If there's anything I can do," each of them said as I staggered up the steps to my building, legs shaking and nose running. I walked past the doorman with my head down, hoping he wouldn't stop me and ask what was wrong.

Safely inside my apartment, I threw myself onto the bed and reached for Rufus's octopus. "Oh, Rufus," I wailed, letting the tears flow.

One hour and a box of tissues later, I took a shower and got ready for work. My mind was foggy from all the crying, but at least I had no tears left for the moment. I promised myself I wouldn't talk about Rufus to anyone that night at work, which would hopefully ensure a tear-free night, at least until I got home.

My phone danced on the desk, vibrating to indicate an incoming call. Stephanie.

"Hey girl," I picked up, trying not to sound as sad and exhausted as I felt.

"Hey, HOT MAMA!" Stephanie said excitedly. "Are you ready for your trip?"

For a moment, I wanted to ask, "What trip?" because my world for the last few hours had been all about tears and tissues.

"You're *still* coming, right?"

"Yes! Yes! Of course," I said, snapping to attention. "Four more days."

A week or so after Rufus died, I decided to book a trip to Denver to see Stephanie perform. I was desperate to have *something* to look forward to, and going to see her play seemed like a great idea.

Stephanie was flattered and excited when I mentioned it to her. "I can't believe you're going to travel all this way to come see me!"

It felt like forever since I'd seen her last, and so much had happened. I needed my friend.

"I'm going to e-mail you my flight info when I get home from work tonight," I told her, trying not to drop the phone while I talked and put on some eyeliner.

It was strange, buying the tickets to Denver. In the past, I'd have to coordinate with my parents first, because they'd watch Rufus while I was away. If they were busy, I'd have to plan my trip around them or find someone else to watch him. This trip, however, was all about me, and not having to worry about anyone else but myself felt kinda nice.

"I just can't wait to get the hell outta here," I said, more to myself than to Stephanie.

"I know, I know. Just a few more days."

I hung up with Stephanie and put the final touches on my hair and makeup. Surveying myself in the mirror, I noticed how *normal* I looked. Amazing what a little makeup and a hair-washing could do. No one would ever know how sad I truly was.

"Let's try and keep it that way tonight—no tears, okay?" I said to my reflection.

I flicked off the light, grabbed my keys and coat and headed out the door. "Bye, Rufus," I called, shutting the door behind me.

23

"How was your trip?" Rachel asked as I settled in behind the bar. It was Thursday night and the first time I'd seen her since Denver.

"It was really good!" I said with a little too much enthusiasm.

The bar was quiet for a chilly night in April, though it was still early. Lately on Thursdays we'd been getting busier in the latter part of the evening, though it still wasn't busy enough for two bartenders.

I'd taken to texting everyone I knew to let them know I was working at Maxie's. A lot of bartenders alerted their regulars and friends on the nights they worked. I'd always been afraid of being too pushy or downright annoying, but Maxie's was the first place where I *had* to do it.

Now my shyness had all but disappeared. The only way I could remain in this job was to make money, and the only way to make money was to build the business. The powers that be were not doing much to promote the place. Plus, a little self-promotion was good practice for someone like me, especially if I ever wanted to get out of the law firm.

Rachel scrunched up her nose. "Hmmm… Doesn't sound that way," she said, passing in front of me to pour a Bud Light draft.

I couldn't get anything past Rachel, which was pretty funny considering I hadn't known her very long. She was one of those people who was just plugged in—she noticed everything—and as much as my trip *was* truly good, it really got me thinking.

"I had a great time, but I gotta be honest," I said, clearing the dirty wineglasses from the service bar. "It made me think about my own life—a lot. It made me feel so aware of how I've got nothing going on in my life. I was so envious and I'm ashamed to admit it!"

"Why? It's not like that's all you felt."

I grabbed some newly washed glasses out of the dishwasher and lined them up to dry. "I know, I know," I said. "But I felt like such a piece of shit! How is it possible to feel such pride for someone else and such disappointment for myself all at once?"

Rachel laughed. "It's very possible. Look, you've just been through some major stuff with Rufus and all. I think it's very normal, now that you've got all this space in your life, to be thinking about what you want to fill it up with."

She was right. It felt good to be away and in a place that held no reminders of my life with Rufus. The air in Denver was crisp, like it gets in the early weeks of October in New York. And the sky felt so low, like I could reach up and touch the clouds. For a few days, I felt like I could breathe again.

Stephanie performed the night I arrived. The play was not quite a musical, but there were a few songs that helped transition each act. Stephanie's voice was clear and soothing as it floated way up above the audience, casting a light glow on everyone.

The second night, her throat hurt and she didn't want to push it, so she opted out and let her understudy take over. She was supposed to refrain from talking, but this was Stephanie.

Sitting on the couch in her temporary apartment, leaning over a saucepan full of steaming-hot water, Stephanie, her voice muffled from the towel draped over her head, said, "You know what your problem is? You are never satisfied. No. Wait. It's more than that. You don't stop to recognize your accomplishments, always moving onto the next thing, never taking the time to acknowledge your progress." She flipped the bottom edge of the towel over her head, like the hood of a jacket. "You've got to stop and give yourself some credit, or else it's never going to be enough. Use your progress as leverage for your process."

You'd think by my response that I was the one with a sore throat. I just sat there and listened.

"Take the law firm, for instance. You needed money and you got a job that sucks and takes up a lot of your time, but you've hung in there. Girl, that's something! Don't you get it? You see it as a failure—*I'm back in the corporate world in a job that I hate.*"

"I don't really sound like that!" I half-joked. "Do I?"

"You're missing my point, Liz," Stephanie continued, her voice squeaking a bit from under the towel. "The law firm is *not* a failure! The law firm is *part* of the journey! It is a means to an end for you, and instead of seeing it as a negative, you should see it as a victory. *You're doing what you need to do to take care of yourself. That* is an accomplishment."

I could always count on Stephanie to break it down, and she certainly didn't disappoint in Denver.

"Your friend is very wise," Rachel said as we continued to talk and work. "I think you're entirely too hard on yourself. It's impossible to do anything—especially when it's creative—when you're struggling with money."

"I know," I sighed. "I just wish I felt like being creative."

"Well, that's a whole other thing," Rachel said, grabbing a martini glass off the top shelf behind the bar. "Actually, I take that back. It's the same thing—this theme of you being so hard on yourself. Helllloooo?! Your dog just died! It hasn't even been that long! Why *would* you feel creative?"

Her words stung me. It was the first time I'd heard someone reflect back to me that Rufus was dead. My mind got all gummy and things seemed to slow down. I felt the tingle in my nose. Damn! And I was doing so well.

The look on my face must've said it all, because Rachel stopped shaking the martini and put her hand on my shoulder. "Oh, honey, I'm sorry... I didn't mean to upset you."

"No, no, it's okay," I said, backing up slightly. I couldn't let her console me. If she did, there was no way in hell I could manage to hold back the tears. Instead I busied myself with re-stocking glasses, and as I did, a few of my friends walked in.

"Heeeeeeeeeey!!!!!!!!!" I said. "How ARE you guys??"

"What's up, Liz? We got your text and figured we'd stop by for a few," Dave said, leaning over the bar to give me a kiss on the cheek.

It had been while since I'd seen Dave and the crew. Dave and Randy were investors at Stella Maris. After I was fired, Dave felt terrible and made sure I got all the money that was coming to me.

I'd met Charlie through these guys; I hadn't heard from him in months, though I did send a text to tell him about Rufus shortly after he died. Since then, thankfully, all had been quiet on his end.

"What are you guys drinking?" Dave's drink never changed: Jameson on the rocks. Randy usually went for pear-flavored vodka, and Lucy, Dave's girlfriend, liked anything sweet. I wasn't too fond of Randy's girlfriend, Kimmi—she tried to play it sophisticated, but people with class don't start their order off with "What's the most expensive drink?" There were two others with them as well, and they usually drank beer.

"You *have* to ask?" Dave said, feigning surprise.

"Yours, I got," I replied, then turned to Randy. "Pear vodka?"

He beamed and puffed up a bit. "Wow. How do you always remember?"

I wish I knew, but it had been my saving grace in all the years I'd been a bartender. "A good bartender remembers everyone's name," my friend Anthony told me when he showed me the ropes almost eight years ago. I was terrible with names, but drinks I remembered. People appreciated that way more.

"I want a martini!" Lucy announced. "OH! How 'bout this white chocolate thing? Is that good? Kimmi! What about you? What are you going to have?"

Kimmi flopped onto the empty barstool next to Lucy and sniffed, "Wine. Something good. *Really* good."

I tried to hold my tongue. Aside from Kimmi, I loved these guys. Dave was a lot of fun, and it was nice to have some action in the bar.

Rachel grabbed two Bud Light bottles for the other guys while I made the rest of their drinks. As I rimmed a martini glass with white chocolate, the new busboy, Carlos, came over to the service bar. "Do you guys need anything?" he asked, cocking his adorable head to the side.

"We're good!" I said.

Rachel, now standing beside me, muttered under her breath for my ears only, "Sooo cute."

I waited until he walked away. "Oh my GOD! Could he be any more adorable?" I said, turning to her and away from the service bar.

"That boy is hot. It's a shame he's so clueless when it comes to being a busboy, but whatever —he sure is nice to look at."

Carlos had started a week before. He'd never worked in a restaurant before and wanted to give it a try. He'd just moved here from California and looked like a mixture of Hawaiian and Spanish, but I didn't know for sure. All I knew was his dark complexion and silky black hair kept making me forget he was so young.

"How old do you think he is?" I asked, dropping a lime in Scott's vodka.

Rachel cocked her head and rolled her eyes upward. "I don't know. Twenty-five, maybe?"

"Yeah," I sighed. "Too young. Damn."

I picked up the drinks and walked over to the crew with Rachel following behind. "What d'ya mean, too young?" she asked, placing Kimmi's wine in front of her. "Here ya go, hun," she said with a smile. "Too young for *what*?"

"You know!" I snorted, snatching the gooey martini glass from Rachel to pour Lucy's drink. "Okay, guys, enjoy!"

"Thanks, Liz!" Dave said, taking a long sip of Jameson. "Ahhh…" he cheerfully growled. "That's good."

Rachel was on my heels at the register. "Too young for what?" she repeated.

"Um, he's 25 and I'm 37! Do the math—he's too young for *any*thing!"

She didn't miss a beat. "You could have some fun, though. Nobody's ever too young for that!"

"Ya wanna know the truth of it? Even if I didn't care about the age thing, I'm just not feeling all that sexual." My hand shot up and covered my mouth. "Oh my GOD! I just realized that. Maybe I'm dried up!"

Rachel laughed. "Easy, girl. Maybe Carlos is just what you need."

The truth of my words had hit me, though. It felt like forever since I'd been with a man. Charlie was the last guy I was with, and that was six months ago! I didn't usually go so long without *something*. My brain kicked into Rolodex mode and scanned all viable options for sex. "JEEsus," I said.

"What?" Rachel asked. Man, this girl didn't miss a thing.

"I just did the hookup scan in my mind and realized there's no one I could actually reach out to for a booty call."

Her eyes grew wide. "NO one?" Pause. "What about your ex?"

"No way. Too complicated," I said, holding my hand up. "And not even all that good."

"Ohhhhhh…"

Before she could say anything else, I cut her off. "DON'T even! I know what you're going to say."

Rachel shrugged her shoulders nonchalantly, "I'm just saying…"

"Just keep that shit to yourself!" I grabbed a bar towel and threw it at her before returning to my friends.

"How's everything, guys?" I said, leaning my elbows on the bar. "How's business at the bar, you two?"

Randy looked like someone had just kicked him in the shin.

"That place is a nightmare," Dave said, rolling his eyes. "I can't even talk about it."

"Sabrina's crazy, and Keith…" Randy chimed in.

"Can't even talk about it," Dave repeated.

"You were lucky to get outta there," Randy said enviously.

I knew they were right. But it still stung, being fired. Of course, if things were rockin' at Maxie's, Stella would be a dim memory.

"How's Rufus?" Randy asked, brightening up.

I stood there, staring at them blankly.

Dave knew about Rufus. He'd actually called me the day I put Rufus to sleep to ask if I'd be interested in being the manager at Stella Maris if he fired Sabrina. I'd completely forgotten about it until then. I guessed they didn't fire Sabrina after all.

I was hoping Dave would tell Randy so I wouldn't have to, but no such luck. Dave just stared into his glass, waiting for me to speak.

"He's gone," I said quietly.

Randy was confused. "Gone? Like staying with other people gone?"

It was all moving in slow motion again. I wondered if there'd ever be a time when I could tell people about Rufus's death without feeling like the walls were closing in on me.

Thank goodness for Lucy, who must've been listening.

"She had to put him down, Randy."

I silently thanked Lucy for being the dog lover that she was and understanding I needed an intervention.

"Ohhhh…" he said, clearly embarrassed. "I'm sorry, Liz."

I mustered a nod.

"Are you gonna get a new one?"

Shock snapped me out of the sadness and my head did that jerky thing as I wondered, *Did I just hear him right?*

"I'm sorry, what?" I practically croaked.

Randy was oblivious to his faux pas and continued. "Another dog," he said, as if I'd missed an important point.

Lucy, equally shocked, was in much better shape to respond. "Why would she get another one? Dude, it's not a car!"

Embarrassment washed over Randy's face as he finally realized his idea wasn't such a good one. "Sorry, I just thought…" he trailed off, trying his best to sink into the background.

I turned away from them and tried to catch my breath, repeating to myself, *Don't cry, don't cry.* Randy's question made me want to leap over the bar, choke him and scream, "Another dog?? Are you kidding me? Would you ask your father if he's going to get another wife right after your mom dies? What the fuck?"

The rest of the night went smoothly as I stuck to lighter conversation with Dave and company. Rachel was the early-out bartender, and she left just after my friends ordered a second round of drinks.

"Remember what I said," she reminded me as she gave me a hug good-bye. "It might be good to just play a little with a guy—take your mind off 'a things."

"Yeah, yeah, whatever," I said, giving her a playful push. "You're just jealous 'cuz you have a husband and you can't play anymore."

"I think we'll take the check, Liz," Dave said, slightly slurring to his words. "I better stop now or else I'll be dying tomorrow."

As they settled the bill, Chris stood in the service bar. "These guys getting ready to go?"

"Yeah," I said, cleaning and talking at the same time. "I just dropped the check."

"Cool," he said, surveying the almost empty restaurant. A table of two in the back corner was the only one left, and they'd just gotten dessert. Aside from my friends, there was no one else in the bar. "Last call in fifteen?" Chris asked, walking away from the bar to the host stand to answer the phone.

"You got it."

With everyone gone and the bar clean, I sat down at one of the empty tables to count my money. Chris locked the front door and sat down across from me. We were the only ones left.

"You wanna drink?" I asked, counting through a stack of singles.

"Nah, I'm good," he said, squirming a bit in his seat.

Not moving my head, I looked up with my eyes. "What's up? You gotta pee or something?"

"I have to tell you something."

Shit. Now what? Was I getting fired? I couldn't take another jolt to my life right now.

"Okay..." I said, putting the money down to give Chris my full attention.

"I'm leaving Maxie's."

My mouth dropped open with surprise, but no words came out.

I could tell Chris had been dying to tell somebody, because like water breaking through a levee, his words tumbled out fast and furiously.

"Another job…leaving restaurants for good…two weeks….maybe a month…you're the only person I've told..."

His words pinged against my mind like sharp hailstones. I caught a few words here and there, but mostly my mind was racing so fast, like one of those bad kung fu movies where the guy's mouth doesn't quite sync up with the words.

I didn't want Chris to leave. I loved working with him! Things were just so easy with him around. What if his replacement was like Sabrina? I'd always known that Chris had my back there, but it wasn't until that very moment that I realized how protected I'd felt by his presence.

"You can't say anything to anyone just yet," he told me when I was finally able to hear the entirety of what he was saying. "I just wanted you to be the first to know."

I let out a long sigh. "Wow. Chris," I said, mustering up as much enthusiasm as possible. "That's really great. I mean it." And I did. "Is it possible to be really happy for you and really sad for me?" I meant that, too.

He stood up and motioned for me to do the same.

"Everything's going to be fine, Liz," he said, wrapping his strong arms around me. As he did this, two things occurred to me: I was getting sick of things in my life always changing. I just wanted some stability. The second thing I noticed was how great it felt to be in a man's arms again. Not that I felt anything other than friendship for Chris, but standing there in his arms shone a harsh light on the reality of my nonexistent love life. And then came thoughts of Rufus. If he were still alive, I'd go home to him, curl up on the floor with him and forget everything for a while.

But he was gone, and soon Chris would be, too.

24

Getting out of bed had become difficult. The bright sun never failed to stir me out of sleep, making it unnecessary for an alarm clock on most days. Today was no different; I'd been up since 8:30. But the thought of getting out of bed was overwhelming.

For the last twelve years I had a reason to get out of bed: Rufus. Now that he was gone, it felt like I could stay there all day and no one would even notice. Only I wasn't so big on staying in bed. Once I was up, I was *up*. I made my bed every day without fail, and unless I was sick, I didn't get back into it until nighttime. Staying in bed all day seemed weak to me, and no matter how sad I was, I'd be damned if I went all weak on myself.

When I opened my eyes that morning, my first thought was, *What day is it today?* This had been my first thought every day since Rufus's death. I was painfully aware of exactly how many days he'd been gone. I'd passed the month marker a couple of weeks ago and could hardly believe it.

Everyone kept telling me that all I needed was time. I watched the clock like a hawk, waiting for it to pass and the pain to go with it. So far, no such luck. Most people wanted me to "move on already," and others would remind me of the time thing, to which I wanted to shriek, "What the FUCK am I supposed to do in the meantime?" I wasn't one to sit in the discomfort of feelings for which I had no solution. Waiting for them to pass was not my style. The worst thing was *not knowing* why I was feeling what I felt. Some people just felt the feelings or, even more commonly, ignored them. I wanted to dig in and figure them out so I could move forward with a new awareness.

My family never understood this. They thought I was dwelling. And maybe I was, but I only dwelled until I understood what was going on inside me. Once I got it, I was done. My sister had the amazing ability to compartmentalize her feelings. I'd always been fascinated by and slightly envious of how she could just decide not to feel something or not think about it for the moment. Though as hard as I tried, I just couldn't fight my feelings.

There was also the guilt. And doubt. Maybe I pulled the plug too quickly. Maybe I misread the situation and Rufus wasn't as sick as I'd thought. What if I'd just waited a little longer? Perhaps he would've gotten better.

I pulled the covers over my head and hunkered down into the softness of my pillow. Being still only made me feel worse. I couldn't stop my mind, and I kept thinking of the e-mail Blair sent me. In it, she told me that although she understood I was going through a difficult time, she was too, and she didn't have the strength and energy to be there for me. "You and I process things differently," she'd written. "It's hard for me to relate to where you're at and I don't know what to do for you."

Her words felt like a hard punch to the gut. This was the same person who'd stroked my hair while I sobbed into her lap over how much I missed Rufus.

Three days after he died, Maxie's made me come into work. It was March Madness, which meant a busy bar, and they couldn't get my shift covered.

"I don't want to go," I'd wailed, while curled up on my sister's couch.

"I know, I know. But maybe you'll be so busy, you won't think about anything..."

It had taken everything I had not to sob into the customers' drinks. I'd wished I could hang a sign around my neck that said "My dog just died, so good service is out of the question."

Chris had been kind enough to let me go the moment things slowed down, but I couldn't bring myself to get on the train back to Brooklyn. I walked around Union Square for an hour and finally called my sister.

"I can't…go…back…" I cried into the phone.

"Come over," she'd said. "You can stay as long as you want, honey."

And I did, for the weekend. Each night, my sister made up the air mattress in her living room and left me an Ambien on the kitchen counter. I felt safe and protected.

And now I didn't know what to feel. In a way, I didn't want Blair to be there for me. Having her pick up my pieces would only embed us in the very dynamic we'd been struggling to get out of for the last few years. I was tired of feeling like a child who needed her sister to protect her, but I wasn't sure it was best time to try and rise above it.

I threw the covers off, bolting out of bed, hoping the sheer force of my movements would shake off the heavy feelings like dead leaves from a plant that was still very much alive. Putting some clothes on, I surveyed the room. "I've got to bring those boxes back downstairs," I said to myself.

The boxes, filled with my winter clothes, were everywhere, cluttering my apartment. It had been almost two weeks since I'd brought them upstairs from storage to make the switch in my closet from winter to spring. I hated clutter, but having the boxes all over the floor covered the empty space Rufus's absence had left behind. At least I'd finally vacuumed. I didn't want to, but after five weeks, I could no longer avoid it. His food, bowls and medication, however, all sat untouched in the kitchen.

I was a little hungover from going out the night before and was not yet ready to tackle boxes. A bunch of us from work had gone out to celebrate Chris's last day at Maxie's. I hadn't planned on going until Rachel showed up toward the end of my shift. "Come on, Liz. Go with us!" she said. "It'll be fun and you could use it."

I started to protest—a knee-jerk reaction of sorts, having always had to get back home to Rufus. But I had no excuse other than not feeling very social, and I couldn't justify not supporting Chris with such a lame excuse.

"Okay, okay," I finally said. "I'll go."

"Yay!" Rachel squealed, her smile wide. She leaned in closer and whispered, "Carlos is coming too."

I rolled my eyes and refrained from telling her I'd already made a decision about Carlos. Sure, he was super-cute, but the idea of being with a man was the last thing on my mind. Instead, I was going to enjoy the apparent crush he had on me and play it safe by being his friend.

It ended up being a fun night. We went to Brother Jimmy's, where Chris used to work. Judy was there, along with Jimmy, the chef. A bunch of servers showed up and so did Carlos, of course. It was the first time I actually got to sit down and talk to my coworkers. I was always so preoccupied with running home to Rufus that I never really gave the majority of the staff the time of day.

Being a bartender, you're involved with everything and isolated all at once. As much as I interacted with the servers, making their drinks, getting them change and cashing them out at the end of the night, I didn't really *talk* to them. Plus, there'd been so much turnover at Maxie's, and I wasn't one to waste my time getting to know someone only to see him go a few weeks later. But it felt good to socialize that night, and in spite of how much I missed Rufus, my newfound freedom didn't go unnoticed.

Speaking of not going unnoticed, my cell phone was dancing on my desk, demanding my attention. Deb was calling. Something had to be wrong. It wasn't even 9 in Los Angeles.

"Hey!" I said, picking up the phone. "What's the matter?"

Deb laughed. "Nothing! I was up early and had this strong urge to call you and see how you were doing."

"You're the best," I said, settling into my comfy chair.

"So?? How are ya?"

"Well," I paused. "Mornings are hard. I just can't seem to get going, ya know?"

"I know," she sighed along with me. "How was Passover?"

Passover had been difficult. It was the first time I'd seen anyone outside my immediate family since Rufus died, and everyone was kind, offering condolences. Aunt Arlene and I spent some time talking on the couch away from the others.

"Death is a part of life, Liz," she said. "The older you get, the more of it you see. It never gets easier, but it doesn't go away either."

"I know," I whispered, my eyes welling. "I just miss him so much."

"I know you do, but you can't dwell on the sadness. You have to get on with your life," she urged, putting her hand on my leg. "It's *your* turn now, Liz."

She was right, but why did people always think I was dwelling when all I was doing was feeling my freakin' feelings? I found myself more pissed than sad about Rufus's absence. I wanted to scream at the top of my lungs, "I want my dog back! Can't I have my friend back just for a little while longer?"

"Oh boy," Deb said when I finally came up for air. "Honey, I'm sorry. They just don't get you."

"I know that. But what's so hard to get? My freakin' dog died last month! If I could move things along more quickly and stop feeling so sad, I would, believe me. It's not like I'm doing this on purpose."

I was definitely wound up, and it was strange that I no longer had to worry about how my excitement would affect Rufus.

"Of course you're not doing this on purpose. It's not supposed to go quickly. Rufus was a part of your life for twelve years, honey. You need to honor his life by giving yourself as much time as you need to mourn his death."

"Yeah. Tell that to my family!"

"Your family doesn't deal with their feelings, so your feeling sad for more than a few weeks leaves them feeling helpless because they don't know what to do for you. They think that something should be done about feelings as opposed to just allowing them to be there."

I pulled my knees into my chest and let my shoulders relax into the chair. "Thank god for you. I'm so grateful to have you in my life."

I could hear the smile in her voice. "Awww. The feeling is completely mutual." She paused for a moment. "What about your sister? What are you going to do about her?"

I let out a long sigh before answering. "I don't know. She's allowed to have her feelings too. I just wish they were the ones I want her to have. I'm mad because I feel abandoned, but I also want to do this on my own, ya know? It's just so damn hard. I can't shake the sadness. I hate feeling so fragile. Maybe I'm finally losing my mind after all these years."

The whoop of laughter on the other end of the phone told me that Deb wasn't buying my journey to insanity. "Uh, hellllloooo?" she finally said. "NOT crazy! You're just working it out. Don't forget that Rufus served as a major force of stability in your life. I think it's quite normal to be feeling so out of sorts with yourself. As for Blair, do talk to her, but do it because you want to say your piece, not because you want to convince her how together you are, okay?"

"Can I bounce something off of you?" I asked, changing the subject.

"Sure!"

"So there's this writing class, and I was thinking of signing—"

"Do it," Deb interrupted. "Do it!"

"You haven't even heard everything!"

"I don't care," she said. I imagined her standing there, phone to ear, her hand on her hip.

"Okay, okay. The only thing is that there's also an astrology conference at the Enlightened Institute in May."

"So go to both," she said.

"That just seems so…extravagant."

Deb wasn't backing down. "*Why?* What's so extravagant about doing for yourself? You're making decent money now, right?"

In spite of the long hours and hating my job, I was finally in a position where I had a little room to spend here and there. But the writing class and the conference were much more expensive than a nice moisturizer from Sephora. It wasn't so long ago I was showing up to Sephora asking for product samples because I couldn't afford to actually buy them. I was smart, though, alternating locations so as not to be recognized as the free-sample frequent flier I'd become.

"I'd be using the money from my tax return, actually," I said, running my finger along the piping on the arm of my chair.

"Duh!" Deb pretty much screamed. "No-brainer!"

"I just wasn't sure if I should put the money aside and build my savings so I can get the fuck out of the law firm sooner than later."

"I don't think putting that money into savings is going to change your life, Liz. Plus, getting back to writing, I think, would make the law firm more palatable until you are ready to make a move. *Give* this to yourself, girl. You deserve it."

Deb's seal of approval was all I needed to convince myself to go for it. After we hung up, I sat down at my computer and signed up for both the writing class and the astrology conference, feeling a lot better than I did when I first woke up.

25

The following week I was working my usual Wednesday night shift, which was shaping up to be pretty decent. The restaurant was getting busier, and I'd built up a small following of customers who came in on Wednesdays just to see me.

Creepy Guy, one of my regulars, had just arrived. I gave him a nod and placed a beverage napkin on the bar where he sat. Creepy Guy liked to settle in before being served, so I hung back while he set himself up: BlackBerry on the bar, iPod and headphones neatly tucked into his bag, and always a wipe of the napkin across the bar before he put his elbows on it. Once he'd done the wipe, I knew he was ready. I saw the guy three times a week, every week, and he'd always start out with a draft beer and then move onto a Bombay Sapphire martini with olives in a chilled glass. And even though I knew it, I'd never assume. Not with Creepy Guy. I think the attention made him uncomfortable, though he didn't want to be ignored either. I'd dote on Creepy Guy just enough to make him feel good.

I walked over, giving him a smile and another napkin. "Bass?"

He nodded with a sheepish grin. I poured his beer, set it down and then left him alone.

He liked to watch, though I'd only been told this by the other bartenders. I wasn't really one to assume people were looking at me—when you worked at a bar, you were fair game for looks and stares. But they were all convinced he had a crush on me because he only came in on my shifts. He'd steal glances at me the whole time, and the drunker he got, the more loving the glances became. Hence the nickname.

The first time he came to Maxie's was on Valentine's Day. He was pretty nondescript: brown hair, pale skin, brown eyes, in his early forties. He did his Bass draft and then moved onto martinis. It was hard to judge a person's capacity for alcohol when you didn't know them, and that first evening, I realized after his third martini that I should probably limit him to two. Creepy Guy confirmed that as he rolled his head back a few times and burst out laughing—silently. He really hit it home when he signed the credit card slip at the very bottom, way below the signature line.

He was a great tipper, though. Not always a redeeming quality, but it certainly helped. I usually charged him just for his martinis. If he ate, his bill was usually around $30. He left me $70 every single time.

His name was Kevin, though he'd never actually introduced himself. He'd just leave his business card in random places every once in a while. Sometimes it was under his plate or in the check presenter. Once he stuck it between the row of pint glasses stacked up on the bar.

Tonight he downed his Bass pretty quickly and gave me the nod to start his martini. As I was pouring it, Scott called me over to the service bar. Since Chris had left, Scott had been covering Wednesdays. It was kind of nice working with him. We had more of an opportunity to get to know each other.

"What's up?" I said, dumping the metal shaker full of ice into the sink.

"Judy's going to be joining you on Thursday nights from now on."

Joining me? What the fuck? They're adding another bartender again? I took a breath and tried not to show my anger. "So," I said gingerly, "there'll be three of us?"

Scott didn't seem to notice my angst. "No. Just you two," he said. He paused for a moment and said casually, "Oh, and I'm going to try and go with just one bartender on Friday nights for the summer. We'll see how that goes."

Things were starting to become clear to me. Thursday and Friday nights were the shifts I worked with Rachel.

"What happened to Rachel?" I asked, a lump forming in my throat.

"Rachel's no longer with us," Scott said with what seemed to be indifference. I guess you kinda had to be detached when you're a manager.

"What?" I said, my mouth open and eyebrows up. "Why?"

Just as Scott was about to answer, Danny, Freddie and Doc arrived. "Lizzy-Liz!" Doc called as they sidled up to the bar.

Damn. Now I had to wait until later to find out about Rachel.

"Hey, boys!" I said, grabbing some beverage napkins and doing my best not to let on that Scott just dropped a small bomb.

"What's up, lady?" Danny said, placing his palms on the bar. "How you doin'?"

"I'm great!" I lied.

"Danny and Freddie are family," Chris had told me when we first opened and all the regulars from the steakhouse were coming over to check us out.

The "family" regulars were in a whole other class. They didn't just come in on an almost daily basis, they were part of the backdrop of the restaurant. I had had a few of these in past jobs. They were the ones I might see outside the restaurant, like for dinner or a drink. The line between personal and professional with a family regular got a bit blurred, and at times I felt strange about taking their money.

Danny and Freddie came in a lot when I worked with Marta. I liked them just fine but got the sense they liked Marta better, so I didn't interact with them as much. Now that she was only working during the day, I saw them a lot more.

Danny was the cool cat of the bunch, always dressed in a suit with a perfectly coordinated tie to match a vibrantly colored shirt. When I first met him I thought he was a player, but since he'd been coming in more often, I realized he was actually pretty shy. I used to think Freddie was just one of those good-looking guys—with his salt-and-pepper hair, smooth Latino skin—who didn't say much, but the past few times he'd been in, I realized he was more reserved and surprisingly deep.

Doc usually came in separately and was more gregarious than the other two. I thought Doc was only a nickname, but when Lara got sick and needed some antibiotics, he took care of it.

Doc's booming voice betrayed his physique. If my back was turned and I heard him talking, I'd spin around expecting to see a 6-foot-tall, 300-pound dude instead of a 5'7", bald black man. Doc liked to talk, and tonight I was grateful, because in light of the news about Rachel, I could barely concentrate.

Once the guys were settled in with their drinks, I scanned the restaurant, looking for someone who might have information about Rachel. I'd hoped Scott would fill me in later, but he was a man of few words, so perhaps that was all I was going to get. If Rachel had been fired or even quit, why didn't she tell me? We weren't just coworkers, we were friends. Or at least she was *my* friend.

I could've asked Jimmy, the chef, but gossip wasn't my thing. When Chris first told me about his decision to leave Maxie's, he asked me not to say anything. I secretly resented that, thinking, *Oh, sure, you feel better now 'cuz you got it off your chest and dumped it on me. Now I've gotta carry it around and suffer in silence?* In the end, Chris told everyone. I should've known he would. He could never keep his mouth shut.

I decided to send Rachel a text. We weren't supposed to have our cell phones behind the bar, but all the bartenders kept them there anyway. With my back to the main part of the bar, I stood at the register and slid out a mesh wire basket that was between the top of the refrigerator and the bottom of the shelf that held the computer. Pretending I was looking for something in the basket, I quickly composed a text to Rachel that said "WTF?"

A couple of hours later, she texted, "Long story. Will tell you when I see you."

Confused and slightly annoyed by all the mystery, I stood there trying to decide whether to leave it alone or push for more information.

"Everything alright over there?" Jimmy called out, leaning his elbows on the service bar. "You look confused."

I threw my phone back in the wire basket and walked toward him. "Just trying to figure something out," I said, deciding to keep the whole Rachel thing to myself. "You wanna drink?"

Jimmy shook his head. "Naw, I'm good." He tilted his chin toward Creepy Guy. "Looks like Creepy Guy's on his third martini tonight."

"No," I said, "he's only allowed to have two." Jimmy snorted as I turned and saw Creepy Guy laughing and muttering to himself. "Fuck!" I said under my breath.

"Yeah," Jimmy laughed. "He's gone."

We stood there watching Creepy Guy, who had thrown his head

back and was silently laughing so hard, I wondered if he would fall off the bar stool.

"You hear about Rachel?" Jimmy asked.

"Yeah, what the hell?" I was relieved that someone else actually knew.

"It's fucked up. All I know is that she walked in, gave Scott her notice and walked out."

"What?" I said tilting my head. "I don't get it. That's so unlike her to just up and quit like that."

"I know, but that's all Scott said. Maybe her husband doesn't want her working here anymore, I don't know. All's I know is she's gone, man."

Now I was really confused. I knew Rachel pretty well, and for her to basically walk out, something major must have happened. I doubted Scott would tell me anything more, so I would have to wait until she told me.

Glancing back at Creepy Guy, I sighed, "I gotta cut that guy off."

It was a challenge to cut anyone off, but regulars were especially tricky. They thought they were beyond the rules, sometimes asking the kitchen to make them special stuff or assuming they could keep drinking even after the bartender had called last call.

There was always the risk that they'd get pissed off and never come back, and in Creepy Guy's case that would be a shame, considering he contributed $120 toward my weekly income. Still, he had to go.

"Here ya go, hun," I said, placing a pint glass of water on the bar and sliding it toward him.

Creepy Guy jerked his head up and smiled at me. He knew he'd had enough. I saw it in his eyes. He was a quiet drunk, and that made it easier to cut him off gently.

He took the glass of water and mumbled, "Thanks."

"Should I take this?" I asked, reaching for the half-full martini glass.

Creepy Guy nodded like a five-year-old who'd just gotten caught doing something he shouldn't have done.

"How are you guys doing over here?" I asked Doc and company as I put the dirty martini glass in the dishwasher at their end of the bar.

"We're good, Lizzy-Liz!" Doc sang.

My assumptions about Scott not giving me any more information were right, and at the end of the night it was business as usual—him running reports, me counting money and then grabbing a cab home.

As I rode back to Brooklyn, my mind ran through all the possibilities that may have contributed to Rachel's departure, and it really sank in that she was gone. I couldn't believe it. She'd truly been my rock at Maxie's—especially through all the Rufus stuff.

First Chris, then Rachel. It was hard to roll with the winds of change when your own life was still very much the same.

I leaned back in the cab and watched Broadway pass before my eyes. It had changed since 1990, when I first moved to Manhattan. My very first apartment was on 8th Street and Mercer, when Antique Boutique was the place to get cheap used jeans. Now it was a Wendy's.

There'd been so much change lately, I felt like the universe was calling out to me, gesturing with its hand, to join in. And I wanted to. But my feet were heavy and I didn't have the strength to lift them and step forward. Crossing the Manhattan Bridge, I rolled down the window in the back of the cab and let the wind blow on my face, hoping it would sweep me up and transport me to a new and better life.

26

"Can you lift yourself up and into the bra a little, Liz?" Loretta asked, looking over my shoulders and into the full-length mirror in front of us. "I want to see if it's the cup or you."

It was Market Week, and things were in full swing. Loretta, the designer, had me trying on some of the bras we'd be showing to see if there were any last-minute changes to be made. As usual, she was also trying to push off any problems with the garment onto me. "Have you lost weight?" she asked, coming around to face me, her eyes fixated on my breasts.

"Nope," I said as nonchalantly as possible.

Just about every Market Week, Loretta asked me if I'd lost weight. You'd think that as a model, it would be good to be down a few pounds, but when you were modeling full-figure lingerie, being too skinny was the kiss of death. A few years back, when I was working at a busy midtown restaurant, I lost a lot of weight. My hours were crazy and I was working double shifts, sometimes three days in a row. Between the physical demands of the job and the long hours, I lost almost eight pounds, and when you weighed only 122 pounds, it made a huge difference.

Alyssa, who was in charge of booking the models, sat me down and said, "Liz, honey, you've got to put on some weight."

I found it funny coming from Alyssa, who probably weighed ninety pounds soaking wet.

"I thought skinny was good," I said, trying not to show my worry. I loved modeling and didn't want to lose the opportunity.

"Skinny's good if you're a 34A," she laughed. "People are saying that because you're so skinny, the bras look like they're swimming on you."

From that point on, I made sure that two weeks before every Market Week, I'd start eating everything from pizza to brownie sundaes, and it seemed to work because nobody said anything about my weight again.

Except for Loretta. She liked to play the weight card whenever she screwed up. Loretta had been designing bras for more than twenty years. When I started modeling, she was the head designer at Lilyette, my very first gig. I didn't work with her directly back then because there was a whole team of designers. At La Jolie, Loretta was the only designer—the "Queen Bee," as the ladies on the sales side liked to call her.

"I think you're a little smaller around the ribs," Loretta pressed on in her thick Westchester accent that made her pronounce things like "cawfee" and "motha." "Teen! Can you bring me the tape?"

As much as I knew she had the right to measure me, I resented the little show she put on each time.

Tina appeared with the measuring tape and handed it to Loretta. I raised my arms without being asked because I'd done this so many times before. Wrapping the tape around my rib cage, just under my breasts and muttering to herself, Linda took a step back. "Hmmph. I just don't get it," she said, shaking her head and staring at me—or, should I say, my boobs.

"How are we doing in here?" Ashley asked, peeking her head into the design area. As usual, Ashley looked great. One of my favorite things about Market Week was seeing what she'd have on. She really knew how to put herself together. Ashley was short and slightly round, but the clothing she chose was always flattering. That day her simple black dress hung loosely against her body, and her chunky necklace and matching bracelet, in vibrant shades of plum and fuchsia, added the perfect amount of color.

Loretta didn't take her eyes off me. "I don't know, Ash," she said, placing her index finger over her lips and cocking her head to one side. "Somethin' just doesn't look right. I don't know if she's lost weight or if the bottom band is a little big…"

"Well, we can't do anything about it now," Ashley said, her eyes flashing my way with a "here we go again" look.

Loretta wouldn't budge. "Yeah, I just don't know if we can show it."

Oh boy. Here we *really* go.

"Not show it?" Ashley snapped. "Why? It's a proto and looks perfectly fine for Market."

Since La Jolie was a relatively small company, it did a large part of the sewing in-house. Other companies farmed that sort of work out, but La Jolie made all its own samples, or "protos." Once the samples were fit-tested, they were sent out for production.

"Look, Loretta," Ashley said, making no attempt to hide her irritation. "I need Liz to be ready for the first meeting." She looked at her watch. "And that's happening in fifteen minutes!"

It was always a bit of an adjustment while modeling to get comfortable with people talking about me like I wasn't in the room. Not my favorite part of the job, but you'd be surprised what you could get used to. Sometimes I just zoned out and pretended I wasn't there, letting my mind wander to laundry, the weather, and conversations I needed to have. It worked especially well when there was tension in the air.

I could tell Loretta wasn't happy with Ashley's tone because she started rifling through the twenty or so bras on her drafting table. "I have another proto here somewhere…maybe we can make a few adjustments…"

"Loretta, we don't have *time!*" Ashley turned to me and calmly said, "Why don't you start getting ready for the first appointment? Loretta and I will figure this out."

I shrugged my shoulders uncomfortably, offering a weak smile in Loretta's direction, and got out of there as fast as I could.

Ashley was the only person in the entire company who had an office, and during Market Week it became my dressing room. It was small and the lighting could have been better, but I made do, dragging the full-length mirror out from behind her door and propping it up on the rolling suitcase she used for the samples when she traveled.

I liked to get myself all set up on the first day of Market Week, but because of the whole Loretta/Ashley showdown, I was behind.

"HOLA, *mami!*" I heard from the other side of the door.

"Hey, Jaz!" I called, laying out my makeup on the small table in the corner. "Come on in!"

Jasmine poked her head in first. "Are you decent?" she asked dramatically.

"Define decent," I shot back, laughing.

Jasmine shimmied through the door, taking care not open it too wide to expose my now topless body. "Did Alyssa bring you your robes?" she asked, going through the bra samples hanging on the rolling rack next to the table.

"Not yet," I said, turning to face Jasmine with my hands over my boobs.

Jasmine rolled her eyes and picked up the phone on Ashley's desk. "Alyssa. Do you have Liz's robes back there?" She waited, feigning a yawn. "No, no. It's too crowded in here. I'll come get them," she said, winking at me. "Fifteen minutes behind? Okay. I'll tell her. The first appointment is running fifteen minutes behind," she announced, hanging up the phone.

"Oh, good."

"Lemme go get the robes."

Jasmine was one of my favorites at La Jolie. A straight-shooting Puerto Rican from Queens, she liked to call me her friend from "the other side of the tracks." She was very wise for her twenty-nine years. At twenty-nine, it was Jasmine who'd talk me off the ledge when I needed it. "Leesten," she'd say, wagging her finger in my direction. "You know Loretta is loco, so don't *you* be going all loco and worrying about what she's saying about you. Everybody knows it's Loretta."

When Jasmine first started working at La Jolie she didn't have any accounts, so she was the one who'd dress me during the client meetings. And even though she was no longer helping me dress, she always looked out for me and made sure I had everything I needed, from robes to a basic black panty to wear when there was no matching one available.

I was always nervous on the first day. The anticipation of kicking off the week really worked my nerves. Plus, there was always a lot of tension shooting around, whether it was Loretta and Ashley or Ashley and her sales team. I bore witness to it all since I was camped out in Ashley's office for the majority of the time. And as much as being a model meant all eyes were on me, I spent a lot of time during Market Week disappearing without leaving the room.

"Let me know if you need anything, okay?" Jasmine said, returning with the robes. "I'll leave you to your thang, Missy."

I was grateful for the time to myself as I sat on the floor and applied my makeup, careful not to apply too much because the lighting in the showroom was harsh, and too much makeup looked garish. I'd be there for the next six hours and didn't want to be all caked up with makeup by the end of the day.

Another knock at the door. It was Yvonne, who was fairly new and had been assigned dressing duties.

"Ya ready, naked lady?" she asked, stepping into Ashley's office. "The clients are here."

Yvonne was cool. When I first met her I thought she was Jamaican, but she laughed after I asked her where she was from in Jamaica. "Oh no, honey. I'm from Trinidad," she'd said proudly, her thick West Indian accent making her words sound like a sweet melody.

"Let's get you into the first look," she said, grabbing a lacy black bra-and-underwear set with shiny brown piping.

I stood with my back to her as she reached over my head, holding out the bra for me to slip my arms through.

"Mmmm, you smell good," I said, leaning over to get my boobs into the cups properly.

Yvonne made a clucking noise with her tongue. "Thas just me hair, gurl," she said, shaking her long dreadlocks from side to side as I turned to face her. "I think you need a little lift," she observed, stepping from behind me and tightening the straps. "There."

We stood together looking at my reflection in the mirror for a moment. I leaned in a little closer to apply mascara and some lip gloss. "Okay, let's do this," I said, tossing my short hair as if it were much longer. "Are my tags in?"

"Yes, ma'am," she sang cheerily, holding out a black silk robe for me to put on. "Go get 'em!"

I wrapped the robe around me, stepping into my heels and out of Ashley's office. I was ready.

The first appointment was The Closet, a small store in Canada. It wasn't one of the heavy hitters like Macy's, which made for a potentially stress-free sixty minutes. But I didn't care for the buyer. She never made eye contact, which always threw me off because I didn't know whether she'd gotten a good look at the garments or not. I always opted to stay a little longer because it was better to be dismissed than to have the buyer calling after me, "Wait, wait! Come back. I haven't even *seen* the panties yet."

"What we have here…" Ashley began as I walked toward the buyer, head high, robe closed and a pleasant smile on my face.

I stood a few feet in front of the buyer, dropping my robe as Ashley described what I was wearing.

Continuing to look as if someone had just told me they liked my shoes, I stole a quick glance at the buyer, who kept her head down while she took feverish notes. Her tight brown bun was bobbing up and down as Ashley continued, "It will be available for 6/25 delivery and will come in a basic black like the one Liz has on."

You'd think this would've made her look up, but no dice. I stood there for a few more awkward minutes, glancing at Ashley, who finally gave me the nod to go.

The meeting went smoothly despite the buyer's seeming lack of interest. With the first of many appointments under my belt, I was feeling more at ease as I sat with Yvonne in Ashley's cramped office, waiting for the next one to arrive.

"How's your doggie?" Yvonne asked, as she arranged sets of bras and panties on the rolling rack.

I had forgotten that some people still didn't know about Rufus. Funny how such a small question could suck the air right out of the room.

I took a deep breath. "He's no longer with me," I said quietly, wondering when and if it would ever get easier to tell people he was gone.

"Oh my goodness! I'm so sorry. I didn't know."

"I know, I know," I said, nodding my head, hoping the movement would prevent any tears from falling.

"What happened?" she said, her big brown eyes searching mine.

"Old age. Do you mind if we don't go there right now? I don't want ruin my makeup."

Yvonne patted my shoulder. "Of course, I understand."

I thought back to the last Market Week, when Rufus was still alive, and wished for the day when my life was no longer measured by his life and death.

27

When I interviewed with Avi and Pradeep, I was clear about my standing commitment to Market Week four times a year. They'd been mostly okay with my absence, though Avi was a bit panicked the week before, firing off things he needed me to do and following up with "Oh, right. You'll be gone next week."

"He's just guilting you, girl," Stephanie said when I told her about it. "They hired you knowing full well there'd be four weeks out of the year that you'd be modeling."

I was a sucker for a good guilt trip and ended up offering to "pop in" between appointments to take care of anything urgent. Avi was happy about this, but when I arrived at 1 p.m. on the first day with an hour to spare, there was nothing pressing to get to.

"I just need you to check and see which Federal Express offices are open late on the weekend in this area," he replied when I asked him what needed to be done.

Again with the damn FedEx offices?

Avi must've been working on a law brief because the only time he cared about how late FedEx was open was when he had to send one out. And although he wasn't quite the procrastinator like Pradeep, Avi was a perfectionist—going over a brief a thousand times, which of course resulted in rushing to get it out for an overnight delivery.

Think of the money you're making, I told myself before stepping into Pradeep's office.

"Hey, Pradeep," I said, trying not to sound weary and unenthused.

"Heeeeey!!!" Pradeep exclaimed, looking up from his computer and leaning back in his leather chair. "How'd modeling go?"

Pradeep had been in a great mood lately, and I suspected he was on medication. Being a former Zoloft user myself, I could tell. He had a lot more energy and focus, he was losing weight, and instead of whining about not getting anything done all day, he seemed pretty motivated. Plus, when a person started leaving the office twice a week for an hour a pop, only one of two things were happening. He didn't seem like the affair type, so my guess was that he was going to a psychiatrist.

Sensing Pradeep wanted to talk, I settled into one of the two chairs that sat opposite his desk and asked, "How's it going?"

"Eh. It's okay," he said, his eyes darting around as if we were planning to blow up the subway or something. "It's been a little tense." He jerked his head back toward the wall that adjoined Avi's office. "*He's* been really tense."

"Mmmmm," I nodded. "He's got a brief due."

I wanted to engage with Pradeep and tell him just how annoying Avi had been, with his snappy comments and incessant keyboard-pounding, but I didn't. They were still partners. As much as Pradeep wanted me to be his ally, I wasn't going to bite. It was too dangerous and so not worth it.

"I don't know why he does this to himself," Pradeep said, leaning his elbows on the desk. "He makes himself crazy with worry each and every time he's got to write a brief." He paused to make sure Avi wasn't standing at the door and listening. "He was here all day on Sunday, but I don't think he got anything done."

I did my best to stay neutral and keep my mouth shut. The last thing I needed was another situation like I'd had with Keith—complaining to me about Sabrina and then standing by in silence while she fired my ass. Pradeep was just going to have to save it for his shrink.

"Yeah, well, hopefully he'll get it done in time." I stood up to indicate the conversation wouldn't be going any further. "Let me know if you need me." I smiled, turning to go back to my desk.

My desk situation had started to wear on me. In the beginning, I didn't mind being in the same office as Avi, but his mood lately hadn't been all that upbeat. He'd taken to listening to Israeli folk music while working. I was all for a musical work environment, but his off-tone, too-loud singing along to most of the songs was distracting.

A week earlier, I'd put my iPod on in the hopes of tuning him and his Jewish Lollapalooza out. Unfortunately, I had to keep my own music low enough so I didn't miss the phone ringing, nixing the opportunity to keep Avi's world out of mine. Plus, he leapt for the phone, picking it up on the first ring, just as I was peeling off my earbuds to answer.

After he hung up, he said, "I didn't think you could hear it with your music on."

That took care of that, and now I was trying to concentrate on paying bills while Avi alternated between humming and singing as he poked at his computer keyboard.

My mind wandered to Rachel as I stretched out the simple task of bill-paying as long as I could. I'd finally caught up with her a few days ago and learned why she had left Maxie's so suddenly.

"I needed to get out from behind the bar," she'd sighed into the phone. "It was getting dangerous for me to be there, and the longer I stayed, the less likely I'd do anything more with my life."

I could totally relate to the part about staying at a dead-end job for too long and was proud of Rachel for taking charge of her life—and a little envious, too. I'd love to make a bold decision like she did and walk in one day to give my notice, declaring to the universe that I was ready to take charge of my life.

The disturbing part about Rachel's decision, however, was that the "danger" she spoke of had more to do with drinking than with becoming a lifer behind the bar.

"Honestly," she said, "I drank so much there, it's ridiculous!"

"Really?" I asked, blinking with the naïveté of a teenager. "I know we do shots and stuff with the customers, but I didn't think it was a problem."

"Shots with the customers is where it *begins!*" she said, exasperated. "The other night, I started drinking at 7 p.m. and kept at it until 4 a.m.! I'm freakin' married, Liz! I have no business stumbling in after 4 a.m. when I've been off work since midnight."

"Ohhhh. What are you going to do?"

"I'm going to get myself to some meetings."

Like AA meetings? I thought, but didn't say. I had no idea it was that bad. "I think that's good," was all I could manage.

"I don't know what Scott's telling people..."

"Nothing! I'll start telling everyone you're pursuing your teaching career. 'Cuz isn't that what you're doing, in a sense?"

"I love you!" Rachel cried with relief. "Yes, that's exactly what I'm doing," she said, sounding as if she were trying to convince herself.

It chilled me to think she had a problem with alcohol. We all drank a lot at Maxie's, and I drank more than I ever had at any bartending job. Working in a restaurant was like working in a vacuum. Excessive behavior could go virtually unnoticed when everyone was doing it. I never got blitzed behind the bar, but a shot of Jack Daniel's every now and again while I was working sure made the shift a lot more pleasant. Did that make me an alcoholic?

"Liz." Avi's booming voice temporarily derailed my mental spinout. "Would you call the process servers we use to find out the prices on serving fifteen subpoenas?"

"Sure," I chirped, happy to have *something* to do.

"Hi, Becky. It's Liz from Levinsky & Gupta," I said, resting the phone on my shoulder. "I need to get some information from you."

One of the things I learned in my assistant days was how to develop a relationship with the people you need. The guys in the mailroom at my old job were my biggest allies, doing whatever I needed, *when*ever I needed it, all because I took the time to get to know them.

Becky had been a doll, never charging us extra when we had last-minute subpoenas to file. As I went over the list of things I needed to know, Avi kept calling out things like "Ask her how much lead time she needs?" and "If we FedEx the subpoenas, can she turn them around the same day?"

His comments were not only annoying, they were distracting, and before I realized it, I turned around and shushed him. "Dude!" I said, glaring at him like he was a bad child. "I can't hear her!"

Now I'd done it. The way Avi started twisting around in his chair made it clear that I'd officially crossed a line.

"Let me talk to her!" he snapped.

I turned my back to him and said pleasantly, "Hey, Becky. Can you hold on a sec? My boss wants to speak with you."

I placed her on hold, the anger burning inside me. I wanted to tell Avi to go fuck himself, but instead said, flatly, "Go ahead."

Avi picked up the phone and started to fire off all the questions I was going to ask had he given me the chance. *This seems like a great time to go to the bathroom,* I thought, pushing myself back from the desk and fighting the urge to grab my purse, turn around and give Avi the finger.

When I got back to my desk, I was happy to see I only had ten minutes to go. Avi was off the phone and back to beating on his keyboard. Still pissed, I sucked it up and asked, "Did you get all that you needed from Becky?" My voice was tight.

"Yup," he said, not looking up from his keyboard.

I sat back in my chair and rolled my eyes, silently repeating what I called my Law Firm Mantra: *I can't wait to get the hell outta this place. I can't wait to get the hell outta this place.*

Pradeep stuck his head into the office with noticeable trepidation. "Uh, hey. Sorry to interrupt Avi, but could I borrow Liz for a second?"

Avi answered Pradeep with a wave of his hand.

"Uh, Liz. I know you've got to go in like five minutes, but I was wondering if you could just scan this document for me real quick. I know it's a little on the thick side, but I'm sure you can get it done before you have to leave."

Oh my god! I was trying so hard not to tell Pradeep to go fuck himself *too*! He did that to me EVERY time I was about to leave, always apologizing about waiting until the last minute, to which I wanted to say, "Then *don't*, Pradeep!"

I was sick of it, and given what had just happened with Avi, it was going to take a lot for me not to throw the damn document out the window.

"I'll do my best, Pradeep," I said, unable to control the edge in my voice. "But I really can't stay past 2 today."

"No, no, I know!" he said, backing up a little. "Ya know what? I'll just do it myself. Don't worry about it. I shouldn't have waited until the last minute."

You're damn right, I thought. "Okay," I shrugged, reaching over to shut down my computer.

In the past, I would have stayed and grumbled about it to myself for days. But I was sick of people taking advantage of me. Although I wasn't raised to say no, it was high time I started setting some boundaries.

"I'll see you guys on Friday!" I called over my shoulder, practically skipping out of the office. My latest clock-watching session was finally over.

I sure hoped Deb was right about doing stuff I loved taking the sting out of doing the stuff I hated and always running from one place to the other. When all was said and done, I'd worked sixteen hours that day! I so wished I had given up my shift at Maxie's. As I walked up Madison Avenue, feeling the spring sun on my face, I tried to concentrate on the good things in my life, like the writing class, my trip to The Enlightened Institute and the fact that summer was coming.

28

It was my first full day at The Enlightened Institute, and the weather, though a little crisp, was spectacular. I parked myself on a large Adirondack chair overlooking the campus, drinking coffee and doing a little writing before the class started.

I'd arrived the night before, after picking up my dad's car in Westchester. The traffic was light, which made the hour-plus drive to western Connecticut quite pleasant. The farther away from my parents' home I got, the cooler the air became, but I didn't care. I had the windows and sunroof wide open, letting the wind have its way with my hair.

The Enlightened Institute was well known among the New Age set and was host to hundreds of famous spiritual teachers like Thich Nhat Hanh and Caroline Myss. The campus was huge and held holistic summits with names like "Getting Off the Emotional Roller Coaster" and "Limitless Minds." Amenities were sparse as the intention of going to a place like the institute was to focus on the healing, not the distraction of luxury.

I was a designer hippie at heart. I liked community-driven experiences with a giant bed and 600-thread-count sheets waiting for me at the end of the day. But at Deb's urging, I stayed on campus. "You'll be more a part of everything," she'd said when I told her I wanted to stay at a quaint little bed-and-breakfast in town. "I get that you want to be in more luxurious accommodations, but this weekend is more about participation, Liz."

So I booked a room with a shared bathroom. The room was as I'd expected—stark and simple, with a bed, a dresser and an oscillating floor fan. Linens and towels were not provided, so the first thing I did was make my bed, hoping there were no bedbugs anxious to go back to Brooklyn with me.

When I arrived, I was told there would be a welcome reception for the general Enlightened population followed by a two-hour astrology class. From the looks of the pamphlet I was given, there were a bunch of different workshops and retreats going on all weekend, and I was immediately curious about who I might meet.

After the orientation, I found my way to the building where I would spend the next two and a half days learning the basics of astrology with twelve others. Classes would take place in a dance studio located on the top floor of a building at the bottom of the hill.

I felt excited and anxious. I couldn't wait to meet Noah in person, but I was also extremely nervous about it. The only contact we'd had was about proofreading and via email. I'd been following his astrology work for almost ten years and the idea of actually meeting him in person made my legs unsteady as I climbed the stairs to the studio.

Inside, there was music playing—it sounded like a cross between Tori Amos and Patti Smith. For a second, I wondered if I was in the wrong place, but I knew I wasn't because the first person I noticed when I stepped inside was Noah Garrett. He didn't look like the pictures I'd seen on the internet. He was much cuter.

"Welcome!" he said. "Have a seat in the circle and we'll get started shortly."

A large circle of chairs was set up in the room, and I took a seat facing the door. Three others were already seated; I nodded hello to each of them and began to busy myself with my notebook, hoping to hide the surprising feelings of self-consciousness when I sat down.

Once everyone was seated, Noah turned off the music and took the last remaining seat in the circle. I liked his energy immediately and felt my body relax. We did the token introductions, going around the circle saying our names and our astrological signs—something I decided I would adopt the next time I had to introduce myself in a group setting. When it was my turn, Noah perked up slightly and said, "Liz Weber.

Hello! It's nice to finally put the face with the name."

The photo Noah had on his website didn't do him justice and was out of date. His head was completely shaved, not long and curly. The lack of hair suited his kind face and small eyes that sparkled when he talked. His lips were full and framed by a perfect smattering of 5 o'clock shadow.

He eased into the material and delivered it in an almost conversational way, saying things like, "My experience with Jupiter has been that although it's an expansive energy, it can also bring up feelings of discomfort, especially if we're not quite ready to expand. Can anyone tell me about their experience with Jupiter?" He was so confident and passionate about sharing his knowledge. It was inspiring and exhilarating. I was glad I came.

When class was over, Noah announced he'd be in the café for a couple of hours and invited us to join him and talk. I was tempted, but I tended to get shy in group situations. Plus, I didn't want to be one of those people who swarmed the teacher, asking all sorts of questions related to themselves, like ticks sucking the blood out of their prey.

I had a thing for authority that made me crave approval and run from attention all at once. Instead of making an honest attempt at my desire to be noticed, I would become the best little student, making sure to prove to the teacher that I was above all of that self-serving bullshit. I stayed off to the side and only engaged when I was supposed to—during class. Afterward, I assumed the teacher would prefer to take a breather from the students and made sure not to hover with the rest of them. It was my own strange way of seeking attention. I figured if I didn't badger the instructor, somehow he'd figure out that I was on his level and we'd form a silent alliance.

My approach, however, usually achieved the opposite result, of me disappearing into the background, wishing to be included in the circle—where those who badgered the teacher got ahead. This weekend, I decided, I wouldn't try to *be* anything. I'd come to learn astrology, and if a natural opportunity arose for me to talk with Noah, I would take it.

The next morning I was feeling less sure of my decision to come and lonelier than I'd ever expected. I didn't sleep well the night before due to the flimsy floorboards in my dorm that registered the comings and goings of my dorm mates. Once everyone was tucked in for the night, the lack of noise kept me awake. I wasn't used to sleeping in such quiet, which only a city person can truly understand. When I woke up, I was intimidated by the notion of going to the dining hall and having to eat with strangers. It was pretty crowded, with three or four different conferences going on at once, and it felt a lot like camp. The astrology workshop had just thirteen people and was a stark contrast to the other workshops that hosted at least fifty or more.

All I remembered about camp that was everyone around me seemed like they were having a great time, while I was missing home and feeling completely out of place. At Enlightened, it felt like everyone knew each other or had come with at least a companion or two.

Sitting alone outside the dining hall, I felt more at ease than I would have been at a table full of strangers doing the getting-to-know-you thing. Being a bartender, I was constantly "on" at work. I didn't want that to be the case all weekend. I didn't feel like being Little Miss Social, walking over with my tray full of macrobiotic food, asking, "Is anyone sitting here?"

And the food—wow! Can we say major gas? Enlightened was known for its great vegetarian cuisine, but I wasn't a fan. The abundance of garlic and onion in everything didn't work for my system. Thankfully I'd opted for a private room, otherwise my roommate would've had to don an oxygen mask in order to sleep.

I needed some coffee before eating anything in the morning, so I decided to sit outside, drink it in peace and do a little writing. On my way out of the dining hall, I noticed Noah and a bunch of others seated at a table in the corner, right next to the Silence table. I couldn't decide what I wanted more—the courage to sit at the table of silence, or the guts to walk up and join Noah and his group.

Sitting on the chair overlooking the lawn and the basketball courts at the bottom of the hill, I was glad I'd made the choice to come outside. I couldn't stop thinking about Rufus, which was quite a surprise. The weekend away was supposed to be a gift to myself, and I felt a little angry that my thoughts were leaning toward sadness, not celebration.

In the past, when I was in a situation where I felt like the odd man out, having Rufus in my life was always a comfort. No matter what I endured, I knew I'd be going home to him. It gave me strength and sometimes even courage to take some risks and join the crowd. Now all I could think about was him being gone, and the more I thought of it, the smaller I felt and the less I wanted to be there. I hated that I wouldn't be going home to him. Once again, I missed my friend. The previous night after class, I walked around a bit, finally giving up and returning to my room because I felt so lost and lonely, I just wanted to make it stop. If I were at home, I'd curl up in my bed with a book or a good movie. Here, I was sleeping in a moderately comfortable single bed with toilets and showers down the hall. Maybe I should've stayed off-campus.

I sat there a little longer, trying to quiet my mind. I knew myself. It was just resistance, sort of like what Noah spoke about the night before: expansion being uncomfortable when you weren't quite ready for it. "Well, I'm *not* ready to expand!" I wanted to scream and run back to my father's car and hightail it out of there.

"Are you heading over to class?" I heard from behind.

"Uh, yes," I said, closing my journal and turning to see who was talking to me.

A woman whose name I couldn't remember stood behind me, her face mostly blocked from the sun's glare behind her. She had sat next to me at the intro class. I remembered that she was a Leo and from Hartford. She looked very Connecticut: blonde, skinny, like she played tennis on the weekends.

"Is it time already?" I asked, standing up.

"Just about. I figured we could walk over together, if you like."

I still hadn't eaten anything and was tempted to tell her I'd just see her over there, but instead I heard myself say, "That'd be great. Do you mind if I pop back into the dining hall and grab a roll? I haven't eaten anything."

"Perfect!" she said. "I wanted to bring some tea with me."

Walking back to the dining hall, I thought to myself, "Okay, universe. You win. I'm staying."

The class was long, and in spite of my disdain for the food, I was happy to have a break for dinner. We had all agreed on a short evening session afterward, so I had a little over an hour to get some dinner. I was going to try the café this time in the hopes that the food would be better. Plus, I could eat alone.

I liked the vibe at the café so much better, and the grilled cheese sandwich I ate wasn't half bad. What an intense day! The astrology stuff was incredible, and I was pleased with myself for being one of the few able to really follow along. That is, when I wasn't getting lost in Noah's magnetic energy.

He was so open and present I wanted to stay in the dance studio all weekend, twenty-four hours a day. I loved the learning, but once it stopped, the loneliness returned. The downtime was not serving me, and I longed to be distracted and engaged so I didn't have to think about how out of sorts I felt or how much I missed Rufus. It was amazing that I could leave class feeling exhilarated and light, only to walk back after dinner with sadness in my heart.

My feet were heavy as I made my way up the hill, away from the café and back to class. The enthusiasm I felt was replaced with dread, while the desire to go back to my room and hide had returned in full force. I could see the studio ahead of me, and the only reason I didn't bypass it and head straight for the dorm was because I was afraid someone might see me. Pride's a funny thing: When all else failed, I could usually count on it to kick my ass into gear.

Inside, I took a seat slightly apart from the few who had already gathered and were talking among themselves. I didn't feel like socializing. I just wanted to get back to learning. I felt a desperate need to make it all stop—the fear, the discomfort, all of it. I just wanted to go home.

"Hi!" It was Heidi, the woman from that morning. Man, this lady had a strong radar. "I looked for you at dinner but I couldn't find you. Did you eat at the café instead?"

Heidi's bright blue eyes searched mine, reminding me that she had no idea what was going on inside me. She just wanted to know where I'd eaten. But I couldn't control myself. I needed to tell someone how I was feeling, and whether she liked it or not, she was it.

"I'm just feeling a little outta sorts," I stammered, my eyes burning. Before I could say anything else, the tears started to fall and all I could manage was, "I'm sorry," to Heidi's "Oh! What's wrong?"

Everything I was feeling tumbled out, including Rufus and my efforts to move forward with my life.

Heidi put her thin hand on my shoulder and said, "You have to go easy on yourself. Grief has its own schedule, Liz. Trust me, I know. When my cat died, I don't think I left my house for a whole month."

"Really?" I said, raising my eyes to meet hers.

"Of course! It sounds like Rufus was a huge part of your life. There's no reason why you should force yourself to move on. The human psyche is very wise. Trust me—when you're ready, you'll know." She patted my shoulder again. "I promise."

Her words were like a ray of light creeping through the darkness. For so long, I'd been needing to be reminded that it was *okay* to miss Rufus. Most people around me seemed to be telling me to do the opposite, and I was too ashamed to let them know that I just couldn't stop. I didn't need people to talk me out of my feelings. I needed them to support me, and a wonderful stranger had just given me the go-ahead to be exactly where I was for as long as I wanted.

29

After class, I was happy it was late enough to justify returning to the dorm. Heidi invited me for a glass of wine from the bottle she had in her room, but I didn't feel much like drinking. For the first time all weekend, I was actually looking forward to being alone. It's amazing how things could shift once you gave yourself permission to feel your feelings without judgment.

The usual suspects were chatting with Noah outside as I sat at the bottom of the steps to put on my sneakers. I could hear their voices, but I wasn't paying attention to their words until I heard, "...catch up with Liz for a minute."

I looked up and Noah was standing in front of me. It took a moment for me to realize that he was talking about me.

"What do ya think, Liz?" he asked, his kind eyes gazing at me. "Shall we take a walk?"

For a moment, I couldn't speak. It was one thing to sit in class and daydream about being singled out by him, but to be alone with him? Just us? I couldn't decide if I was thrilled or terrified, but somehow I stood up, brushed off the seat of my pants, and said "Sure!"

As we walked away from the others, I could feel their envy burning into my back. Had I not been so nervous, I would have reveled in the fact that I was going to have quality time with the man I'd once hoped would be my mentor.

"I wanted to talk with you last night, but you disappeared so quickly," Noah said.

"Yeah, I was tired," I lied. Then I added, "Everyone was bombarding you with questions after class. I figured you had enough people to talk to."

"Well, I've got you now," he smiled, turning to me as he stopped in his tracks. Man, he was cute and alarmingly sure of himself.

I tried to focus on anything but the energy I felt just standing next to him. It wasn't as much sexual as it was magnetic. Like I said, authority got me every time.

That's how I fell for Charlie. I'd met him several times before we started dating, and each time, he'd made no memorable impact on me. It wasn't until I'd asked him to come and look at the floor in my newly purchased apartment in Brooklyn. He was a contractor and I needed advice on what to do about the water damage that was hidden under the carpet by previous tenants.

He'd shown up in his work gear—faded jeans, a tight T-shirt that hugged his muscular upper body and dusty work boots. As he stood there with his clipboard, surveying the damage, a switch flipped in me, and for several weeks after that I couldn't stop thinking of him. "I can't hire you to fix my floor," I finally told him. "I'd rather you ask me out instead."

My feelings for him faded as soon as he started showing signs of being anything but in charge.

Noah was in charge, and it felt good to be in his company.

"I'd love to show you my portfolio," he said. "Maybe we can smoke a little first?"

Getting high sounded great to me due to the fact that I was feeling like a nervous schoolgirl. Noah was totally at ease, which made me even more aware of my edginess. I wanted to relax and forget about the fact that he was not only a world-renowned astrologer but a talented photographer who took pictures of women in the nude.

I guess that was another reason why I was so enamored by him. Noah was compiling a book of photos of women masturbating in the nude. The premise was about the shame behind masturbation. The women in the photos wanted to claim their sexuality and document it to release themselves from the shame and the secrecy of self-induced sexual pleasure.

When he'd first emailed me about it, I was full of judgment. I had nothing against masturbation but was unaccustomed to someone talking about it so freely. But then my resistance switched to intrigue, and I even entertained the idea of letting him photograph me, if he ever offered.

"You don't happen to have any papers with you?" he asked.

"I do, actually!" I said, thrilled to contribute.

As we walked toward the dorm, I realized that Noah seemed completely enamored with *me*! He had been looking forward to meeting me just as much as I had him.

I continued, "Yeah, I found them when I was looking for my toothbrush, and I was so bummed that I didn't have any weed to go with them!"

"I am at your service, madam," Noah replied, bowing like a butler.

As we walked, I silently pleaded with myself to get my shit together and stop chattering like an awkward teenager. Noah's energy was intense and very sexual, so much so that it made me aware of my own sexual energy and how cut off and shut down it was. Being in the presence of someone reflecting that back to me was unnerving.

I was also a little afraid of relaxing into the energy for fear of giving him the wrong idea. Once I tuned into his interest in *me*, I felt uncomfortable, almost responsible for him. And while he wasn't necessarily coming onto me, I didn't feel comfortable being in the position to let someone down. Despite my desire to be noticed, I shied away from situations where I was the object of a man's desire. Chasing was much easier because I never lost control. Charlie was the first guy who I knew liked me more than I liked him, and look how that ended up.

I grabbed the papers from my room and we made our way back to his. I focused on keeping my nerves at bay, reverting back to what I'd learned as a meditation student: staying in the moment and out of my mind. I didn't feel unsafe with Noah at all. On the contrary! I felt completely at ease, but the voices in my head still warned of being careful and staying on guard, just in case he got the wrong idea. Those voices were not my own, but, they were still strong, and I was hoping a little weed would quiet them down and help me relax.

His room was smaller than I'd expected. I figured that being a teacher, he'd have a more elaborate setup. Instead, it was closer to what I had, with a bed, some built-in shelves on the wall and a bathroom. But his room had been renovated, and its flax-colored walls and deep brown furniture gave it a warm feeling.

Noah dropped his stuff on the bed. I realized we were going to there to look at the photos.

"Make yourself comfortable," he said over his shoulder, then disappeared into the bathroom.

I felt like a six-year-old who'd had way too much sugar. I reminded myself to focus on the moment, which meant listening to Noah pee just a few feet away.

You know he wants to fuck you, right? My mind screamed, knocking me right out of the moment. *What are you going to do if he tries something?*

Standing in his small room, looking at his bed, I was pretty sure he wanted to fuck me. How could I explain that I was attracted to his power and not his penis? My first instinct was to make up some excuse and back out gracefully without having to deal with the whole potentially messy confrontation of polite rejection. But Noah's energy, though intense, was also very comforting, and I didn't feel threatened at all. In fact, it wasn't about trusting him—it was about trusting *me* to take care of myself even in the presence of someone whom I totally admired.

I was still standing close to the front door when he came out of the bathroom and flopped himself onto the bed.

"So, here it is…the Book of Blue," he said proudly, producing a large black leather portfolio.

I edged closer to the bed, battling my fears and curiosity. I wanted to be comfortable here. Why shouldn't I be? Nothing had to happen unless I wanted it to. And who knows if it wasn't all in my head anyway?

Looking through his book, I realized his photos weren't about women taking their clothes off. I was looking at their souls and was struck by their courage to be vulnerable.

"They look so peaceful," I said, sitting down on the bed and quietly turning the pages.

Noah passed me a freshly rolled joint and I took a long pull.

"They're really beautiful," I said, exhaling a waft of smoke.

It was through the photos that I began to relax. If those women could bare their souls and end up okay, why couldn't I? I let go and accepted that the man sitting across from me on the bed wasn't going to hurt me.

Yeah, but what if he wants to have sex with you? Damn those nasty little voices.

I sat there caught between the space of comfort and panic. The comfort represented who I really was, while the panic was all about who I used to be. I didn't want to be a scared little girl anymore, I thought, studying the faces of each woman. I wanted to be bold and unafraid of the power within me.

I was definitely getting stoned, and through the haze I noticed that Noah had shifted himself on the bed. His back rested against the headboard while I remained at his feet, focused on the book. I didn't have to look at him to know he was getting turned on. I felt slightly panicked and my shoulders tensed as I sensed he was touching himself.

My instinct was to assume the maternal position and pat him on his shoulder or make a gesture that screamed, "I am uncomfortable, and if I retreat from the energy in this room I'll be safe." He must've known this because he reached over and grabbed my hand, holding it gently. As his breathing grew deeper, I felt my own become shallow. I was ready to reach over and give him a pat, but I didn't. Something else in me spoke up.

You're safe. You are fine. Feel this person. Connect with him. You won't be taken advantage of. You will have your voice, your right. It will not turn out badly. Feel. Breathe. Love. Let go. Trust.

The voice was calm and grounded and it eased my panicked mind. It reminded me to open up and allow his energy into my heart. And I did. I sat there and held his hand, feeling his energy by breathing into my own. I felt it all, fear included, and just sat with it.

When he asked if he could undress, my mind went ballistic. *Here we go! See, see, I told you. This guy is a freak! Oh my god, what are you going to do? You're so not in a sexual place with yourself and this guy wants to get naked? What the FUCK have you done? I never should have trusted you to take care of us!*

I sat for a moment while thirty-plus years of voices battled it out in my head and finally looked him straight in the eye with surprising clarity.

"I want you to take your clothes off. But I'm keeping mine on."

He was openly touching himself now, his breathing shorter and faster. "Okay."

He removed his pants and for the first time, I saw the fear in his own soul. I saw this beautiful being standing there in need of something from me. I wasn't quite sure what it was yet, but I saw beyond my own fear and ego and understood that it was bigger than fucking or student/teacher worship.

And without hesitation or fear, I said, "I'd really like to watch you masturbate. I have no desire to masturbate or take my clothes off, but it would really turn me on to watch you come."

And there it was. I waited for the panic and the notion to take it back, but nothing—just the sound of crickets outside, talking among themselves.

My mind gently wandered, and I realized this was what it really felt like to be a woman. The little girl inside was quiet and content with my ability to handle things. She trusted me. And I trusted myself.

It felt natural and so okay. I wanted to open myself up to this experience as wide as possible and stay present throughout. I leaned into the wind and let it carry me wherever it was supposed to, knowing I could stop at any time.

The best part of all was that I was so turned on by watching Noah stroke himself to full hardness that I wanted to stand up and dance on the bed and scream, "I'm alive! I'm alive!" I could still feel aroused and desired. How about that? Still, no matter how hot for him I felt, I knew there was no need to do anything more than just sit there and take it all in, allowing myself the ultimate balance between receiving and giving all at once.

The next hour consisted of a lot of talking and a lot of watching. Noah told me about his own needs and what masturbating in front of me would give him.

"I'm intimidated by you, Liz. By your beauty. You sitting there, watching me, makes me feel special and scared all at once. I want to share my vulnerability with you and feel your acceptance as I do."

I realized I could give this man something more than just a hot, wet pussy to fuck. It seemed irrelevant to whip my clothes off and sit on top of him. I saw the vulnerability in his heart, the fear and the years of shame peeling away, as we sat and shared in the energy. Most importantly, I didn't feel turned off by his departure from so-called authority. I felt responsible on a soul level to help him through and over to the other side.

"I'm right here with you," I said evenly when he seemed close to climax.

His breath was fast and furious as he stroked himself with vigor. My breath caught in my chest as I waited for him to come. As he did, he let out a loud, almost primal wail. The rush of emotion was so intense that upon his release, I felt something letting go within me as well.

"Thank you," he breathed, slumping against the headboard and smiling.

"Thank *you*, Noah," I said.

I wasn't sure exactly what he had given to me, but I knew it was something big, and as I walked back to my room under the glorious sky crowded with stars, I felt at peace for the first time in a very long time.

30

"Is it too early to do a shot?" Doug called out from behind me.

"I'm not starting before 8 o'clock," I said, turning around to face him.

It'd been a few months since Chris's departure. Scott had moved into the GM position, and instead of someone new being hired, Doug came over from the steakhouse next door to be the assistant manager at Maxie's. I didn't like Doug at first. Our first encounter was about six months ago, when a bunch of the staff came over to have some drinks after the steakhouse closed. I'd never seen Doug before but he was clearly drunk, continuously demanding shots of Patron Silver tequila. "Gimme another shot," he yelled out. No "please," no "thank you." I disliked him immediately.

Sensing my disdain, he stepped closer to the bar and asked, "Do you know who I am?"

I didn't have a chance to answer, which was a good thing because I'm not sure I would have been all that polite.

"I run this place!" he announced, slamming his empty glass down onto the bar.

When Scott told us he'd be joining our side, I was less than thrilled, fully expecting repeat performances of that first night. Thankfully that night was a fluke because Doug turned out to be a really nice guy.

He did like his drink, though, and occasionally he liked to do a little coke—not unusual for people in the restaurant business. Coke was not my thing, so it never occurred to me over the years that my former happy-go-lucky-managers were just amped up on the stuff. Judy was the one who got me hip to what was going on behind the scenes at Maxie's.

"I can't believe you didn't know about it!" she laughed when she realized I wasn't playing dumb.

"I just thought everyone was drunk."

"Oh my GOD, no WAY!" she snorted, amused by my naïveté.

Even though I still missed Rachel, I was glad Judy and I were working Thursdays together. Judy was on the quiet side and had a tiny frame. Her long, dark hair and olive skin made people assume she was Indian.

"You're so exotic-looking," I once told her.

"Ugh, I know!" she said, rolling her eyes. "I hate it!"

Most people hated what they had. I hated my nose and always wished for a smaller one. A photographer once told me she loved it because it had so much character. I suppose Judy felt the same way when people envied her uniqueness. Though she was born in Russia, she made a point to tell people she was Canadian—technically true, considering she grew up there.

Doug was still standing in the service bar, cocking his head like a dog waiting for a treat. "Come on…just a small one…"

"No!" I laughed, throwing a dry bar towel at him. "And don't be giving me those eyes either, mister."

Doug had the most incredible blue eyes, clear and bright like the Caribbean. His fair skin made them even more pronounced, and trust me, Doug worked those eyes. I'd watched many women fall for them, but I didn't. As attractive and charming as he was, we shared the same kind of sibling vibe that Chris and I had.

"I'll be back," he said, doing his best Arnold Schwarzenegger impression.

There was so much power in bartending, and it always struck me as funny when I realized it. Doug was my boss, yet I had the final say in whether he got a drink or not.

"These guys over here wanna do some shots with us," Judy said, passing in front of me to grab some shot glasses off the shelf.

"What is *with* everyone tonight? I just fought Doug off for a half hour."

"I don't know. But I'm doing water. It's too early to start drinking."

I never had to do the water trick until I started working at Maxie's. It was one of the plays in the book where you poured shots of something clear, like vodka, for the customers and water for yourself. The secret was to do the pouring away from everyone so nobody noticed. You just had to keep track of the water shot. Rachel once mixed them up and ended up doing twice as many "real" shots to make up for it.

"Cheers, guys!" Judy and I sang in unison as we downed our fake shots, making the appropriate faces to solidify our performance.

"They just threw us a hundred bucks," Judy said, putting the money in our tip jar while I loaded glasses into the dishwasher.

Things at Maxie's had improved considerably since my trip to Enlightened a couple of months earlier. It was getting busier, and having the bar to myself on Wednesday and Friday nights made a huge difference financially. I was able to quit Smokehouse and finally have two days off in a row.

Noah and I continued to keep in touch, and it was really nice to have shared such intimacy with someone and not feel any residual awkwardness. Our connection continued to be intimate, but not in a sexual way. He'd become a good friend.

"I'd really like to start writing again," I told him on the phone. "I have this writing class and it's almost over. For the whole time, I've played it safe, handing in edits of stuff I'd written years ago. When I signed up for the class, I thought I was going to write about Rufus, but when I tried, it was just too painful."

"Why don't you try again?" he asked, letting the question linger for a moment before he continued. "Just *tell* me about him, Liz. What did he look like? How did he smell?"

I was afraid to do it. But I was also completely grateful that I had someone whom I respected gently urging me toward the thing I needed and wanted to do. "Whenever you're ready," he'd said when I promised to get him something by month's end.

There was something about having him in my corner that made me feel more confident, and self-assured. I'd even flirted a little with Carlos the other night, telling him, "Damn, Carlos, if only you were just a little older…"

He blushed and grinned sheepishly. "Yeah, I know…bummer."

The weekend at The Enlightened Institute didn't completely change my life, but something had definitely shifted in me. I continued to struggle with my grief and loneliness, but I'd gotten really good at hiding it, allowing myself to be sad only in the privacy of my own home. The day I finally got rid of Rufus's meds, which had been sitting on the counter untouched since his death, I felt strangely excited by the fact that I was beginning to let go. But grief's a funny thing, because the very next day I could hardly make it through the morning without succumbing to the urge to dig through the garbage and put it all back to the way it was.

Baby steps had become my new mantra, and with the help of the people around me, I was determined to continue taking some every chance I got.

"Yo, Liz! Are we really out of Amstel?"

Sully's voice brought me back to the present. Walking toward him, I smiled, thinking about how far David Sullivan had come since he first started at Maxie's.

"Yes, sir," I said, grabbing a drink ticket that had just come out of the printer.

"Man, I shoulda asked before I rang it in. Let me see what else they want."

Sully started right around the time Rufus died. He had been so sweet, offering his heartfelt condolences on my first night back to work. Recently out of college and doing some sort of internship with a hedge fund, Sully worked at Maxie's to subsidize the small income from his day job. He'd never worked in a restaurant before and was willing to work his way up from the bottom, starting out as a busboy, then a barback, and now a full-fledged waiter. Sully was like the little brother I never had, and I was always on him when he wasn't doing his best.

It was finally after 8. Doug was happily liquored up, and Judy and I were able to chat without being interrupted by thirsty customers and/ or managers.

"Soooo, Judy. I have an idea."

"Okay!" she replied, tossing her long brown hair and turning to me expectantly.

"I've been thinking about starting a women's group," I said, surprised at the sudden flutter in my stomach. "And, um, I was wondering if you'd like to be a part of it."

Still smiling, she raised an eyebrow. "What kind of women's group?"

I don't know why I felt so self-conscious about it. I'd been wanting to do this for months, but Rufus's death kind of threw a wrench in things.

"I want to get a few people together—women—who are like-minded and create a sort of support group where we discuss our goals and obstacles, and offer each other ideas on how to reach those goals."

"Ohhhh," was all she said, and I could feel my face getting hot. Maybe it was a stupid idea. Who was I to think anyone would want to do something like that?

"I like it," she finally said. "Though, I'm not the greatest in groups."

Relieved, I reassured her, "No! No! It will only be four people, including me. My friend Stephanie, who's really cool and an actress, you, me, and I'm going to ask Rachel."

"Rachel! Oh…okay! Why not?"

"Excellent!"

I didn't know what I was more excited about—the group or the fact that Judy thought it was a good idea. I never really thought of myself as an organizer, but I felt like the group thing could be really great.

"What are you girls whispering about?" Doug stood at the bar with his arms folded, like a father who had just caught his daughters smoking a cigarette.

"Just girl talk," Judy said, walking to the other end of the bar to check on the customers.

"Yeah," I sighed with delight. "Girl talk."

31

Avi had hadn't spoken to me in almost two months. Gone were the days when we'd sit and bullshit about cool new restaurants in Manhattan. I liked Avi back then. Somewhere along the road, though, he'd spiraled into a dark place, and I had become the target of his daily irritation.

Pradeep, unfortunately, was in the middle of it all. He knew there was tension between us, and early one morning, while Avi was at his son's school for a conference, I finally said my piece.

"It's getting to the point where the tension with Avi is distracting. I don't know what to do," I said when Pradeep asked me how things were going on my side of the wall.

Seated across from me in the other comfortable chair that faced his desk, Pradeep was sympathetic. "I know how difficult he can be. And I'm not really sure what's going on with him. I just know that he's stressed. He's even been giving me shit lately."

I wanted to roll my eyes and say, "Dude! You guys are partners! I'm your employee. I'm coming to you to *fix* the solution, not to commiserate!" Instead, I was more direct than I'd ever been with a boss. "I just don't know how much more I can take of this."

This got Pradeep's attention, and he sprang up with worry. "No, no. I'll take care of it. Maybe we can move you out into the hallway area, next to Carla. Maybe create some distance between you two."

"I think that would be a great idea," I said, happy at the prospect of sitting closer to Carla. In the time that I'd been at the law firm, she was one of the few people I talked to. Though much older than me, she was a kind person with a young energy. I could tell by the way she complimented my outfits that she longed to be more hip and fresh in her look. The week before, she'd gotten her hair colored at the same place I did and was thrilled with the auburn and bronze highlights in her chestnut-brown hair.

"Now if I could just do something about this helmet," she'd laughed, touching her slightly dated hairstyle. "It's just so boring."

Carla worked for Paul, Avi and Pradeep's landlord. Like me, she disliked like her job, and the crazy thing was she didn't even need it! She lived with her partner in a rent-controlled apartment in Chelsea. Her partner was older, and from the way Carla told it, they could easily live off her pension money. In the meantime, it was nice to have someone to roll my eyes at when Avi or Pradeep were driving me crazy.

"I don't know how you do it," she'd said to me a while back. "You guys are cramped into that office, and he's so loud on the phone. How do you even concentrate? I'd shoot myself."

I had a high tolerance for strange situations but it wasn't until Carla pointed out the ludicrousness of my seating arrangement that it occurred to me how unbearable it had become.

"Do you think he's still pissed about the FedEx thing?" Pradeep asked me.

"If he is, it's ridiculous. That was *not* my fault."

On the heels of the day he was all up on me about the process server, I had given Avi a list of FedEx offices that were open late on the weekends. He waited until the very last minute to prepare the affidavits, and when he went to the FedEx office that was, according my list, open, it wasn't. It was also raining like crazy that day, and Avi was not happy about trekking back to the office on a Saturday evening to call FedEx to find another location.

In the end, he hand-delivered the affidavits, taking a car to and from the process server offices in Long Island. When I came in a few hours later, the receipt for the car and the envelopes I had prepared for FedEx lay crumpled and rain-stained on my desk. It didn't take much to figure out that something had gone wrong.

"How come the envelopes are still here?" I asked.

"The FedEx office you told me was open wasn't," was all he said, not even looking up from his keyboard.

"What? That's impossible!" I cried. "I called the office myself to double-check on Friday."

"I took a car and delivered them myself," Avi replied, a hint of arrogance in his voice.

I don't know what I was more pissed about—FedEx giving me the wrong information or Avi treating me as if I'd done it on purpose. I kept my mouth shut and didn't push it any further but the damage was done, because from that day on, Avi stopped talking to me except for when he had no other choice.

Since then, I spent my days at the office happy the moment he left for lunch or an appointment. Today was an extra-special gift because after the school meeting, he was going to lunch with his wife. Pradeep, who assured me he'd talk to Avi about the seating situation, had gone to lunch as well, and I was thrilled to have the office to myself.

As usual, I had nothing to do. It was fun to be able to check my e-mail freely without worry of Avi asking, "Do you need something to do?"

Blair had sent me an e-mail with the subject "Club Getaway," asking me if I'd be interested in going to a sleepaway camp for adults:

> Sounds like it could be fun...it's like camp/a cruise. Constant activities if you want...dance classes, yoga, hiking, boating, wine tasting, archery. The activities are all over the place, so there is definitely something for everyone, or you can just chill at the lake. The cabins have bathrooms and a/c. It's $369 plus $25 to have a cabin for just two people. Do you think you'd wanna do it?

Archery? Jeez, I hadn't done archery since I was a kid! A weekend away might be really nice, and the price was certainly right. With things picking up at Maxie's, I could swing it. But I wasn't sure how Blair and I would do going away together.

Since her e-mail, I'd stuck to mostly superficial stuff, and I didn't know if I could maintain that for an entire weekend. And what if I had the same experience of missing Rufus terribly, like I did at the Enlightened Institute? I couldn't hide that from strangers, let alone my own sister. Still, it could be fun, something we hadn't had together in a long time.

"What the hell!" I said to no one in particular and shot an e-mail back to her saying, "I'm in!"

A few hours later, I called Deb to share the news.

"*Camp?*" she squealed. "Oh my GOD, I *loved* camp!! I'm so jealous."

"I know, right? It's crazy. They have everything! Even archery."

I could feel her excitement despite the 3,000 miles between us. "WHERE is this place? Give me the website. I wanna check it out."

I gave Deb the address and poured myself a glass of wine. It was an unusually cool evening for mid-July, and my plan was to take Deb, my wine and my lawn chair up to the roof and watch the sunset. Grabbing the blue-striped nylon chair out of my hall closet, I clomped up the two flights of stairs between my apartment and the roof, chair slung over my shoulder, wineglass in hand and phone squeezed between my ear and shoulder. I spent a lot of time on my roof that summer. The views were incredible, spanning all the way to east Brooklyn, midtown Manhattan and the Financial District. I could breathe up there; the space and the vastness of the view reminded me that there was more than just me in this world.

"This place looks a–MAY–zing!" she said as I unfolded the chair to face west the soon-to-be-setting sun.

"I'm just glad they have cabins with air-conditioning," I laughed. "I'm sooo not a camper."

"You said you're going the weekend of the 8th, right?"

"Yep."

Deb's voice dropped an octave. "Uh, honey, you realize it's singles weekend, right?" She paused. "A Jewish singles weekend."

"WHAT?" I shoot up in my chair, wine sloshing all over my feet. "What the fuck?"

Deb burst into that deep, belly-shaking laughter reserved specifically for the ridiculous. "Oh yeah, you goin' to the 'Club Getaway J–Date Singles Weekend,'" she read from the website between whoops of laughter. "It really *is* like summer camp! Jews included."

"There's got to be some mistake."

"Nope. It says right here on the site. August 8th, singles getaway. August 15th, family getaway."

"OH MY GOD. What was Blair *thinking*?"

"Maybe she was thinking you'd have a little nosh and get a little *meshuggah* in the dance hall," she giggled.

I wasn't laughing. "I can't go to a singles weekend! Let alone a Jewish singles weekend. I don't even like Jewish men. Plus, it puts a whole different spin on the experience. Ugh," I said, putting my glass on the ground and my head in my hand. "The pressure."

"Come on. It'll be f–UH–n! Just go and have a good time."

I couldn't just *decide* to have fun. Something had to *be* fun in order for me to enjoy it. I couldn't believe I had agreed to do this.

"This is a disaster," I whined. "I know how it's going to go, too. My sister will be all gung ho and I'm going to feel pressured to be just as excited, and there is nothing about this weekend anymore that is exciting."

"Oh come on, Liz. Think of the archery. Just because it's a singles weekend doesn't mean you have to go there to *meet* someone. You can just enjoy the camp experience."

"I guess," I said, biting the inside of my lower lip. "I just hate the idea of going someplace that is centered around meeting people. It's so freakin' contrived. I'm not in a dating place, and going to a camp where the entire theme of the weekend is dating…" I needed more wine.

"You're going to be FINE. Just focus on the time away with your sister and the fact that you're going to a new place with all this fun stuff to do. Seriously, if your sister wants to do stuff that you don't want to do, then you don't do it." She paused for effect. "It's your weekend too."

It *was* my weekend, too, but I knew myself. I wasn't good at saying "I'm going to do my own thing and meet up with you later." It just wasn't my way, especially with Blair. I had always been following her lead. And most of the time, I was okay with it. I'd rather follow than deal with the pressure of choosing something, making her do it and then feeling crappy if she didn't like it.

The sun sank slowly behind the tallest building in sight. As it dipped lower into the horizon and the wine began to take effect, I started to relax.

"Maybe it won't be so bad. At least there's waterskiing."

"Thatta girl," Deb cheered. "Mazel tov!"

32

"*This* is *perfect*," my sister murmured from beneath the baseball hat resting on her face. "Good call on the inner tubes."

Blair and I were floating in the middle of a lake at Club Getaway on our first full day of camp. I'd always been more of a beach person, but the lake was really spectacular. The whole campus was amazing, set on a few hundred acres of the Berkshire Mountains, whose lush green trees reminded me of stalks of broccoli waiting to be picked from the earth. The weather couldn't have been more beautiful that day, with the sun flying solo in the sky and just a hint of humidity, rare for an early August weekend.

After a good hour in the sun on less-than-comfortable plastic lounge chairs, we decided to cool off with a dip in the lake when I spotted two lone inner tubes floating near the dock by the shore.

"Ya wanna float in those tubes?" I asked, pointing to the large red and yellow doughnuts bouncing around in the water. "We can take them out to the far dock and just chill for a while."

Blair was right. It *was* a great idea, sitting in the tubes, dangling our fingers and toes in the cool lake water. "Sure beats speed dating," I said, paddling over to the dock, extending my legs and resting my feet on its edge.

"OH GOD!" my sister snorted with laughter. "FUCK camp!"

"STOP!" I wailed, trying to not to fall off my tube. "I can't laugh and balance at the same time."

When we arrived at Club Getaway the night before, Blair and I were definitely on different pages. She, the eternal optimist, had decided to make the best of the situation, telling me days before our trip, "Maybe it'll be fun. Ya never know. We might meet some nice people."

I wasn't so sure, but Blair was indignant. "I'm going to force myself to be social and join in on the activities because, I gotta tell you, I need some single friends." That was a continuous complaint of my sister's, being that just about every one of her friends was married with kids.

I, however, had plenty of single friends and didn't share my sister's optimism. I feared she'd be all gung ho about everything camp while I'd be watching the clock, waiting for the weekend to end. I'd never been much of a group person and despised the team-building types of fun where some peppy person with a clipboard and a whistle yelled, "Mingle!" or "Turn to your neighbor and introduce yourself!"

The night before, after we'd settled into our no-frills single room with a bathroom, two beds and a shared porch out front, we were instructed to go to the main tent, where there would be a welcome reception. Sure enough, there was Sven, a tanned Swedish man holding a clipboard, who greeted us with enthusiasm and a sheet full of activities for which we could sign up.

My sister was all over it. "Oh my god! I want to do everything," she cried, scanning the sheet. "Look! They have wine tasting and poker!"

I was mildly excited about the archery and waterskiing. The rest of the stuff sounded interesting, but the idea of having to sign up in advance and be on a schedule for the entire weekend was less than thrilling. Plus, I'd slept wrong the night before, and my neck was hurting.

"We need a pen," Blair announced, jumping up from the table we'd sat down at to plan our fun. "I'm going to see if anyone has one."

With Blair off to find a writing utensil, I sat back and had a good look at my fellow campers. There seemed to be a helluva lot more guys than girls, and they were all pudgy or gangly. I'd yet to find one with a full head of hair. They looked expectant and awkward, walking around in their nicely pressed khaki shorts, golf shirts and running sneakers. I'm pretty good at sizing up a situation and seeing it for what it is, and I didn't think Blair and I would be meeting our future husbands at Club Getaway.

Blair signed up for wine tasting, Texas Hold'em, trapeze and archery, while I just stuck to archery. Waterskiing and stretching didn't require advance sign-up. "I heard there's a late bus coming with a bunch of people from the city," she said as we walked to the dining hall after the welcome reception.

"Ohhhh, okay," I said, wondering if maybe I'd been wrong.

"Hopefully we'll meet some interesting people at dinner."

Dinner would be served in the building directly across from the large tent where we had our meet-and-greet. Several round tables of ten were arranged in an airy room that smelled slightly of mildew and sawdust. Each table was manned with a "counselor," a volunteer who stayed at the camp for free in exchange for acting as a social ambassador for the weekend.

I let Blair take the lead in choosing a table. She chose an empty one near the door.

"Ladies! Hello!" a guy wearing a blue Club Getaway shirt called to us as we neared the table. "Sit down, sit down! I'm Adam."

"Hi, Adam!" Blair and I sang in unison.

Adam was a good-looking guy in his mid-thirties. His blue eyes had a kindness to them, and I liked his energy. He was bubbly and completely comfortable in his own skin, which put Blair and me at ease instantly. The three of us became fast friends, laughing as if we'd known each other for years rather than minutes. From the corner of my eye, I saw a short, nerdy-looking guy in a blue oxford shirt and khaki pants making his way to our table. His wide-open eyes and frozen smile made me silently scream, *Keep going! Keep going! Don't sit here. Don't!*

Fat chance.

"Hi, I'm Seth," he announced, his face still frozen with a smile.

"Hey, Seth! How ya doin', buddy?" Adam got up from his seat between us to shake Seth's hand, while Blair and I stole a look at each other that said, "Oh no!!"

When Seth decided to sit next to me, Blair's eyes urged me to come and sit next to her, but it was too late. A guy who looked like something out of Sha Na Na, wearing a shiny cotton shirt unbuttoned to expose a thick, gold rope chain swimming in the sea of dark hair on his chest, took it. "Hiya! I'm Yuri," he announced, sitting next to Blair and running his hand through his slicked-back hair.

"Hi Yuri!" my sister said with enthusiasm that only I knew was fake.

There we were, breaking bread with our fellow campmates. Adam was a great host, joking and telling very funny stories about everything from a crazy ex-girlfriend who never cleaned up the dog shit in her house to the prior weekend at Club Getaway, where a bunch of people went skinny-dipping in the lake.

Unfortunately, I could barely participate in the fun because Seth would *not* stop talking. "And then I had to tell my partner that he was bringing the company down, and if he didn't shape up I'd have to terminate the partnership…"

I sat there nodding and smiling, inserting "Wow, really?" into the mix a few times, my eyes completely glazed over. At one point, I thought we might be getting somewhere close to a conversation, as opposed to the never-ending Seth Show, when he asked, "So, where are you from?"

"New York."

"I'm from New York too!" he cried, eyes bright with delight. "Not New York City, though," he continued. "No, no. I'm from Rockland County. Ya know, over the Tappan Zee Bridge…"

"Mmm-hmm," I said, turning my head toward Adam and the laughter I was missing out on. I felt like a kid with my nose pressed against the candy store window, watching my friends gorge themselves on jelly beans and Swedish fish.

Seth didn't get the hint that I no longer wanted to talk to him, and I was starting to lose patience. Plus, the free bottle of wine had been drunk—mostly by me. Blair seemed to be having a good time and I didn't want to ruin it by announcing I'd had enough, so instead I pretended to listen to Seth, hoping dinner would end soon.

"That was pretty brutal," I said, when dinner had finally ended and we were walking back to our room. I didn't want to spoil it for Blair by going all negative, but after two long hours with Seth, I had to get it out.

"I know! Adam is great, but the rest of them…" She looked around and lowered her voice. "Kind of nerdy."

"Riiiight?" I said, relieved. "What's up with that?"

"I don't know," she sighed. "It's like nobody had anything interesting to say. All they cared about was where people are from. If it wasn't for Adam, I'd be asleep on my plate."

The visual of Blair facedown in her kosher chicken and mashed potatoes was too much for me, and I practically tripped over a loose rock on the ground, whooping with laughter.

"Careful!" she called, laughing too.

Back in our cabin, we changed clothes to get ready for the disco. I was glad I'd splurged a bit on some new clothes for the weekend, because the current state of my wardrobe was pretty sad. Plus, I knew Blair would have ten different outfits for the weekend, and I didn't want to feel like the poor and dowdy sister.

It wasn't a competition thing—I was just envious that she had the money to buy whatever she wanted. Blair loved clothes, and I did too, though I had given up the luxury of buying new stuff every season when I decided to pursue my creative passions. My sister, on the other hand, had the perfect white shirt for every single outfit. She had *everything!* And she also had the patience to search for that perfect black belt, whereas I lost interest after the third store.

In spite of my irritating dinner experience, I was enjoying myself, singing along to the music from Blair's iPod, drinking the wine she'd brought out of a little plastic wineglass.

"I wonder what the 'disco' will be like," I said, making air quotes.

"I just hope they play good music," my sister replied, putting the final touches on her makeup. "You ready?"

The disco was in a large building facing the lake. Inside, there were two rooms split by a retractable divider. On one side of the room was a stage, apparently for the shows the camp put on. The other side had a bar and a few small tables lining the perimeter. Blair and I went straight to the bar, where we got ourselves a drink and checked out the scene.

"It feels like more of a barn, not a disco," I said, my eyes darting around the room.

From the look of it, the party had yet to get started because the place was half empty. We took our drinks toward the center of the room, in search of interesting people.

I spotted a very tall, very dark-skinned black man standing alone in a corner, bopping his head along to the music. He looked like a basketball player in his nylon breakaway pants and gray hoodie. All I could see was the back of his head—or shall I say hood.

Blair and I stood beside him with about five feet between us. She was digging the music, dancing in place and singing along, while I moved my hips and tried to look nonchalant while checking out the guy in the hood. At the same time, Adam showed up and came over right over to us. "It's the sisters!" he said, giving each of us a warm hug.

Hoodie Guy looked over at us, and Adam reached out to grab his hand and do that handshake guys do when they shake and snap their hands apart. I figured that was it, but Hoodie Guy stayed close.

"Hi," he said, extending his big hand. "I'm Derrick."

He was facing me now, hood off his head, and wow—he was hot! Chiseled face, warm eyes, smooth bald head. I was in trouble.

"Hi," I said, leaning in so he could hear me over the music. "I'm Liz."

The night turned out to be a lot of fun. We danced and drank and danced some more. Derrick stayed with Blair and me the whole time while Adam popped back and forth between us and the rest of the crowd. "They make us mingle," he'd told us earlier.

It was too loud to talk, so Derrick and I stuck to dancing, and he could definitely move. I'm always a little nervous when dancing with strangers. What if we dance close and they get the wrong idea and expect to continue the party once the music stops? The thought had crossed my mind that night, but between the wine and the Jack Daniel's I'd had in my hand all night, my inhibitions were low.

"I think I'm gonna go," my sister whispered in my ear as I spun around and shook my ass toward Derrick's hips. "I don't want to be tired for tomorrow."

While I was definitely having fun, I had no intention of staying while my sister went back to the cabin alone. I bid Derrick goodbye and got a preview of his tight body as he hugged me and wished us good night.

"Derrick was cute," she mused, taking the lead up the narrow walkway toward the cabin.

"I know, right?" I said. "Probably a player, though." He had a great body, the face of a model and the ease and confidence of someone who was used to being popular with the ladies.

"Could be fun for the weekend…" she said, her voice trailing off.

"Nah, I don't think so," I said, walking up the three stairs to our room, confident that someone like Derrick would never go for me—and if he did, he'd definitely be trouble.

33

"Will you ladies be joining me in my stretching class this morning?"

The next day, Derrick, even better looking in daylight, found Blair and me seated at a table in the dining hall, drinking our coffee, trying to wake up. It was early for me—like 8 a.m. early—and the idea of moving my body was so unappealing.

"I don't know," I said, wrapping my hands around my coffee mug. "My neck is kind of messed up."

Derrick tilted his head and put his large hand on his narrow hip. "Well, then you'll just have to let me give you a massage later."

In my sleepy haze I wondered if he was flirting with me.

"I have a massage class in the afternoon," he explained.

"Oh," was all I could muster, disappointed and instantly annoyed with myself for buying into the notion he'd be interested in me.

"I think he likes you," my sister said once he was gone.

"He's just 'mingling,'" I reminded her, ignoring the twitch of excitement in my stomach. But in the end, I decided to join his stretching class. I was already awake. Why not get my blood flowing?

Class took place on top of a hill facing the lake on the main lawn. Derrick, dressed in shorts and a tank top, led the group with ease. I was proud of myself for staying focused on the stretches and not his broad shoulders and strong chest.

Archery was next on the schedule for the day, but when I met up with Blair, she had a different idea.

"Speed dating?" I said. She had to be kidding.

"Come on, it could be fun," she said. "I met this girl who seems nice and she's going to do it...Why not, right?"

I didn't want to do speed dating but I also didn't want to be a downer, and if Blair could be a joiner, why couldn't I? "Let's do it," I said, forcing a smile, eager to please my sister.

It was just as lame as I'd figured it would be. Twenty-six men and twenty-six women had three minutes to forge a connection until one of the counselors blew a whistle indicating it was time to move on to the next person. It was quite a scene: The ladies stayed put and the men switched seats each time the whistle sounded, like something out of musical chairs at a seven-year-old's party.

I went into bartending mode, putting on my best bubbly version of myself. The fruit punch laced with alcohol certainly helped, because after the tenth round of "Hi! How are you? What's your name? Where are you from?" I just went with the flow.

Blair was on the other side of the room, something she'd suggested when we first walked in, saying, "Let's not sit together. This way we won't be tempted to get all judgmental, looking at each other and making faces the whole time."

When it was over, I was exhausted and teetering on laryngitis. Blair was already outside. When I caught up with her, it was like someone flipped a switch on her.

"That was HORRIBLE!" she ranted. "I had to leave. I did."

"What?" I couldn't believe my ears. She didn't even stay for the whole thing? "What the hell happened?"

"NOTHING!" she said. "That was the biggest waste of time. I just couldn't take it anymore. I'm done with this bullshit. I'm finished with trying to be a good sport and giving people a chance." She paused, trying to find the right words. "FUCK camp," she finally said.

"Noooo?!?!" I said, unsure of why I was trying to talk her out of this newfound attitude.

But Blair had made up her mind. "No way. I tried. I came here and gave it a shot. All I want to do for the rest of our time here is relax, participate in a few activities, and that will be that."

I wanted to dance. I was sorry she was so stressed out, but all the pressure I'd been putting on myself to match her enthusiasm had lifted like a curtain. *Now* we could be real.

"I want to stay here all day," she said later, as we floated on the lake.

"Ohmigod, riiight?" I said, careful not to lose my balance. "It's like you can't even go to the bathroom without somebody walking up to you and saying, 'Hi, I'm so-and-so. What's your name? Where are you from?' Don't people here know how to have *natural* conversation?"

"Exactly! I'm done being nice. I'm just going to start ignoring people."

After a few hours of floating and soaking in the lake, Blair and I returned to our lounge chairs. "I think I'm going to try and water-ski," I said, squeezing the water from my hair and eyeing the ski dock on the far end of the beach.

"Great!" my sister said, getting comfortable on her chair. "Maybe after, we'll do some archery." She leaned over and grabbed the cold beer we'd stopped to purchase on our way back to our chairs. "Or... not," she sighed happily.

"Ha! Suddenly *I'm* the joiner."

"And how are my two favorite sisters doing this afternoon?"

Derrick came up behind us looking like he'd just had an intense workout, sweaty and shirtless.

"Hey!" I said, wrapping a towel around the lower half of my body.

"What have you all done today?" he asked, sitting on the edge of my lounge chair.

"Not a thing!" my sister announced with pride. "We're a little peopled out."

Derrick laughed. "Yeah, I get it. When I'm not 'on,' I sit right there on top of the hill, by myself, with a book." He pointed behind us to a lone green plastic chair that looked like it could use some company.

"I'm thinking about waterskiing," I said, trying to keep my eyes off the tattoo on his chest. Derrick didn't miss a thing. "Oh, this? You like it? I got it in Mexico."

I was trying not to size him up, but I couldn't help it. He liked to read, was gorgeous and fit, and traveled! *Marry me!* I silently pleaded.

Blair and I chatted with him for a bit longer until he got up to leave. "Well, hopefully I'll see you both later," he said, looking at me.

"Will you be at the disco?" my sister asked.

"If you ladies promise to be there," he laughed.

"We will!" my sister exclaimed while I nodded, trying not to punch her.

I knew she was trying to play matchmaker. Once he'd left, I turned to her and said, "Will you stop?"

Blair feigned surprise. "What? He's cool. I just want to make sure we see him later." But her smile said it all. I knew my sister. "Besides, he's totally flirting with you. It's so obvious."

Even if he was flirting, I wouldn't know what to do. It had been so long since I'd flexed that muscle. There was Noah at Enlightened, but that was a totally different scenario. Derrick was hot, and hot guys intimidated me.

Sven, the guy from the welcome reception, was standing near the dock, shirtless and wearing loud Hawaiian-printed shorts. He was still perky even though he was no longer holding a clipboard.

"You wanna ski?" he asked, bending down to pick up a few life jackets that were scattered on the dock.

"Yes," I gulped, not sure I truly wanted to.

"Ever skied before?"

"Uh, yes," I said, tilting my head and checking to see if my neck was really up for it. "But not since my twenties."

"Not too long ago, then!" Sven jumped to his feet, smiling. "Let's get you into a jacket and some skis."

I grabbed a life vest and shuddered as the cold, wet nylon hit my skin. Snapping the clasps into place, I could feel heart pounding. What if I can't do this? What if I hurt myself? It had been a really long time, and I hadn't worked out in at least three years. I looked back toward Blair, the beer and our lounge chairs, contemplating whether to abort my mission.

Sven and three others zipped off into the lake while the skier before me readied herself, looking like a frog with her skis sticking out of the water. I sat down and put my skis on, dangling them over the edge of the dock.

A petite girl in a bikini sat on the dock with her knees pulled into her chest, calling out to her friend in the water. "You can do it, Sher! Just remember to put your weight on your heels." Her enthusiasm made me wish I'd taken my sister up on her offer to come down to the dock to watch.

The girl turned to me. "It's really hard out there. I mean, I skied in camp, but this is no joke."

I smiled weakly and once again considered giving up. "Yeah, I'm worried I'm too out of shape."

After three failed tries, her friend was ready to call it a day, removing her skis and pushing them in front of her as she swam back to the dock.

"You're up!" Sven yelled to me from the boat. I eased myself into the water. I was self-conscious, wondering if Derrick was watching me from his chair.

"Grab the rope," Sven yelled.

I got in position, knees bent, ski tips up and out of the water, the rope positioned between my legs. My life vest was creeping up, making it feel like I was being lifted by my collar. I questioned for the last time if this was a good idea and realized it was too late, so I took a deep breath, fought the urge to squeeze my eyes shut and said, "READY!"

The boat hummed with acceleration, the rope went taut and I felt the weight of the pull urging me up and out of the water. Suddenly I was nine years old again, with my camp instructor calling out to me, "Arms straight! Knees bent! Lean back, lean back! Weight on the heels!"

And then I was up! My first attempt and I was doing it. Sven was motioning to me from the boat to bend my knees more and straighten my arms. I'm sure there was a stupid grin on my face as the boat pulled me around the lake, making wide circles toward its far edges.

After my first lap, Sven rotated his finger in the air to let me know we were going around again. I looked to the shore to see if I could spot Blair among the dots of people. We were too far out, so I enjoyed the moment privately instead.

As we neared the end of our second lap, Sven motioned to me, sliding his index finger across his neck. I nodded and threw the rope as far to my left as possible to avoid getting it caught on one of my skis as I sank slowly into the water.

Sven and the others in the boat clapped and whistled as I removed my skis and vest. I was shaking. I wasn't cold or scared; I was *exhilarated*! Thirty minutes ago, I was standing on the dock nervous and afraid, thinking I'd made a terrible mistake. But I faced my fears and I felt taller and stronger—like I could do anything.

I caught up to Blair. "Did you see me?" I asked, panting.

"YES!" she squealed. "You were great!"

I savored my triumph and tucked it into a warm, safe place where only I knew it existed and no one could take it away from me.

34

"I have a date tomorrow night," I said, popping a tortilla chip in my mouth.

"Whaaaaaaaaaaaaat??" Judy and Stephanie exclaimed in unison. Stephanie scrunched up her face and said, "Whatchu talkin' 'bout, Willis?"

We were gathered around the coffee table in my living room. I was sitting in my comfy chair, while they sat at either end of the couch. It was our third meeting of the women's group I'd initiated almost two months ago. After Rachel declined my invite, I was worried about it being awkward with just three people, but Judy and Stephanie hit it off immediately. Since then, we'd managed to meet every two weeks at my apartment.

Tonight, just back from camp, I was giving them the lowdown on Derrick.

"So yeah, I wasn't sure if he was just being nice or if he was really into me, but on the last night of camp..."

Judy and Stephanie stifled and then snorted laughter upon my reference to "camp."

"Blair kept telling me he was flirting with me, but I wasn't sure," I continued. "He was so nice to *every*one, and I'm not one to assume the whole world is in love me. On the last night, we were at the disco..."

More stifled laughter.

"And we just got to talking. I don't know," I said, my eyes wide. "We just hit it off and talked for hours!"

"That's great!" Judy said, clapping her hands together.

"I know! But I felt so bad. I totally missed my sister riding the mechanical bull."

"What the hell kinda camp did you go to?" Stephanie asked, donning the same dramatic face scrunch. And then more seriously, "I'm sure Blair understood."

"She did, but still."

"Is that when he asked you out?" Judy piped in.

"No! It was so crazy because at the end of camp, we exchanged numbers and talked about my reading the screenplay he's working on."

Judy raised an eyebrow. "Ohhhh…a writer, too?"

"Not really. I mean, he's got this screenplay, but he's a personal trainer, a model and an actor in real life." I ignored the looks of wonder and approval from Stephanie and Judy. "He asked me out to lunch. I thought it was a date, but I don't know, it was just me and him, eating lunch and him giving me his script."

"And?" Stephanie asked, leaning forward.

"Nothing!" I said, throwing my hands in the air. "After that I thought, well, maybe he's not interested, ya know? But then he calls me a few days later and says in that crazy, deep, Barry White voice"—I tucked my chin and dropped my voice several octaves—"'Lemme take you out on a real date.'"

Stephanie and Judy erupted into simultaneous squeals. "Niiiiice!!"

"I guess he was interested," I said with satisfaction, leaning back in my chair and taking a sip of wine.

Stephanie was all over it. "You're damn right he's interested! He was interested at LUNCH, girl!! *When* are you going to *get* that?"

"No, but I did say I'd read his script," I protested.

"Script, schmipt." Stephanie said, waving her hand around. "He is *interested*. Period."

"I agree," Judy said from her corner of the couch.

There was a great balance of energy among us. Stephanie was the most animated while Judy was more reserved, sometimes shy. I seemed to flit back and forth between the two.

"Where are you guys going?" Judy asked.

"That's the thing," I said, laughing. "He lives in Brooklyn and clearly doesn't do much hanging out in Manhattan."

"What do you mean?"

"He suggested we go to Halo."

"So?" Stephanie asked.

"Halo closed like five years ago!"

"Okay," Stephanie replied. "So he's not Mr. Hipster. Big deal."

"But it *is* a big deal," I said, shifting uncomfortably in my chair. "I hate going out with a guy who's always looking to me to choose the places."

That sparked a flurry of comments from Stephanie and Judy all at once.

Judy pushed forward. "Who cares about the superficial stuff? If he's a nice guy, that stuff won't matter."

My head knew that she was probably right. But all my life, I'd been taking care of people, especially men. I was the one choosing the place for dinner, deciding whether we stayed in or went out, and picking up the check too many times. I liked being the one to teach back then because it gave me a sense of worth that I hoped would ensure loyalty. If he needed me, he'd never leave.

Charlie was the first guy who really tried to take care of me, never letting me pay for a thing, picking me up from work whenever I wanted him to and always being available, even if it meant neglecting his construction business. Charlie was me in all my other relationships, and when I got a taste of it myself, I vowed never to be that girl again.

"Just have a good time, Liz," Judy urged. "Ya never know how it will turn out."

The next evening, I suggested to Derrick that we meet at Merc Bar, an oldie but goodie in SoHo where the front windows retracted into the ceiling like a garage door to expose dark velvet couches and small leather squares for seating. It was a beautiful summer night. As I walked from the subway toward SoHo, I was nervous. It felt like forever since I'd been on a date.

I knew I looked good that night. I was wearing the lemon-yellow halter dress that I'd bought for Club Getaway but never wore. My brown wedge sandals rounded the outfit out perfectly. I was even having a good hair night, my curls framing my face perfectly. So what was the problem?

I contemplated it as I turned onto Mercer Street. Maybe it was just the anticipation. Or that I was out of practice. Whatever it was, it vanished like a chocoholic's resolve in a sweetshop when I saw Derrick leaning against the brick façade just outside the front entrance. He looked fantastic, of course, wearing tan linen pants and a cream-colored cotton sweater.

"Hello, beautiful," he purred, that deep voice putting me at ease instantly. He leaned over and down to kiss my cheek.

"Shall we go in?" I asked.

The place was crowded and we were only able to get a seat at a table in the back. As much as I liked the idea of being up in front with the open windows, I was glad to be in the back, where it was a bit more private.

The unease I'd felt had completely disappeared, and we talked comfortably about everything from where we grew up to funny stories about our past.

"There are two things people are surprised to know about me," he said at one point in the evening.

Oh, great. This was it. Probably jail or something.

"The first thing is—" Derrick took a sip of his pinot grigio—"that most people think I'm a player, ya know, 'cuz of the whole modeling thing. But," he paused, putting his wineglass on the table and waving his free hand, "that's all nonsense. I'm a normal guy and so *not* a player. It's frustrating because I think sometimes people don't give me a chance."

I was relieved to hear him proclaim a lack of player-ness, but it was going to take more than that to convince me. How did a guy that good-looking *and* nice not walk around thinking he could have any woman he wanted?

"What's the other thing?" I asked, leaning my elbows on the table and clasping my hands under my chin, thinking, *One down, one to go… Please let there be no crazy baby mamas.*

"Oh! I'm also fifty-four years old," he said matter-of-factly.

"Whaaaaat??" was all I could manage. Derrick laughed a slow, deep chuckle, shaking his head.

There were so many things about that little slice of reality that my mind didn't know where to go first. "Pardon me while I pick my jaw off the floor," I joked. "You look so good!"

"Well, thank you," he grinned, raising his glass to me.

I'd never dated a guy in his fifties, and the idea of dating one made me feel like I was crossing a certain threshold, one where it was actually *okay* to date someone of that generation. What would be next—a subscription to *AARP* magazine?

Derrick didn't look a day over thirty-five. And his body—forget it! I knew twenty-seven-year-olds who didn't look as good. He seemed mature and like he had his shit together, so my suspicious mind wondered, *What is* wrong *with this guy?*

After a couple of glasses of wine, Derrick offered to drive me back to Brooklyn, grabbing my hand as we walked to his car. The shock of his age had worn off, and the smile on my face was radiating from within. I liked this guy and I was pretty sure he liked me. If I thought I could get away with it, I'd do a little jump, with a joyful squeal for effect.

In the car, Derrick pulled out a cigar-like joint. "My one and only vice," he said, reaching for a lighter in the ashtray, its flame illuminating his strong jawline. "Would you like some?"

"Sure."

After a few hits, we drove over the Manhattan Bridge to my apartment. There was an easy, slightly stoned silence between us. I was happy to just groove to the light jazz playing on the radio and let the wind blow through my hair.

Derrick pulled up in front of my building and jumped out of the car to open the door for me. I'd always found this gesture endearing and silly all at once. He reached in to take my hand, easing me onto the sidewalk. Once outside, I realized how tipsy and stoned I really was, and I started to worry that I'd fall off the curb.

"I had a great time tonight, Liz," Derrick said, leaning against the car, his voice sweet.

"Me too."

"I hope we can do it again real soon."

"I'd like that." I knew what was coming. Or at least I thought I did. But then again, he was fifty-four. Maybe he would shake my hand, take a small bow and say good night.

I really wanted him to kiss me. Finally, after what seemed like an hour, Derrick stood up tall and moved closer to me, placing his large hand on the arch of my back. He pulled me toward him and put his soft lips on mine.

We kissed, small ones to start, our lips getting acquainted. Derrick's grip on my back tightened slightly as his lips lingered and his tongue urged my mouth open slightly.

Suddenly I was scared. I could feel the intensity between us. If I could have stopped him and screamed, "Wait! Wait! I don't know if I'm ready for this. I'm not sure I can do this! It's been so long," I would have. Instead, I stood there, trying to gather myself and lean into the kiss, not away from it. And once I did, I knew I'd turned a corner and given something to this man.

"I should go," I murmured when we finally came up for air.

Walking away, my mind was racing and my legs unsteady. After months of inward existence, I had reached the tipping point. Something in me was coming undone as a result of our kiss, and the mixture of elation and fear was overwhelming. I just wanted to get inside.

Reaching the front steps, I gripped the railing and focused on trying not to trip *up* the stairs. I could feel Derrick's eyes on me. When I got to the top, I turned around and he was still standing there, leaning against his car and smiling. I managed a wave because it took everything I had not to dash inside and lock myself back up where it was safe and familiar.

By the time I got to the elevator, my chest was tight and my breathing shallow.

It's time, my mind urged. Time to let go and trust myself. *But how?* Riding in the elevator alone, I tried to steady my nerves by repeating silently, *All I need to do is get inside. If I can get inside, I'll be fine.* Key in the door and knob turning, I was back in the safe zone.

If Rufus were still alive, I'd get down on the floor with him and hold him until I felt grounded again. But now, it was just me and a potentially fresh start in love. I wanted the chance, I really did. I just wish I had something to hold me steady while I forged new territory. I kicked off my shoes, dropped my purse and myself onto the floor, letting its density stabilize my nerves.

Twenty minutes later and still on the floor, my cell phone beeped with a new text message. I sat up, woozy, and reached for my phone.

"Just got home. Had a great time. Sweet Dreams. —Derrick."

Smiling, I held the phone to my chest and exhaled. Everything was going to be okay, I told my now quiet mind. It was already okay.

35

My first date with Derrick ushered in feelings of excitement and anxiety. I was trying to cultivate the excitement and embrace the fact that it felt like someone had thrown open the curtains after a long, dark winter, letting the warm sunlight burst into the room and shine light on things I'd forgotten were there.

The anxiety, however, was like a sneaky cat, swooping in when I wasn't looking to wreak havoc, unraveling rolls of toilet paper or shredding tissues in the garbage—completely messing with my well-executed efforts to keep things under control. I wasn't sure I entirely trusted Derrick. He'd told me that people automatically thought he was a player because of his looks. Maybe I couldn't get past them. Was I really that insecure? I wanted to think I wasn't, but it'd been so long since I'd been with a guy, especially one so attractive. And I couldn't decide if he was emotionally remote or not that deep or, worst of all, one of those guys who came on strong but didn't stick around.

Dating is tricky because it's hard to separate the past from the present, especially in the beginning. There were so many times in my love life when the signs were clear and I ignored them, all of them. Since then, I'd learned my lesson, vowing to never let my guard down and pretend the red flags weren't waving in front of my face. The only problem with that methodology was I found myself *looking* for signs of deception as opposed to trusting that I'd see them when and if they appeared.

"You have to trust your instinct," my sister told me when I voiced my apprehension. "If you feel like he's not being completely honest with you, you'll know. You're not stupid, Liz."

Derrick seemed interested. He was always asking me "When do you have time for me?" which I loved. He was on time and called when he said he would, so what was the problem?

I wished Rufus were here. At least I knew what I was getting with Rufus. He never let me down and was always there when I needed him. Sure, he was a dog, but he was the first thing in my life I loved who loved me back just as much, if not more. Shortly after he died, it became clear to me that his unwavering presence was probably the main reason I never got serious with anyone.

Lisa and I joked about not needing men for the ten-plus years we'd had our dogs. "At the end of the day, I preferred Jake's company over a man's," she'd said one warm afternoon over drinks at the Maritime Hotel in the Meatpacking District.

"I don't know, girl," she'd said, stirring the ice in her white sangria. "Sometimes I feel like I missed the boat with the whole marriage-and-kids thing. Let's face it, I got Jake when I was twenty-six and had him through my mid-thirties. Most people meet someone during that time. Now I'm almost forty and alone. I wonder if it would have turned out differently had I not had Jake…"

"You don't regret having a dog?" I asked, surprised at how betrayed I felt. We were the girls with dogs. We'd been through everything with them. She couldn't possibly regret her time with Jake! Lisa's candidness sparked something in me—perhaps recognition of the fact that I'd had the same thoughts since Rufus's death, never truly acknowledging them, stomping them out like a small fire in the woods, ridding myself of all evidence of regret.

"It was too easy, Liz. I had my dog. I didn't need anyone else, ya know?"

"Yeah," I sighed, leaning back in my chair. "I know."

Derrick's presence in my life and my waterskiing victory at Club Getaway gave me a renewed sense of confidence and clarity. A week after my return from camp, I finally got rid of Rufus's food, the last remaining evidence of his presence in my home. I'd long since put his bowls and toys away, promising myself that at some point I would donate his food to a local shelter. It had been six months since he died, and taking the case of canned dog food from the very spot it occupied in the kitchen, next to the garbage can since that sad day, was a big step for me. But I was ready to move on.

Maybe having a dog all those years really did prevent me from falling in love. With Rufus gone, it was time to get on with this love thing in spite of my fears. I told myself I was ready to give Derrick a chance—and hoped I really was.

Sexually, he was amazing. His large, strong hands moved expertly all over my body as if he knew instinctively where to touch me, how long to linger and when to move on. He was more than a generous lover, which sometimes made me uneasy as my sexual comfort zone had always been that of the provider and rarely the receiver. But Derrick was patient, so very patient, taking care to put me at ease with hours of massage and foreplay.

On our second date, he invited me to his place in Brooklyn for a night of "pampering," as he proudly put it. Walking into his apartment, I thought it was probably a bit too soon for me to be in his home. I hardly knew him, and seeing how he lived felt odd and intrusive.

"What are these?" I'd asked, running my hand over the plush heads of two stuffed bears.

"My stuffed animals," he replied, as if this, at the age of fifty-four, was the most normal thing in the world.

Derrick's apartment was modest in size, with a small living room filled with a partial sectional and a desk, and an even smaller bedroom where he slept on a pullout couch, the remaining piece of the sectional. He lived in a gated community just past Coney Island where, once inside, it was like entering another world of large houses and manicured lawns. We'd stopped to get some Chinese food close to his house in an obviously rougher section of the neighborhood. The place smelled of sesame oil and soy sauce. Oversized photos of beef and broccoli and pork fried rice lined the walls. I didn't have the heart to tell him how much I disliked Chinese food, so when he asked what I wanted to order, I answered casually, "Just some shrimp fried rice. I'm not crazy hungry."

While I watched Derrick place our order through the thick plastic window as if he were making a bank deposit, I was aware that this wasn't the safest of neighborhoods. The few people waiting for their orders looked like they could be in a gang, with baggy jeans and blue bandannas tied around their heads à la Tupac Shakur.

"Knuckleheads," Derrick sighed, standing behind me and slipping his arms around my waist.

I felt my body tense up and was aware of feeling oddly out of place with a man so incredibly handsome. I assumed the people throwing stares in our direction were wondering, "Why's he with *her*?"

Back at his place, he'd set up a picnic of sorts, laying the food, some napkins and two glasses of pinot grigio on the carpet. His apartment was quiet and smelled heavily of pot. I wondered why he didn't open a window to air it out.

Sitting alone on the floor, I waited for Derrick to join me as he sat at his desk, rolling a thick joint identical to the one we'd smoked in the car on our first date. There was a quiet confidence about him, and the density of his energy made me twitchy and too aware of myself.

Once we'd had some weed, I began to relax, though my mind offered some clarity on what exactly was contributing to my nerves. There was so much anticipation to that evening. We hadn't had sex yet, and there we were, in his home, sitting on the floor with candles flickering and soft, sultry music playing. I wondered what he expected of me. I also wondered what I expected of myself.

After dinner, Derrick took my hand and led me to the couch. "I hope you're ready for your massage," he purred, clearing the plates and arranging a blanket on the floor.

I sat on the couch, my mind buzzing from the weed, waiting for further instruction and fighting the urge to help. I wanted to *do* something! I hated being so out of control.

Are you going to have sex with this guy? You don't have condoms, do you think he has condoms? Do you think he'll massage you naked? Are you ready to get naked in front of this guy?

Temporarily lost in the traffic jam in my mind, I didn't even hear Derrick the first time when he'd summoned me to the floor.

"Are you ready?" he said again, this time standing over me and reaching his hand out to ease me off the couch.

"Uh, should I take my clothes off?" I stammered as I moved onto the blanket.

"No, baby," he murmured. "You are in my hands. Just lie back, relax and let me pamper you."

I felt the need to make a joke to quell my nerves, but it didn't seem appropriate, so instead I did what he said, laughing nervously as he began to remove my shoes.

Derrick slid his hands lightly down my legs and removed my jeans, stopping to massage my feet before continuing onto my shirt. In spite of myself, I began to relax because as nervous as I was, it felt really good to be touched like that.

When I was completely naked, Derrick stood up for a moment and just looked at me, clucking his tongue with delight. "Sexy," he said, grabbing a bottle of oil from the bookshelf next to the door to his bedroom.

I bet he does that a lot.

Before I could buy into the voices, Derrick's hands were easing me onto my stomach and massaging the last remaining bits of tension from my body.

He took his time, starting with my back, kneading the stress free with gentle urgency. When his hands reached my hips, I held my breath, wondering if he'd reach down to feel the moistness between my legs. Though he lingered near the area, giving each butt cheek equal attention, he continued down my legs, rubbing my thighs, calves and toes vigorously.

By the time he'd finished on my backside, my body felt like a wet noodle and my mind was in a state of cautious relaxation. I heard Derrick get up and what sounded like credit cards being thrown onto a table. My mind made the connection once the music stopped and Sade's sensual voice filled the room that the credit cards were just CDs.

More rustling behind me, and just as my mind was stirring itself to attention, Derrick said from above, "Time to turn over."

I rolled onto my left side with the laziness of a dog waking from a deep sleep. On my back, I opened my eyes. All but one of the candles had burned out. It was hard to make out Derrick's location, but I could feel his presence close to me.

"Here, put this on," he said, his mouth whispering softly in my ear.

I looked up. In the dim light of the remaining candle and bluish hue from the stereo, I saw a black sleep mask in Derrick's hand.

Kinky.

"No, I'm good," I said, suddenly feeling less than relaxed and not ready to submit fully to this man by covering my eyes completely.

He didn't push, thankfully, and I settled back down, closing my eyes and allowing Sade to ease me back into comfort.

At some point Derrick had taken off his clothes, because as he worked his hands down the front of my body, I could feel his bare leg brush against mine. My mind fought to stay alert as he edged closer to my hips. I wanted him inside me. I wanted him to touch me and play with the wetness between my legs.

As Sade's "Lovers Rock" began, Derrick eased my legs apart and explored the hidden parts of my body.

"Mmmm," he said, his breath like feathers dancing across my inner thighs. "You taste so good."

As good as it felt, I knew I wouldn't be able to come, and the more I thought about it, the more uncomfortable I got.

"I can't come on my back," I said quietly, hoping he could hear me.

"Just relax," Derrick murmured, reaching up to play with one of my nipples. "There's no rush."

I didn't know what to do. Though I was telling the truth about not being able to climax in my current position, I was unsure whether I'd be able to come at all. It was a trust thing, and when I was with a man to the point of orgasm, it was like something was being exchanged and I gave him a small piece of myself. Was I ready to do that with Derrick?

Derrick was good. Really good. As he worked his tongue and fingers simultaneously, I realized that I was very close to coming. Rufus came to mind for some odd reason, and as I felt myself edging closer and closer to climax, I decided I would take this offer of pleasure and allow myself to fold into it.

Relax, girl. Just lie back and relax. You can do this. Let yourself go. Let go.

"I'm going to come," I breathed. Derrick moaned with encouragement. Closer. Closer. I was nearly there, my breath shallow and legs tense. I wanted this and I was going to have it.

I came loudly, arching my back and pushing my pelvis into Derrick, my insides feeling like a lotus flower opening up to full bloom. My head was spinning in ecstasy as I dropped my hips back to the floor and lay there, completely spent.

"Wow," I murmured. "Thank you."

"Thank *you*," Derrick said, taking me in his arms.

We stayed on his floor for a while, not talking, wrapped in each other's arms. I became restless, and once the post-orgasm haze faded I was ready to get up. I weighed my options and wished Rufus were still alive. I'd used him many times to get out of uncomfortable situations. "I have to go home and walk my dog," I'd say smoothly, getting out of bed and into my clothes. It was fail-safe. Who would ever argue against the comfort of an animal?

On that night, it was clear to me that it was time I started choosing myself. Rufus knew that, and I believed that was why he let go in the end. No more excuses. No more hiding behind my obligations to him. It was time for me to assert my needs without apology.

I waited a little longer, practicing what I'd say in my head and anticipating what Derrick would say back. I hated that I was in the middle of nowhere and couldn't just get up and hail a cab. If I wanted to go home, Derrick would have to take me.

Finally, I took the plunge.

"Uh, I think I'd like to get going." Pause. "Is that okay?"

"Why wouldn't that be okay?" Derrick laughed. "It's not like I planned on kidnapping you."

And just like that, I'd said my piece. Nobody died, no one got hurt. Rufus would've been proud.

36

It was Monday, and Stephanie, Judy and I were gathered in my apartment for our bimonthly ladies' night. We'd been meeting at my place consistently for the last two months, drinking, laughing and sharing our hopes and fears about everything from men to art to money. I loved how honest and open we were with one another. It was the first time in my life I felt supported by my friends without feeling helpless.

It was my turn to be the first to share. Each of us were in our usual spots, Stephanie and Judy on the couch and I in my comfy chair, gathered around my coffee table where snacks had been laid out. Stephanie was nursing a gin and tonic, while Judy and I were almost finished with the first of two bottles of wine.

Taking a somewhat dramatic deep breath, I began. "Okay, so…things are good. Yeah, good. Work's been busy and I'm finally making good money at Maxie's, the law firm still sucks…" I trailed off, knowing the girls weren't buying my superficial download.

"Very compelling stuff," Stephanie said sarcastically with a penetrating stare.

"You know how she is," Judy snorted. "She's got to warm up."

"Okay, okay…fine. Let's see. I think I'm going to keep things casual with Derrick. After what happened at Ideya, I'm just not sure he's boyfriend material. I like his company, but he's just not that social and I'm such a social person. I can't be with a guy who's such a dud."

Judy set her wineglass down and sat up tall. "Wait. I think I missed something. The *camp guy* who was Mr. Personality is now suddenly a dud. I don't get it. I thought he was like the nicest guy ever!"

"He was," I replied. "He is! It's just that I saw an odd side of him at Stephanie's restaurant a couple of weeks ago, which made me think that he's only social in situations he's in control of."

"Well, what happened at Ideya?" Judy asked.

"Actually, Ideya was icing on the cake," Stephanie interjected, since she had already heard the story.

"Long story short, we met up in the afternoon last weekend. Things were cool. We walked around and ended up in the Meatpacking District. I suggested we get a drink, to which he replied, 'I'm easy. Whatever you wanna do.' Cool. So I'm thinking maybe Pastis or something, when we pass the place on the corner of 9th and 14th and he says, 'How 'bout here?'"

"The *diner*?" Judy blinked.

"Exactly!" I practically screamed. "He wants to go in because they have *pinot grigio*—ugh, him and that fuckin' pinot grigio. I'm like, 'Eeeeew...not a diner!' I suggest an Italian spot around the corner, thinking they'd have some pinot grigio. He gives me the 'I'm easy' reply and we head over."

I paused to take a sip of wine. (*Not* pinot grigio.)

"We get to the Italian spot and they don't have pinot grigio," I continued.

"Oh jeez."

"Yep. He's all pissed off because he doesn't know any of the wine.' I'm like, 'Dude! You're with a bartender! I can help you find something good and different—ya know, change it up a little.' I suggested a Vernaccia."

Both Judy and Stephanie murmured with approval.

I scrunched my nose up like I'd just smelled sour milk, imitating Derrick. "'It's fine,' he sniffs, and basically spends the whole time sulking. We finish our wine," I continued. "Correction: *I* finish my wine, and we decide to walk over to the water 'cuz Derrick wants to smoke some weed. Things are less tense as we find a spot on the grass overlooking the late afternoon sun and I'm thinking, *Okay, cool, we're good now.* We smoke, and as the sun is setting it starts to get chilly. We weigh our options. I don't feel like going home—we're *always* staying home—so I suggest we go and visit Stephanie at Ideya. It's a lively place and there's always a good group of people. Plus, I want her to meet him, ya know?"

Judy nodded. "Right!"

"We start walking toward SoHo and he's like, 'How far is this place anyway?' all cranky and shit. I suggest a cab or the subway, but he's not having it. Finally I lose my patience and say, 'I'm not sure what you want me to do here, Derrick. It's not around the corner, but it's not a million blocks away either.' We walk to Ideya, pretty much in silence. Now, mind you, my feet are KILLING me because my sandals are digging into my toes, but I don't complain. At this point, I just want to *get* there."

More murmurs of agreement as I continued, "Once we're there, I'm rarin' to go. There's a bunch of fun guys to my left and we all strike up a conversation—except for Derrick, of course."

"What was he doing?" Judy asked, wincing at the potential answer.

"Nothing!" I yelled. "He just sits there in silence, looking bored."

"Reeeeeal bored," Stephanie said, pursing her lips.

"I was so annoyed, but I kept asking him if he was okay, was anything wrong?"

"Did he have his pinot grigio?" Judy mocked.

"Ha! Nope. He had water," I replied with a sour look. "He barely spoke to Stephanie, and after a while, I just didn't care. Especially when I asked him again if he was okay and he got annoyed at *me*, acting as if I'm the crazy one and he's just Mr. Normal."

"What the fuck?"

"Exactly. *Finally,* he's like, 'I'm gonna get going,' and I practically jumped for joy, offering no protest or polite gesture to leave with him. Fuck that shit. I wanted him to take his ass home, which he finally did after asking me, 'Is there a train around here?'"

That was too much for Judy, who practically spit out her wine. "Where did he think he was? Rochester?"

"Riiiiight?" I said, raising my wineglass in agreement. "So yeah, that was that and he didn't call for a few days, and to be honest, I'm kinda done with the whole dating thing and him. I'd rather just have sex with him and keep it simple."

"Okay, good!" Judy said.

"Nothin' wrong with that, girl," Stephanie added, raising her gin and tonic.

"Plus," I said, biting my lip, "I may have met someone else."

Stephanie and Judy whooped with laughter like they'd just won the lottery.

"What do you mean, *might have*?" Stephanie narrowed her eyes. "Spill!"

I told them about Marcus, a guy I'd met at Maxie's the week before. He was there with one of my regulars, having dinner at the bar. He certainly wasn't hot like Derrick, but he was attractive in a more low-key, conservative way, with big brown eyes, milk-chocolate skin and a very easy energy. The thing I liked most about him was his quick wit. We spent a good part of the evening throwing bits of sarcasm back and forth like volleying tennis players.

"At first I didn't even realize he was flirting with me," I said, returning from the kitchen with a new bottle of wine. "So when he asked me out—"

More whoops of excitement from the couch.

"Actually, he asked me to marry him, to which I replied, 'Do you have health insurance? I'm not interested in love—only health insurance.' He said he had great health insurance and would be happy to start with a date."

"Oooooh…smooooooth," from the couch.

"I was so caught off guard and a little flustered, I walked away and busied myself with the dishwasher so I could think."

"About what?" Stephanie asked, challenge dripping from her voice.

"Yeah, what's the problem?" Judy chimed in.

I positioned myself in the chair like I was stating an important case to the grand jury, both feet on the floor, back straight and hands clasped together. "First off, I don't date customers."

Stephanie and Judy failed at an attempt to stifle their disapproval, snorting and making faces. "Plus," I said righteously, "I'm not exactly finished with Derrick. I'm not gonna date two guys at the same time."

Stephanie could no longer contain herself. "*WHY* not, girl? You said yourself that you want to keep it casual with Derrick. As far as I'm concerned, this is a perfect situation. You've got a pair and a spare, baby!"

Acknowledging the quizzical looks from Judy and me, Stephanie continued, "A pair and a spare! I've never told y'all about this?" She clucked in surprise. "I got it from a dating book I read. It's better to keep a few guys going at once; takes the pressure off, ya know? If guy number one stands you up, nooooo problem," she said, waving her hand like she was directing traffic. "Call up guy number two. That way you're never putting all your energy into one guy."

Judy and I silently considered this.

"It's not like you're being dishonest," she said, as if reading my mind. "Until a man tells you, 'Hey, I'd like to see you exclusively,' you've got no obligation to anyone but yourself, so why not play the field a little? It's not like you're lying. Plus, who's to say he's not seeing a couple of women at the same time as well?"

She had a point. What would be so bad about seeing Derrick and Marcus at the same time?

"I've never done that before," I said.

"Which is precisely why I think this would be good for you! Liz, you're always all about *reacting* to other people's behavior. Why not call the shots for a change? I think it would be a great experience for you, especially having to set boundaries with these guys and say, 'I'm sorry, I can't see you tonight, but I can see you on Friday.' Make these guys work a little for your company. It's worth it!"

"She's right, ya know," Judy finally added. "I love having a few guys going at once. It keeps it interesting and gives you an opportunity to really get to know them without the pressure of 'Oh my god! Is he the *one*?!'"

Still not completely convinced, I asked, "What about sex?"

"What about it?" Stephanie deadpanned.

I felt like a schoolgirl, blood rushing to my cheeks. "I've never done that—ya know, sex with two different guys at once. It's so slutty, no?"

"Come on!" Judy laughed. "You're a grown woman!"

"Which is why, again, I think this would be very good for you," Stephanie said, slowing down her next thought for emphasis. "It's time to date like a woman, Liz—not like a girl."

37

By the time Thanksgiving rolled around, we had a new president, and I had three men in my life. Derrick and I fell into a casual once-a-week thing where he'd come to my place and we'd smoke some weed, order some food and spend several hours having fantastic sex. He never overstayed his welcome, leaving shortly after some post-coital cuddling. It was the perfect arrangement.

Marcus, the guy I'd met at Maxie's, was more traditional. He was a great dater, taking me to different places around Manhattan or offering to cook dinner for me at his apartment in the Financial District. He too was easy to be around, and I loved how comfortable I felt with him.

Marcus was almost forty and worked in the banking industry. I appreciated his stability and reliability. He loved to go out, whereas Derrick liked to stay in. I had the best of both worlds. Sexually, Marcus was a good lover, though it was hard to beat the chemistry between me and Derrick. He was always asking me to stay over, insisting that the weather outside was perfect for "snuggling."

"Are you coming over tonight?" Marcus asked the week before, after we'd polished off a bottle of cabernet franc at WineBar in the East Village.

Giddy from the wine, I didn't want the night to end. "I'll come over," I said, touching my hand to his face and looking into his eyes, "but I'm not going to stay, okay?"

Marcus took my hand in his and sighed, "Yeah, yeah, the snoring.

I know."

I'd stayed over a few times, but Marcus snored so loud it reminded me of the suction the dentist uses to keep the saliva in your mouth under control.

As we split a final glass of wine, I marveled at how easy it had become for me to set my boundaries. There were no rehearsals in my head in preparation for what he might say, or worry as to whether he'd push himself on me. It was simple. Easy. And the power I felt was incredible.

"That's because you're putting you first," Stephanie reminded me when I gave her the rundown the night after my date with Marcus. "Plus, having a couple of guys in your life takes the pressure off, too."

She was so right. My life had slipped into a nice rhythm: Marcus on Mondays and sometimes Saturdays, and Derrick on Tuesdays. There wasn't much time for myself, but I liked it that way. The distraction was welcome after months of feeling lost and lonely from Rufus's absence.

I also liked the confidence I felt having these men in my life. It wasn't so much about "Wow! Look at how many guys I can get to like me!" as it was about the empowerment of finally being in charge of myself.

With Charlie, I thought I was in charge because he was constantly pursuing me. The only problem was he never took no for an answer, and I got tired of his pleading and guilt trips, which ultimately pushed me into a position of non-power. With these guys, I got questions like, "So when can I see you next?" or "You got any time for me this week?" It was like finally riding a bike without the training wheels. I was zooming around the streets, loving the independence of it all.

"Is Future Husband coming in tonight?" Sully asked.

It was an unusually slow Wednesday night, and Sully, Lance and I had congregated around the service bar.

"I don't know," I said, leaning against the refrigerators. "I doubt it."

"Ha! You should've seen it last week," Lance piped up. "She had Future Husband *and* Trainer Guy here at the same time."

"Whaaaaaaaaat?" Sully said, standing up and spreading his arms wide like a rapper. "Lizzzzz with the skills! Did they know it?"

"Of course not," I snorted. "That would be bad."

Sully clapped his hands together. "Oh man! You are awesome. Such a play-ah!"

"Sull, it was great," Lance said. "At one point, Trainer Guy was just watching Liz work, right? And Future Husband was across the bar with some of Liz's regulars. It was so obvious that Trainer Guy was checking her out, I thought for sure Future Husband would figure it out."

"Did he?" Sully asked, eyes wide, dropping his jaw for effect.

"NO!" I said, smacking at the two of them with a bar towel. "I can't help it if they *both* decide to come and see me on the same night."

It was the first time both Derrick and Marcus showed up. Until that point, I'd gotten pretty good at managing their visits. As much as I loved the excitement, I had no intention of being disrespectful to either of them.

"It's not disrespectful!" Judy cried when I told her what happened. "They're coming into your bar, girl! You guys are not exclusive so hey, it's fair game."

Judy, who was normally low-key, was so adamant about this, I had no choice but to agree.

"You're right. I just don't want anyone to get hurt."

"I get it, but if either of these guys wants you all to himself, let him step up and say so."

The truth was that I didn't want anyone to ask for my hand in exclusivity. I liked things the way they were.

"Who's better boyfriend material?" Lance asked.

"DUDE!" Sully jumped in. "Future Husband guy, of *COURSE!*"

I let them go at it for a while like two younger brothers fighting over my virtue. Lance, a bit more blatant with his genteel manners, reminded me of a young boy at times, whereas Sully tried to play it off like he was a tough guy, getting all street when trying to prove a point.

"Yeah, but Trainer Guy's so *nice.*"

Sully smacked his head with his hand. "That's 'cuz he's *stoned* all the time!"

"He's not stoned *all* the time," I said. "He just likes his weed."

That cracked Sully up and got me thinking about which one it would be if I had to choose between the two of them.

"I don't want either of them to be my boyfriend," I finally said. "I'm just having fun, ya know?" But I was done with boy talk. I exhaled dramatically. "Guys, I need a vacation. It's been sooooo long."

"Where would you go?" Sully asked, holding out a twenty. "Can I get change for this? No singles. Just fives."

I headed over to the register. "I don't know. I was thinking about Mexico," I called over my shoulder.

"Mexico? Dude, isn't there like a bunch of crazy shit going on down there?"

"Not where I'd go," I said, handing him a handful of fives. "My friend has a place in Tulum. It's about ninety minutes from Cancun and reeeeeeally chill. Everyone does yoga, and all the hotels are eco-friendly."

"Sounds very crunchy. Very you," Sully said.

Lance returned to us after dropping the check on the last occupied table. "Who's crunchy?" he asked.

"Liz here wants to go to Mexico for vacation."

"Ooooooooo, nice. How long would ya go for?"

"I don't know. My friend's got a new place, and she said I could stay for free in exchange for helping her get the apartment ready for prospective tenants."

"Sweet," Lance said, grabbing a pint glass and filling it with water. "I say go for it."

It sure would be sweet. I was dying to get away. I just didn't know how I'd swing it: It wasn't like bartenders, let alone part-time office assistants, got paid vacation.

"Let's start wrapping it up, guys!" Doug called from the back of the restaurant.

Doug was talking to Marcelles, a waiter next door at the steakhouse... and guy number three. I'd had a thing for Marcelles ever since I started at Maxie's. Besides the fact that he was a genuinely nice guy, he was totally hot. I loved his short little dreadlocks poking out of his head like a forest of trees. Though he'd been out of college for ten years, the football he played during that time still showed in his husky build.

Nobody at work knew about Marcelles and me. I was pretty determined to keep it a secret after we first hooked up. It was nobody's business, and keeping it quiet meant I didn't have to entertain the notion that a third guy in the mix potentially made me a whore. Of course, Stephanie and Judy felt differently, whooping with approval when I told them about our first encounter.

"I'm jealous!" Stephanie said. "You're getting enough play for the three of us!"

I tried not to go there. Sure, I protected myself, and Marcelles actually knew about the other guys, but there was a large part of me that felt dirty and loose.

"Whuuuuuut???" Deb shrieked over the phone the other day. "Wa–EYYYYE?? You're a sexual being and you deserve the pleasure that is out there available to you. It's not like any of these guys are asking you to be with them and only them. You're saying yes but still sleeping with other guys."

"True. But still, it's not my usual M.O."

"I know! I love it! This is good for you. Have fun."

"Hey you," Marcelles called to me from the middle of the bar.

"Hey!" I said walking toward him, peeling off my rubber gloves. "How was your night?"

"Eh, slow," he said putting his bag down onto one of the empty bar stools. "What about you? Doug said you guys were slow."

We went back and forth for a few minutes, warming up to what I knew was coming—grabbing a drink after work, and then heading my place.

"So, ya wanna grab a drink after you're done?" he said.

Aside from the sex, I loved *talking* to Marcelles. A musician and a fellow creative soul, he understood passion. When we talked, it was deep and philosophical and way more interesting than any conversation I'd had with Derrick and Marcus combined. If I were able to mix the chemistry I had with Derrick, the stability of Marcus and the creative stimulation I felt with Marcelles, I'd have the perfect man.

"Give me about twenty minutes," I said, grabbing my cash drawer out of the register. "I'll meet you at our spot around the corner."

For now, I guess I'd just enjoy each of them and hope that no one got hurt.

38

Marcus and I finally had "the talk" in February. We'd been seeing each other since November, and the subject popped up unexpectedly at dinner one evening.

We were sitting in the back of a small, dimly lit French bistro in the West Village, glad to be far from the cold air bursting through the front door each time it opened. Somehow we'd gotten onto the subject of relationships, and Marcus joked about us growing "old and gray" together. This was the first time he had ever mentioned anything remotely close to our getting serious, and I must have looked surprised. "Look at you," he mused. "You're getting all nervous!"

"I am not!" I lied. I was hot and feeling the need to check for the nearest exit.

Marcus wasn't buying it. "You are! Your eyes are darting around like you're planning a quick getaway."

Rather than continue my lame attempt at an award-winning performance, I decided to be straight. "Well, it's just that, I don't know, you never mentioned 'us' and 'the future' before."

Things were going well with us. In the three months we'd been together, there'd never been any arguments or tension. We saw each other once or twice a week without fail. It was fine. Just fine. Taking it to another level had never even occurred to me. I liked Marcus and spending time with him, but if I had to give up the other guys and commit solely to him, I'd be bored. He was stable for sure—something I'd learned was extremely important to me in a relationship. But I also realized that stable didn't have to mean boring. And Marcus, in many ways, was boring, always answering, "Not much," and meaning it, when I asked him what he did on the days we didn't see each other.

I certainly wasn't ready to break up with him. I liked what we had, and as long as he did too, I saw no reason to change a thing. Until now.

"So are you saying you want to grow old with me, Marcus?" I reached for my wineglass and took a long sip, waiting for his answer.

"Not necessarily," he said. "But I do wonder where you stand on the whole relationship thing."

That was tricky because I really didn't know where I stood on relationships. "I like things as they are," I finally said.

In the end, we didn't resolve much. He never told me straight up that he didn't want me to see other people anymore. He never asked if I was seeing other men. He never said anything about me actually *becoming* his girlfriend. And because I had no intention of messing with my house of cards, I didn't push it, though I knew it would be just a matter of time before another one of these conversations popped up again.

My plans for a vacation, on the other hand, were shaping up nicely. I decided to put my apartment on Craigslist in the hopes of renting it out for the three weeks I'd planned to be away. A guy who lived in my apartment complex answered the ad, and I agreed to let his visiting parents stay for eighteen days.

With my rent covered, I needed to come up with money for the actual trip, and like a gift from the universe, that money came walking into Maxie's a few days later.

Her name was Lorraine, and while she sat my bar sipping a glass of cabernet, we struck up a conversation. "I love your sweater," I said, eyeing the pale yellow angora cowl-neck that clung to her small frame. "It looks so soft!"

"It totally is," she said. It was early in the night and not that busy, so we were able to immerse ourselves in a conversation about fashion and how hard it was to find well-fitting clothes.

Lorraine was in her forties and looked good for having had two children. She had small features, wavy blonde hair that fell to her delicate shoulders and a slightly raspy voice. After five minutes of talking to her, I felt like I'd known her for years.

"Forget about jeans," she said. "I can't find a good bra!"

"Really?" I said, dropping my eyes to her very small breasts. "What size are you?"

"I know, sad, right?" She laughed. "Two children and I'm not even a full A-cup anymore."

"No, no!" I said. "I'm a bra model, and I was hoping you could wear our sizes, but…"

"Yep. Too small, I know." She took a sip of wine and switched gears. "Bra model, huh? Fit?"

"Sometimes. Mostly show," I answered, impressed that she even knew there were fit models in the world.

"Oh, cool. I'm in the shoe business. Kids' shoes."

"Nice!" I said. "I used to shoe model a million years ago until they changed the sample size."

"Yeah," Lorraine sighed. "The whole industry has changed so much."

When her husband showed up, they went to a table where I sent them a round of drinks to show my gratitude for such good conversation.

When I walked into Maxie's the following day, Rebeca, my favorite hostess, greeted me with her usual smile. Rebeca was from Mexico and had big brown eyes, full lips and a heart-shaped face. Her tight red jeans showed off her slim, twenty-year-old figure, while her simple earth-toned shirt and chunky wool scarf rounded out her bohemian-chic style perfectly.

"Hey, mama!" she said cheerily, shuffling through the drawer in the host stand. "Someone left a note for you." She handed me a piece of paper with a business card attached to it.

"What the hell?" I said.

Rebeca shrugged her shoulders. "I don't know. Some lady came in earlier to see if you were working. When I told her you were coming in at 5:30, she left that for you."

I dropped my bag on the cushioned banquette beside the coat check and unfolded the note to reveal a business card from Ralph Lauren:

Dear Liz,

I hope you remember me. We met the other night here at Maxie's. You mentioned that you used to shoe model, and my friend, who's a

shoe designer, is looking for a size 7 fit model. Any interest? If so, give me a buzz. Great to meet you!!
    —Lorraine

"Oh my GOD!" I said, clapping my hand over my mouth.

"Whuuuut?" Rebeca asked, sliding up to me.

"This lady just offered me a job as a shoe model."

"That's awesome!" Rebeca squealed, her long braids dancing on her shoulders. "I didn't even know they *had* shoe models."

Still in shock, all I could muster was a nod.

"So random," she said, returning to the host stand to pick up the ringing phone.

Two days and a couple of shoe try-ons later, I was officially hired to be the size 7 fit model at Faryl Robin. Lorraine came through and put me in touch with Jill, a young, very sweet designer there. Jill had me try on a few different styles, asking questions about each one: "How are the straps? Do you feel like you're *in* the shoe? What about the back? Does it feel like your heel is slipping off?"

After half an hour, she introduced me to Faryl, the owner of the company and Lorraine's friend. Faryl was a petite woman in her early forties. "I'm so glad Lorraine found you!" she cried, shaking my hand, her bangle bracelets jingling melodically.

The job was on an as-needed basis, which, depending on how much they needed me, could be a great gig. It would be a stretch, fitting yet *another* job into my already packed schedule, but I didn't care. With the extra money, I could go to Mexico.

"Wow! Three weeks," my mother said. "That's quite a trip."

I decided to wait on calling my parents to tell them about Mexico until after everything was in place. I'd just gotten the last of my shifts covered at Maxie's and was finally ready to give them the details.

"When do you leave?" my father asked.

"February 18th."

"Oh, that's soon," my mother said.

As parents go, mine were pretty liberal. Sometimes I forgot that until I heard someone's story about how their parents were all up in their business. Mine didn't meddle, though I knew when they were not happy about something. This conversation, I suspected, was going to be one where what they *didn't* say would speak volumes.

Cutting into the awkward silence lingering on their end of the phone, I launched into the details of my trip.

"What about work?" my father asked, trying to sound casual, though I knew he was worried.

"I got my shifts covered at the bar, so that's cool." And then, "I still have to work it out with the guys at the law firm."

My mother was all over that. "What do you mean? Haven't you already booked your ticket? What if they say no?"

My parents tended to live on the conservative side, and I'd always been the one in the family to do things that didn't always align with their approach. Over the years I'd gotten much more comfortable with standing alone in the choices I'd made, and sitting in the discomfort of not always having their full approval.

I was also good at omitting certain details until *after* the fact, for the best interests of all. "They'll be cool with it," I lied. "I kind of mentioned it in passing the other day."

"Liz," my father said, his tone serious. "You don't want to mess that up. It's been a good situation for you."

"Yes," my mother agreed. "And they've been very good at being so flexible with your modeling and all."

I was considering leaving the law firm altogether. It would be great to make a clean break and come back from Mexico renewed and ready for a fresh start. When I mentioned it to Stephanie and Judy the other day, they were all for it.

"I love that idea!" Judy cried. "Sometimes you have to make space in your life for things to happen. You've been working *so* much, there's been no room for anything!"

"I'm just worried about money. I don't want to go back to that place of not having enough money."

"You won't!" Stephanie said. "You have to have faith, Liz. Look at how your life has changed! You're making good money at Maxie's. You've got this new shoe modeling gig. It's time to take a leap. You will be *fine!* You already are."

My parents didn't need to know about my potential departure from the law firm. Telling them this on top of my plans to go to Mexico might just put them over the edge. Besides, wasn't it time I started making my own decisions, not looking to everyone else for their approval?

"Is it safe there?" my father asked.

He was being the more vocal of the two. My mother would usually go silent whenever I made a decision that was more radical in nature. I could smell her disapproval and wished she'd just say, "Good for you!" or "Go for it!" Instead, my excitement was overshadowed by the mental gymnastics needed to penetrate the density of her silence.

Today, however, I wasn't biting. I had no idea what it would be like to go away, alone, for three weeks, but I did know I was ready to do it, and if my family didn't get it, then so be it.

"Dad! Tulum is a total yoga town!" I laughed. "It's really small and really chill. So yes, it's safe. On another note, did I tell you I got hired to be a fit model for a shoe company?"

"Shoes?" my mother said, her voice coming back to life.

"Yes," I said, happy to be on more neutral ground. "It's good money and the work seems to be steady."

"That's great!" my father said. "It sounds like things are really turning around for you, Liz."

Smiling on my end of the phone, I said, "Yeah, Dad. They really are."

39

"*Ladies and gentlemen, welcome to Continental Airlines Flight 1709 with connecting service to Cancun, Mexico. At this time, we ask that you turn off all electronic devices as the door to the main cabin is now closed.*"

Rising above the rows of snowcapped New Jersey homes, I felt a mixture of excitement and anxiety. The excitement, of course, was simple: For the next eighteen days, I would be in Mexico. My nerves, however, were doing a number on my mind, and despite the early-morning hour, I couldn't help but give in to the clamoring of the need to know.

What if I hate it? What if two and a half weeks is way too long to be away? What if I'm lonely? What if? What if.

Shifting in my window seat, I reminded myself of the intention I set for this trip. *Be open,* I told myself as I packed the last of my things into my suitcase. The very thought of that calmed my mind, and I was able to settle back down.

Before I left, everyone kept asking, "Soooo? Are you excited?" I wanted to tell the truth and say, "Nope, I'm scared shitless because I'm traveling solo with a hand-drawn map and I've got no clue what to expect." Instead, I spent the week leading up to my departure smiling and saying, "Yeah, sure! You bet!"

But I did confide in Matthew, a newer regular at Maxie's who'd become a fixture at my bar and a friend. He was a fellow writer, a little older than me, and just that type of guy you felt comfortable telling most anything to. "You're just afraid of the unknown," he said when I mentioned how phony I felt pretending to be excited when all I really wanted to do was cancel the trip and stay put.

"It's not that you don't want to go. You just want to *know* that's it going to be okay, and it will."

"Yeah," I sighed. "I know me. I'll be excited when I'm actually *on* the plane."

My excitement, just like my plane, was delayed, and it wasn't until the flight attendant welcomed us to Cancun that I started to feel it.

Mother Nature unkindly dumped a foot of snow on the East Coast, causing my flight to be canceled. I was able to get out a day later, but the storm had residual effects. When I arrived at the airport earlier that morning, the first leg of my flight was delayed. The panic lay in wait like a lion ready to pounce. As I stood in line at the gate, waiting to hear if I could get on another flight so I wouldn't miss my connecting flight in Dallas, I wondered if it was all a bad omen.

Thankfully, the panic started to lose ground and the excitement began to stir when I was seated on the surprisingly empty flight from Dallas to Cancun. My early-morning mind-fog had cleared, and I was able to focus on the trip.

The first item of business was getting *to* Tulum. I'd heard there was a bus you could take from Cancun to Tulum, about a ninety-minute trip, for around $18. As I walked through the crowded airport upon my arrival, I looked forward to the adventure of finding my way to the bus depot.

Cancun was totally Americanized, so asking about the bus and where to board was a cinch. Bus ticket in hand, I rolled my suitcase past the slew of tour operators to an empty corner where I traded my sneakers for flip-flops and stuffed the residual winter layers into my bag.

The whoosh of the sliding glass doors reminded me of the first time I visited Cancun. It was 1989, spring break, and the airport was not yet renovated. There were no automatic doors like the ones I was walking through today, nor was there the little outdoor bar I noticed when I stepped out into the warm, dry Mexican air.

The sun felt so good that I stopped for a moment and tilted my head up, drinking in the warmth and the brightness. The guy who sold me the ticket had answered "soon" when I asked him when the bus left, so I decided against stopping for a beer and searched for my bus instead.

Tons of buses were awaiting arriving tourists. I walked toward to the far end of the depot and spotted the bus, large and white with tinted windows and "ADO" written in big red letters on its body. For $18, I suppose I expected a rickety old van, but this bus looked modern and luxurious.

The air was hot, and I was glad I'd changed into more suitable attire. The people standing beside the bus hadn't shed the clothes from wherever they'd come from, and they looked uncomfortable. Judging from their practical style, I guessed they were from the Midwest.

I was the only one traveling solo, and I could feel the discomfort rise as I rolled my suitcase past the large group and stood off to the side, doing my best not to appear as awkward as I felt.

A short, pudgy woman dressed in khaki shorts, a floral blouse and bright orange Crocs waddled toward me.

"Do you mind watching my stuff?" she asked, dumping her red tote bag on top of her matching rolling suitcase. "I want to get a beer for the ride." She seemed cheerful and nice enough.

"Oh," I said. "You can drink on the bus?"

She laughed, her frosted dirty-blonde curls dancing on her head as she said, "Of course! It's Mexico! You can drink *everywhere!*"

She was right, I remembered, laughing along. "Sure, I'll watch your stuff," I said, reaching for my purse. "Would you mind getting me a beer as well?"

"Absolutely!" she said, glad to have to a drinking buddy.

It seemed only natural that we sit together on the bus, and for the next 45 minutes my new drinking buddy regaled me with stories of years past in Mexico.

"We used to go to Cancun," she said, sipping her cold can of Corona. "But we like Playa del Carmen much better. It's less touristy."

I found that funny because looking at her, I had to admit that my first thought was "typical tourist." But I was on a mission to be open, and if it meant hanging out with a woman from Wisconsin who wore

Crocs and drank beer from a can, so be it.

In Playa del Carmen, I bid my new friend good-bye and boarded the bus to Tulum for another forty-five-minute ride. That bus was older and smelled of stale cigarette smoke. The portly driver looked more like a rancher in his brown polyester pants, rodeo shirt and weathered cowboy boots.

"Hola!" he said, smiling widely as I handed over my suitcase and got on the bus.

The bus wasn't full, and apart from a French couple in the very back, the rest of the passengers appeared to be locals. Some were dressed in hotel uniforms, while others wore clothes more suitable for manual labor. Everyone smiled and offered a friendly "Hola!" as they talked in Spanish among themselves.

Once we were out of Playa del Carmen, the ride was fairly uneventful. We traveled down a modern two-lane highway surrounded by miles and miles of untouched jungle. The lack of scenery gave me time to sit back and relax into the faded velour seat. With nothing much to look at and no idea of what was to come, I had plenty of time to digest all that was behind me.

Avi and Pradeep were surprisingly disappointed when I finally gave notice a couple of weeks before I left. "I think we'll have to get two people to replace Liz," Avi said. After a year of working for that man, I knew it was his way of saying he'd be sorry to see me go.

I, of course, was anything but sad about leaving. I felt such joy cleaning out my desk on my last day that I had to remind myself to not show it out of respect for the guys. I was definitely worried about income, but I'd decided that along with my intent to be open, I would adopt a mantra of "all will be fine" and see how it went.

Marcus wasn't happy about my departure, and from the looks of it, he'd be moving back to Texas not long after I returned to New York. He and I had a good run, and there was no talk of maintaining our relationship while he was in Dallas, so that was that.

Derrick was his usual chill self, kissing my forehead as he wished me a great trip two nights before my departure. I realized, as the bus slowed down to exchange passengers on the side of the highway, that I didn't even get to say good-bye to Marcelles.

No big deal, as all of it was already starting to feel so far away. I couldn't believe how content I felt in just a few short hours. *Content.* There's a word I hadn't used to describe my life in a long while. Distracted and busy, yes, but not content.

All the things in my life had been more of a source of distraction rather than contentment. Even the guys in my life kept me from myself. I liked them all just fine, but I wasn't in *love* with any of them. I wasn't even sad about Marcus leaving. It was amazing to me that I could spend all that time with someone and not even feel much more than a deep like for him.

By the time I would make the journey from Tulum back to Cancun, Rufus would be gone for a year. Thinking of it that day still made me sad, but the feeling was distant, more of a habit than something I could reach out and grab onto. I guess this was what people meant when they told me to give it time.

It was less about time and more about choice. When you lose something close to you, you have two choices: The first is to stay immersed in the pain and emptiness of the deep crater left behind by the absence. The second choice is more fluid and requires you to find the space in the loss. In that space, many other things can be gained or cultivated—love, creativity, a new dog, whatever you want. And for the first time in a year, I could feel the possibility in my life.

Rufus was a wise soul. I think he saw the possibility long before I did. He knew it was my time to fly. As his body began to tire, he was ready to stop carrying me because he knew I could stand on my own.

"*Señorita?*" the bus driver leaned in close to me, snapping me back to the present. "*Estamos aquí.*"

I felt disoriented, like I'd been sleeping, and it took me a minute to realize we had arrived at the bus station in Tulum.

Outside, I gathered my bag and got a taxi with ease. Kara's hand-drawn map didn't do much good as the taxi driver turned to me and shrugged his shoulders in confusion when I showed it to him.

"She said it's at the end of town," I said, more to myself than to the driver.

With some exaggerated hand gestures and a lot of pointing, we managed to get going. We drove through the small town, and just when I wondered if perhaps we'd gone too far, I saw a small sign in the distance on the right.

"Premir Amore!" I squealed, pointing over his shoulder.

"*Si, si, si,*" the driver said, pulling into the unpaved driveway. My heart pounded when I saw a cluster of buildings set at the end of the driveway, all of which were painted a bright and creamy yellow and crowned with *palapa* roofs. Upon opening the taxi door, I heard a woman's voice from somewhere within the gated community. "Hi, Liz! I'll be right down!" It was Joanna, the caretaker of the property, who Kara said would give me the keys.

I started to get out of the car when a huge, Lab-looking dog came bounding out of the gate, jumping and barking happily.

"Yeller!" I heard a different woman call from inside. "Sorry!"

Yeller ran straight to the car and stuck his large head into the backseat.

"Hello!" I said. "Are you my welcome committee?"

Yeller gave a small bark and leaned in closer to give me a full-on face-lick, his tail wagging wildly behind him.

I sat back and happily conceded to the message in it all. I didn't know what was in front of me, but I did know that if I left enough space, good things were bound to come.

"*Gracias, señor,*" I said, closing the door to the cab and petting Yeller's head while I waited for Joanna.

Kickstarter Contributors

Meet the wonderful people who helped make this book happen:

Abby Freeman	Cindy Levine
Alex Dempsey	Colette Lelchuk
Alice Chera	Cynthia Ehrenkrantz
Allison Mays	Daniel and Joan Rosenfeld
Amanda Bhalla	Danielle Carver
Amanda White	Danny Millan
Andrea Demetropoulos	Daphne Gaines
Andrea Ivey Harris	David Sherin
Andres Nicholls	David Sullivan
Angelica Heppe	Debbie Brown
Anthony Peterson	Debbie Mistretta
Anya Hoffman	Deborah Kagan
Arlene and Marvin Levine	DJ Eldon
Arthur Chu	Donna Hadfield
Baron Santiago	Elinor Franco
Barry Bertram	Eloy Trevino
Becca Saxon	Emily Beaver
Benjie Theodore T	Ernest Kolaj
Beth Kliegerman Tafuri	Evelyn Howard
Bettina Faltermeier	Felix Feliciano
Brian Merker	Hanif Sean Perry
Brian Rosenberg	Harold Cook
Carrie Dobson	Hector Pottie
Cat Lee	Iran Daniel
Catherine Calderon	Jonathan Kaufman
Catherine Lowe	Jake Perten
Ceara Murtagh	Jared and Pam Weber
Charles Salzberg	Jen Dicker

Jennifer Barron

Jesse Purewal

Jessica Staley

Jimena Garcia

Joan Ullman

Joan Weber

Josh Meyer

Karen Flannery

Karen Pancholi

Karin Kelly

Kathleen Higgins

KC Weakley

Kimberly Mitcham

Kristina Jenkins

Kyrsten Musich

L.ynda and Michael Grauer

Laura DeNatale

Laurie Santos

Lenore Perry

Leslie Barahona

Linda DiVito

Lucy Lomellin

Maris Weber

Marissa Haro

Marje Wagner

Mark Chambers

Mark Lewis

Mat Zucker

Matthew Wells

Melinda Tracy

Michael Brenner

Michael and Debra Levine

Myles and Avonne Seideman

Nicole Monaco Johnson

Omar Abiera

Patricia Pappagallo

Peggy Rubel

Peter Dixon

Quentin Vidor

Rebeca Ibarra Calabrese

Renee Lyn

Robbie Tucker

Robert Lascaro

Roberta Carver

Roberta and Paul Marshall

Robin Ely

Ron Lane

Ron Weber

Sally Fisher

Sara Hruska

Sarah Carr-Locke

Scott Elliott

Scott and Lori Levine

Scott Schneider

Seana Eileen Anderson

Shani Wright

Sloane Farber

Stan & Paula Popeil

Stefanie Bradley

Steven Getchell

Steven Whalen

Sylvia Lee

Tiffani Donelli

Todd Sinett

Tommy Connolly

Tracy Riordan

Trinae Leshaun Thompson

About The Author

Liz Weber is a freelance writer
living in Brooklyn whose work has
appeared on national websites such
as *Narrative.ly*, *Apartmenttherapy.
com* and *Planetwaves.net*. She's
been a regular contributor for
lifestyle website *Citypath.com* and
Boredandthirstynyc.com and has doled
out dating advice to the urban
female set on the popular website
Thefatwhiteguy.com. Her short story
about working in a male strip club
for women was featured in the
2009 Staten Island Arts Festival.

More at: Lizweber.com